Lecture Notes in Artificial Intelligence 3048

Edited by J. G. Carbonell and J. Siekmann

Subseries of Lecture Notes in Computer Science

Peyman Faratin
David C. Parkes
Juan A. Rodríguez-Aguilar
William E. Walsh (Eds.)

Agent-Mediated Electronic Commerce V

Designing Mechanisms and Systems

AAMAS 2003 Workshop, AMEC 2003
Melbourne, Australia, July 15, 2003
Revised Selected Papers

 Springer

Series Editors

Jaime G. Carbonell Carnegie Mellon University, Pittsburgh, PA, USA
Jörg Siekmann, University of Saarland, Saarbrücken, Germany

Volume Editors

Peyman Faratin
Massachusetts Institute of Technology
Computer Science and Artificial Intelligence Laboratory
Massachusetts Avenue, Cambridge, 02139, USA
E-mail: peyman@mit.edu

David C. Parkes
Harvard University, Division of Engineering and Applied Science
33 Oxford Street, Cambridge, MA 02138, USA
E-mail: parkes@eecs.harvard.edu

Juan A. Rodríguez-Aguilar
Institut d'Investigació en Inel.ligència Artificial (IIIA)
Spanish Scientific Research Council (CSIC)
Campus de la Universitat Autònoma de Barcelona
08193 Bellaterra, Barcelona, Spain
E-mail: jar@iiia.csic.es

William E. Walsh
IBM, T.J. Watson Research Center
19 Skyline Drive, 2S-K15
Hawthorne, New York 10532, USA
E-mail: wwalsh1@us.ibm.com

Library of Congress Control Number: 2004113028

CR Subject Classification (1998): I.2.11, K.4.4, C.2, H.3.4-5, H.5.3, I.2, J.1

ISSN 0302-9743
ISBN 3-540-22674-5 Springer Berlin Heidelberg New York

Springer is a part of Springer Science+Business Media

springeronline.com

© Springer-Verlag Berlin Heidelberg 2004
Printed in Germany

Typesetting: Camera-ready by author, data conversion by Boller Mediendesign
Printed on acid-free paper   SPIN: 11301516   06/3142   5 4 3 2 1 0

Preface

The design of intelligent trading agents, mechanisms, and systems has received growing attention in the agents and multiagent systems communities in an effort to address the increasing costs of search, transaction, and coordination which follows from the increasing number of Internet-enabled distributed electronic markets. Furthermore, new technologies and supporting business models are resulting in a growing volume of open and horizontally integrated markets for trading of an increasingly diverse set of goods and services. However, growth of technologies for such markets requires innovative solutions to a diverse set of existing and novel technical problems which we are only beginning to understand. Specifically, distributed markets present not only traditional economic problems but also introduce novel and challenging computational issues that are not represented in the classic economic solution concepts. Novel to agent-mediated electronic commerce are considerations involving the computation substrates of the agents and the electronic institutions that supports, and trading, and also the human-agent interface (involving issues of preference elicitation, representation, reasoning and trust). In sum, agent-mediated electronic trade requires principled design (from economics and game theory) and incorporates novel combinations of theories from different disciplines such as computer science, operations research, artificial intelligence and distributed systems.

The collection of above-mentioned issues and challenges has crystallized into a new, consolidated agent research field that has become a focus of attention in recent years: *agent-mediated electronic commerce.*

The papers in this volume originate from the 5th Workshop on Agent-Mediated Electronic Commerce (AMEC V), held in conjunction with the 2nd International Joint Conference on Autonomous Agents and Multiagent Systems (AAMAS) in July 2003. The AMEC V workshop continued with the tradition, and built upon the success of the previous AMEC workshops.

The workshop was intended to explore research in the principled design of economic agents, mechanisms, and systems. Along this direction, areas of particular interest included:

- mechanisms, negotiation protocols, and auctions (especially advanced designs such as multi-attribute auctions)
- bidding and negotiation strategies
- integration of negotiation with broader decision making
- economic-based theory and design methodologies
- market-based problem solving
- trading and pricing
- eliciting human preferences and requirements and ensuring that they are represented in automated agent behavior
- significant new problem domains

- systems that support bidding and negotiation
- simulation and evaluation of properties of novel and complex mechanisms

The workshop received a total of 22 submissions, from which 9 were selected for full presentation during the workshop. After the workshop, the authors were asked to submit their revised versions for publication in this volume. The result is that this volume contains 9 high-quality papers that can be regarded as representative of the field.

We have arranged the papers in the book around three major topics:

- *automated negotiation*;
- *mechanism design*; and
- *multi-agent markets*.

The first section contains four papers dealing with a variety of issues on automated negotiation. Somefun et al. elaborate on bargaining strategies aimed at the trading of bundles of information goods. Similarly, Feng et al. examine automated strategies for trading agents, but in a rather different negotiation scenario: stock trading. Complementarily to these works, Luo et al. turn their attention to a central HCI problem of automated negotiation: how to capture a user's preferences so that his agent can adequately represent him. This section ends with the contribution by Hoen et al., who analyze the convenience for trading agents to decommit after a negotiated contract has been settled.

The second section compiles papers focusing on computational mechanism design. Firstly, Sandholm et al. introduce a new allocation mechanism (take-it-or-leave-it auction) that generates close-to-optimal expected utility for the seller while allowing buyers to hide much of their private valuation. Elaborating further on auction design, Likhodedov et al. design a dominant-strategy auction mechanism aimed at maximizing expected social welfare. A rather different approach is taken by Walsh et al., who offer methods designed to sample the strategy profile that is expected to provide the most value of information, measured in terms of beliefs about the effect that one more sample might have on the current decision about the equilibrium of the system. These methods are said to be relevant to *experimental mechanism design*, in which computational methods are used in a closed loop to evaluate alternative designs for electronic markets.

Finally, the third section contains two papers dealing with upcoming issues in digital markets. Firstly, the work by Brooks et al. develops a model of an information goods duopoly to empirically support the hypothesis that a producer using some knowledge of a problem's structure can outperform a producer employing knowledge-free forms of learning. Secondly, Klein et al. address the problem of emergent dysfunctions in open markets where consumers select providers among competing providers. The authors offer a method for coping with such dysfunctions based on selective stochastic resource request rejection.

We would like to conclude by thanking the members of the program committee. They were able to produce a large number of high-quality reviews in a very short time span. Furthermore, we would also like to thank the authors for submitting their papers to our workshop, as well as the attendees and panelists for their valuable insights and discussions. Needless to say that these helped authors to improve the revised papers published in this book.

May 2004   Peyman Faratin
                                              David C. Parkes
                                   Juan A. Rodríguez-Aguilar
                                              William E. Walsh

Workshop Organization

Organizing Committee

Peyman Faratin	Massachusetts Institute of Technology, USA
David Parkes	Harvard University, USA
Juan A. Rodríguez-Aguilar	IIIA-CSIC, Spain
William E. Walsh	IBM T.J. Watson Research Center, USA

Program Committee

Chris Brooks	University of San Francisco, USA
Rajarshi Das	IBM Research, USA
Frank Dignum	Universiteit Utrecht, The Netherlands
Boi Faltings	EPFL, Switzerland
Maria Gini	University of Minnesota, USA
Amy Greenwald	Brown University, USA
Robert Guttman	IBM Research, USA
Nick R. Jennings	Southampton University, UK
Jayant Kalagnanam	IBM, USA
Jeff Kephart	IBM Research, USA
Sarit Kraus	Bar-Ilan University, Israel
Kate Larson	Carnegie Mellon University, USA
Kevin Leyton-Brown	University of Stanford, USA
Joerg Muller	Siemens, Germany
Julian Padget	University of Bath, UK
David Pennock	Overture Services, USA
Chris Preist	Hewlett-Packard, UK
Antonio Reyes-Moro	iSOCO, Spain
Jeff Rosenschein	Hebrew University, Israel
Onn Shehory	Carnegie Mellon University, USA
Liz Sonenberg	University of Melbourne, Australia
Katia Sycara	Carnegie Mellon University, USA
Gerry Tesauro	IBM Research, USA
Steven Willmott	Technical University of Catalonia, Spain
Peter Wurman	North Carolina State University, USA

Table of Contents

Automated Negotiation and Bundling of Information Goods

D.J.A. Somefun[1], E.H. Gerding[1], S. Bohte[1], and J.A. La Poutré[1,2]

[1] Center for Mathematics and Computer Science (CWI), P.O. Box 94079, 1090 GB
Amsterdam, The Netherlands
{koye, Enrico.Gerding, S.M.Bohte, hlp}@cwi.nl

[2] Eindhoven University of Technology, School of Technology Management,P.O. Box
513, 5600 MB Eindhoven, The Netherlands

Abstract. In this paper, we present a novel system for selling bundles
of news items. Through the system, customers bargain with the seller
over the price and quality of the delivered goods. The advantage of the
developed system is that it allows for a high degree of flexibility in the
price, quality, and content of the offered bundles. The price, quality, and
content of the delivered goods may, for example, differ based on daily
dynamics and personal interests of customers. Autonomous "software
agents" execute the negotiation on behalf of the users of the system.
To perform the actual negotiation these agents make use of bargaining
strategies. We decompose bargaining strategies into concession strategies
and Pareto efficient search strategies. Additionally, we introduce the orthogonal and orthogonal-DF strategy: two Pareto search strategies. We
show through computer experiments that the use of these Pareto search
strategies will result in very efficient bargaining outcomes. Moreover, the
system is set up such that it is actually in the best interest of the customer to have their agent adhere to this approach of disentangling the
bargaining strategy.

1 Introduction

Personalization of information goods becomes more and more a key component
of a successful electronic business strategy [1]. The challenge is to develop systems that can deliver a high level of personalization combined with, whenever
possible, a high adaptability to changing circumstances. In this paper we develop
a system which can attain these properties through the manner in which it sells
information goods.

We consider the novel approach of selling bundles of news items through a
system that allows for bargaining over the price and quality of the delivered
goods. Bundling of information goods has many potential benefits including
complementarities among the bundle components, and sorting consumers according to their valuation (cf. [2] and the references therein). The advantage of
the developed system is that it allows for a high degree of flexibility in the price,
quality, and content of the offered bundles. The price, quality, and content of the

P. Faratin et al. (Eds.): AMEC 2003, LNAI 3048, pp. 1–17, 2004.

delivered goods may, for example, differ based on daily dynamics and personal interest of customers.

The system as developed is capable of taking into account business related constraints. More specifically, it tries to ensure that customers perceive the bargaining outcomes as being "fair" by having customers end up with equivalent offers whenever that seems fair. Partly because of this fairness constraint the actual bargaining process is not really one-to-one bargaining between seller and customer but instead is one-to-many (i.e., between seller and customers).

To accelerate the negotiation process, customers can initiate concurrent negotiation threads for the same bundle with differences in the quality of the delivered bundles. The thread in which the agreement is reached first determines the final bargaining outcome.

In the developed system, autonomous "software agents" perform (part of) the negotiation on behalf of the users of the system. These software agents bargain over a multi-issue price (the price is actually a tariff with a fixed and variable component).

To enable efficient multi-issue bargaining outcomes, we decompose the bargaining strategies into concession strategies and Pareto search strategies. Additionally, we introduce the orthogonal and orthogonal-DF strategy: two Pareto search strategies. We show through computer experiments that the respective use of these two Pareto search strategies by the two bargainers will result in very efficient bargaining outcomes (i.e., these outcomes closely approximate Pareto-efficient bargaining solutions).

In the system the seller agent uses a Pareto search strategy (i.e., the orthogonal-DF) combined with a concession strategy. Although the customer is free to choose other bargaining strategies, the system is set up such that it is actually in the best interest of the customer to have their agent also use a Pareto search strategy (i.e, the orthogonal strategy) combined with a concession strategy.

In Section 2 we discuss the developed system at a more conceptual level. In Section 3 we discuss the customer and seller agent in greater detail. Furthermore, we discuss the type of bargaining strategies these agents use. In Section 4 we study in greater detail the Pareto search aspects of bargaining. Through computer experiments we investigate the efficiency of the introduced bargaining approach. (Note that for this purpose it is not necessary to simulate the entire system as developed, it suffices to consider one-to-one bargaining only.) In Section 5 we discuss the results of the paper and relate the paper to the relevant literature. Conclusions follow in Section 6.

2   A System for Selling Information Goods

2.1   Problem Statement

The goal is to develop a system for the sales of bundles of news items where customers bargain over the price and quality of the delivered goods. The negotiated contract applies to a fixed time interval, which is typically a short period of time, e.g., a single day. There are roughly three possibilities for implementing the starting time of the negotiation process: customers can negotiate a contract before the news arises, after the news arises, or while the news arises. The system is set up in such a way that all three possibilities can be implemented.

The value customers attach to news items may fluctuate heavily due to daily dynamics. Moreover, there may be wide differences in personal interests of customers. The advantage of the developed system is that it allows for a high degree of flexibility in the price, quality, and content of the offered bundles. The price, quality, and content of the delivered goods may, for example, differ based on daily dynamics and personal interest of customers.

2.2   Bundles of Information Goods

The system sells bundles of news items which become available during a predefined and fixed time interval (e.g., a day). Within the system, prices vary based on the content and "quality of service" of the bundle. A *bundle content* defines which types of news categories the bundle contains. The system distinguishes between k categories. Within a category the system distinguishes between two quality of service levels: i.e., a customer pays a fixed price for either receiving headlines or complete news articles. In the former case we speak of a category with low quality of service, whereas in the latter case we speak of a category with high quality of service. Moreover, with the quality of service (or just quality) of a bundle we actually mean the quality of service specified per category.

A customer bargains with the seller over the bundle tariff. The negotiated tariff is a two-part tariff with a fixed and variable price. The fixed price (p_f) is the price a customer pays for receiving the bundle content with the specified quality of service. Moreover, the variable price (p_v) is the price the customer pays for reading a full article whenever the quality of service only specifies delivery of the article headline.

Consider, for example, the bundle content religion, culture, and politics, where the category religion has a high quality of service and the other two have a low quality of service. Then the customer pays a fixed price for receiving all the full articles in the category religion and only the headlines of all the articles which do not belong to the category religion but do belong to the other two categories. Moreover, the variable price is the price the customer pays whenever she wants to read the full article of a news item that belongs to the categories culture or politics (and does not belong to the category religion).

2.3   Bargaining with Software Agents

We employ the paradigm of "software agents," where pieces of autonomous software perform (part of) the negotiating on behalf of the users of the system. Customers and seller instruct their agent through a user interface (UI). The agents conduct the actual negotiation. Figure 1 depicts, at a high abstraction level, the bargaining process between a customer and the seller.

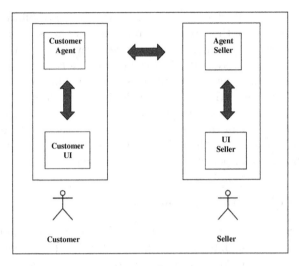

Fig. 1. The one-to-one bargaining process

2.4   Bargaining Process

Bargaining occurs in an alternating exchange of offers and counter offers, typically initiated by the customer. An offer specifies the fixed price, the variable price (uniform for all low quality of service categories), the bundle content, and also the desired quality of service of the information for each category separately. The bargaining process continues until an agreement is reached or one of the bargainers terminates the process. Based on this bargaining process, figure 2 draws the bargaining protocol the customer agents and seller agent use to do the actual bargaining.

To accelerate the negotiation process, we allow concurrent negotiation threads for the same bundle content with different quality of service. The customer can therefore submit several offers at the same time. In order to discern between threads, each thread must have a different quality configuration for the categories where a quality configuration specifies the quality of service for all the bundle categories. The seller can only respond by varying the fixed and variable price. The thread in which the agreement is reached first determines the tariff and quality configuration for the desired categories.

2.5   Fairness & One-to-Many Bargaining

A possible drawback of bargaining is that two customers may end up paying a substantially different price for very similar bundles. Customers may perceive this as unfair. This is an important concern for the seller, since customers may become dissatisfied or stop using the system altogether.

In the system a notion of fairness is incorporated into the bargaining strategy the seller agent uses. More specifically, within a limited timeframe the seller agent

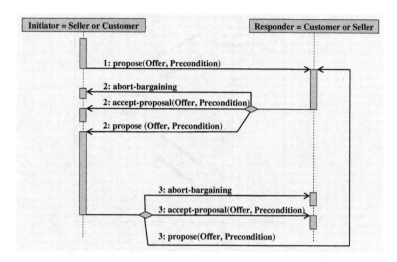

Fig. 2. The agents bargaining protocol

makes equivalent offers to customers who are interested in identical bundles. For offers that specify identical bundles, the actual tariff may still differ from customer to customer. Fairness, however, ensures that the expected revenue of these tariffs is identical for all (counter) offers submitted by the seller agent; the expected revenue (R) of a tariff (p_f, p_v) for a particular bundle is defined as follows:

$$R = p_f + p_v \cdot \rho, \tag{1}$$

where ρ denotes the expected number of articles read in the low quality of service categories (for the average customer). The expected revenue can, however, vary through time. The offer equivalence therefore only holds within a limited time frame. Note that beside "fairness" also other business side-constraints may be implemented. The actual way in which side-constraints, such as fairness, are implemented may be important because it can alter the strategic behavior of customers. It is however beyond the scope of the paper to discuss these issues.

The actual bargaining process between seller and customers is not really one-to-one bargaining between seller and customer but instead is one-to-many. On the one hand, the seller can use his experience in other ongoing bargaining processes between customers to adjust his bargaining strategy; under true one-to-one bargaining the bargaining strategy only depends on the moves of the direct opponent. On the other hand, fairness and/or other side-constraints limit the bargaining options of the seller. These limitations do not apply under true one-to-one bargaining. Figure 3 depicts the one-to-many bargaining process and the possibility of parallel negotiation threads between a customer and the seller.

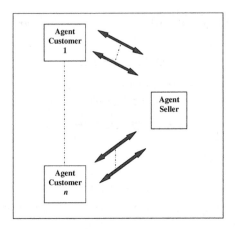

Fig. 3. The one-to-many bargaining with parallel threads

3   Agents & Bargaining

3.1   Agents

Seller Agent Bargaining with a customer is done based on the seller agent's desired aspiration level expressed in expected utils. We define the expected utility u of the seller agent as the expected revenue from selling a bundle given p_f and p_v (see also equation 1), i.e., $u(p_f, p_v) = p_f + p_v \cdot \rho$. We assume that all costs are sunk, i.e., there are no transaction costs. Recall from section 2.5 that ρ denotes the number of expected articles read in the low quality of service categories. The agent can assess the expected number of articles read based on, for example, aggregate past sales data.

Due to the fairness constraint, the seller agent cannot charge different prices to different individuals for identical bundles (within the same time frame). The seller agent can indirectly discriminate between different customers, however, based on differences in the preferred bundle content and/or quality of service. In the system, the seller can discriminate by varying for example the desired expected utility for different combinations of quality of service and bundle content.

Customer Agent The customer agent acts on behalf of the customer. The customer can indicate her preferences by specifying, for each information category she is interested in, the amount of articles she expects to read. The customer can furthermore select between several negotiation strategies to be used by the agent and specify a maximum budget b_{max}. The budget provides the agent with a mandate for the negotiation; the total expected costs should not exceed b_{max}.

Given a tariff (p_f, p_v) for a particular bundle, the customer's expected utility is defined as $u(p_f, p_v) = b_{max} - (p_f + p_v \cdot \rho)$. The second part of the equation is identical to seller's expected revenue (see equation (1)). However, ρ, the number of expected articles read in the low quality of service categories, refers now to the expectation of the individual customer. Given the utility the agent is able to translate the customer's preferences into offers and also respond to the seller's offers as to maximize the expected utility.

The negotiation protocol allows for multiple negotiation threads for the same bundle content (see Section 2.4). Given a bundle content with n categories, in principle 2^n threads are possible (by varying the quality of service for each category). The customer agent, however, selects only a limited number of combinations based on the customer's preferences, to reduce the amount of communication. In the current system the customer agent initiates $n+1$ threads. In the first thread the quality of service for all categories is set to low. In the second thread, only the quality of service for the category with the highest expected articles read is set to high. In the third thread, this is done for the two categories with the first and second highest expected articles read, and so on. Within a thread, a fixed price and a variable price are negotiated.

3.2   Decomposing Bargaining Strategy

The customer agents and seller agent contain various bargaining strategies to do the actual bargaining over the two-part tariff. These strategies make use of the notion of a utility function to represent the bargainers' preferences for the various tariffs. We decompose bargaining strategies into concession strategies and "Pareto search" strategies.

Concession strategies determine what the desired utility level of an offer will be given a particular sequence of offers and counter offers. Algorithms that implement Pareto search strategies determine, given a particular utility level and a particular history of offers and counter offers, what the multi-issue offer will be, i.e., the fixed price p_f and the variable price p_v of the two part tariff. In terms of a multivariable utility function a counter offer entails both a movement off the iso-utility line and a movement along the iso-utility line. (Given a specified utility level, an iso-utily line specifies all the p_f and p_v points which generate identical utility.) Concession strategies determine the movement of an iso-utility line; Pareto search strategies determine the movement along an iso-utility line.

Pareto search strategies aim at reaching agreement as soon as the respective "concession" strategies permit this. Therefore it may be good for both parties to use it. In more economic terms a negotiated tariff is called Pareto efficient if it is impossible to change the tariff without making one of the bargainers worse off, i.e., one of the bargainers will always attach a lower (or equal) utility to the adjusted tariff. From a system design perspective Pareto efficiency of the negotiated tariffs is clearly desirable.

In Section 3.3 we introduce a particular class of Pareto search algorithms. The experiments in Section 4 show that if the seller agent uses this Pareto search algorithm and customer agents use a similar Pareto search algorithm, then the bargaining outcome will closely approximate a Pareto-efficient solution given a wide variety of concession strategies.

In the system the seller agent uses an instance of the Pareto search algorithms combined with a concession strategy. Although a customer is free to select other bargaining strategies the system is set up such that it is actually in the best interest of customers to have their agents use Pareto search strategies combined with a concession strategy. We elaborate on this issue in the discussion in Section 5.

3.3   Orthogonal Strategy & DF

Both customer agent and seller agent may use— what we call— an orthogonal strategy as the Pareto search algorithm. This strategy is probably best explained through an example. Suppose, the customer (with whom the seller bargains over the tariff) placed the tth offer of $(p_f(t), p_v(t))$. Moreover, the seller's concession strategy dictates an *aspiration level* of $U_s(t+1)$: i.e., in utils the (counter) offer should be worth $U_s(t + 1)$. Based on this information the orthogonal strategy determines $(p_f(t + 1), p_v(t + 1))$, the counter offer of the seller, by choosing a (p_f, p_v) combination that generates $U_s(t + 1)$ utils and lies closest (measured in Euclidean distance) to the point $(p_f(t), p_v(t))$. Figure 4 gives the graphical representation of the orthogonal strategy.

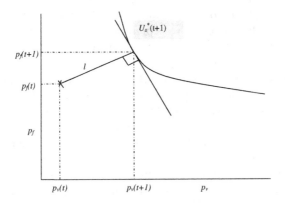

Fig. 4. Example of Orthogonal Strategy

The use of the orthogonal strategy by both parties results in a mapping f from a bargainer's aspiration level at t to the aspiration level at $t + 2$. Given convex preferences (cf. [3]) and fixed aspiration levels the mapping f can be shown to satisfy the Lipschitz condition $||f(x) - f(y)|| \le ||x - y||$ for all x and y in the domain of f.[3] Thus, given fixed aspiration levels and convex preferences, the orthogonal strategy does imply that consecutive offers do not diverge. (Note, that

---

[3] The proof is a straightforward application of convex analysis (cf. [4]) given that without loss of generality we can assume that the preferences are bounded. That is, negative and extremely high $(p_f(t), p_v(t))$ combinations can be discarded, without loss of generality.

convex preferences do not rule out changing preferences it only means that at some point in time—i.e., during the bargaining process— the preference relation is convex.) Figure 5 illustrates the use of the orthogonal strategy by both parties for the case of tangent iso-utlity lines. It draws a sequence of two offers and counter offers with convex preferences and a fixed aspiration level. (U_s and U_c denote the iso-utility lines of the seller and customer, respectively.) The figure illustrates, for instance, how the customer's offer at time 1 (with aspiration level $U_c(1) = U_c$) is transformed into an offer at time 3 (with aspiration level $U_c(3) = U_c$).

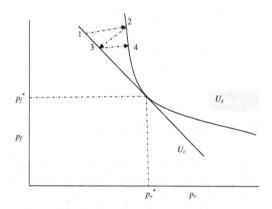

Fig. 5. Sequence of two offers and counter offers with fixed aspiration levels and convex preferences, where (p_f^*, p_v^*) denotes a Pareto-efficient tariff.

The use of just the orthogonal strategy by both parties may lead to very slow convergence to Pareto-efficient bargaining outcomes. To speed up the convergence process we can add an amplifying mechanism to the orthogonal strategy. As the amplifying mechanism we use the derivative follower with adaptive step-size (ADF). (Henceforth we will call this the orthogonal-DF.)

The derivative follower (DF) is a local search algorithm (cf. [5]). It adjust the variable price p_v found by the orthogonal strategy by either subtracting or adding δ to it depending on the result of the previous two adjustments, where δ is called the step-size of the DF. Consequently also the fixed price p_f changes because the adjusted offer still needs to generate the same utility level (specified by the concession strategy). The difference between ADF and DF is that the step-size δ becomes adaptive [6, 7]. We use the ADF proposed by [7]. Intuitively, the idea is to increment the step-size relatively far away from a Pareto-efficient solution and decrement it in the vicinity of a Pareto-efficient solution. Consequently, a quicker and more accurate search of the solution space becomes possible. Algorithm 1 specifies the orthogonal-DF in greater detail and figure 6 illustrates the use of the orthogonal-DF by the seller (the customer uses the orthogonal strategy only).

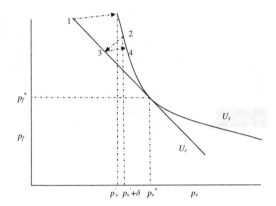

Fig. 6. Sequence of two offers and counter offers with fixed aspiration levels where the seller uses the orthogonal-DF and the customer only uses the orthogonal strategy.

4   Experimental Setup & Results

The previous sections outlined the general system for selling bundles of news items to several customers through negotiation. As discussed in Section 3.2, negotiation essentially consists of two strategic aspects: the concession of the agents and the Pareto search method. In this section we focus on the latter aspect of the negotiations. By means of computer experiments we investigate the effectiveness and robustness of the orthogonal and orthogonal-DF approach, to find Pareto-efficient solutions for a wide variety of settings. We evaluate the robustness of the search strategy by experimenting with various concession strategies on the customer side.

Although the system enables customers to initiate several concurrent negotiation threads, within a thread the Pareto search strategy operates independently from the other threads. For researching the efficiency and robustness of Pareto search strategies it therefore suffices to consider only a single negotiation thread in the experiments.

Furthermore, the bundle content in the experimental setup consists of a single category with a low quality of service. The experimental results generalize to negotiations involving multiple categories: Only the shape of the iso-utility curves is affected by the number of categories. In the experiments the shape is varied using different parameter settings.

A general specification of the customer agents and the seller agent was provided in Section 3. Sections 4.1 and 4.2 describe the agent settings which are specifically used within the experimental setup. In particular the agents' preferences and concession strategies are specified in detail in Sections 4.1 and 4.2 respectively. The experimental results are discussed in Section 4.3.

Algorithm 1 The orthogonal-DF algorithm

The following is given: (a) the opponent's last and before last offer $O_1 = (p_f(t), p_v(t))$ and $O_2 = (p_f(t-2), p_v(t-2))$ respectively, (b) bargainer's utility function $u(p_f, p_v)$ and next aspiration level $U(t+1)$, (c) the step-size δ, and (d) the search direction $s_{dr} \in \{-1, +1\}$. Based on this information the orthogonal-DF computes the next counter offer $O = (p_f(t+1), p_v(t+1))$.

1. Use the orthogonal strategy to compute $O_1' = (p_f'(t), p_v'(t))$ and $O_2' = (p_f'(t-2), p_v'(t-2))$, i.e., the points in the (p_f, p_v) plane which generate $U(t+1)$ utils and lie closest to O_1 and O_2, respectively.
2. Compute d_1 and d_2 the distance of the opponent's last two offers, i.e., $d_1 = ||O_1 - O_1'||$ and $d_2 = ||O_2 - O_2'||$ ($|| \cdot ||$ denotes Euclidian distance).
3. Update s_{dr}: whenever $d_1 > d_2$ the orthogonal-DF "turns", i.e., $s_{dr} = -1 \cdot s_{dr}$, otherwise $s_{dr} = s_{dr}$.
4. Update δ: decrease δ whenever the orthogonal-DF turns. For a number of periods directly after a turn δ is not increased, and otherwise δ is increased (cf. [7] for the details).
5. Compute the counter offer $O = (p_f(t+1), p_v(t+1))$: set $p_v(t+1) = p_v'(t) + \delta \cdot s_{dr}$. Next choose $p_f(t+1)$ such that given $p_v(t+1)$ the counter offer generate $U(t+1)$ utils.

4.1 Agent Preference Settings

We simulate the negotiation with a variety of customer and seller preferences, expressed by the agents' utility functions. The *customer agent*'s expected utility depends on ρ the total number of articles the customer expects to read in the low quality of service categories (see also Section 3.1). The value ρ is assumed to be a constant, set randomly between 1 and 20 at the beginning of the experiment. Note that this results in a linear iso-utility curve in the (p_f, p_v) plane (see e.g. Fig. 5). Furthermore, since the purpose is to demonstrate the efficiency of the final deals reached, we set the customer agent's mandate b_{max} for the bundle such that an agreement is always reached.

The expected utility (i.e., expected revenue) for the *seller agent* is based on ρ, the expected number of articles that the customers will read *on average* in the low quality categories. In contrast to the customer agent, the expectation is not a constant but a function of the variable price p_v. It is assumed that customers who are willing to pay a high variable price are expected to read less than customers with a low variable price (i.e. we assume the law of demand holds cf. [?]). In the experiments we use the linear function $\rho(p_v) = b - a \cdot p_v$ with $b = 20$ and a set randomly between 0.03 and 0.07 at the beginning of an experiment. Note that the seller's iso-utility curve is now convex (towards the origin).

4.2   Concession Strategies

The customers and the seller can each select their own concession strategies. Although a seller's concession in the main system can depend on the behavior of all customers (i.e., one-to-many), in the experiments the seller agent's strategy is simply to decrease the desired utility level or *aspiration level* with a fixed amount each round. The initial aspiration level is randomly varied. Note that the number of customers and their behavior does not affect the seller's concession when this strategy is used.

On the customer side, on the other hand, we implemented four classes of concession strategies to investigate the robustness of the Pareto search strategy:

1. *Hardhead.* The customer agent does not concede when this strategy is used; the aspiration level remains the same during the negotiations.
2. *Fixed.* A fixed amount c in utils is conceded each round.
3. *Fraction.* The customer concedes the fraction γ of the difference between the current desired utility level and the utility of the opponent's last offer.
4. *Tit-for-tat.* This strategy mimics the concession behavior of the opponent, based on subjective utility improvement. If the utility level of the seller's offers increases, the same amount is conceded by the customer. Note that it is the increment in the utility level perceived by the customer. The seller's actual concession is shielded from the customer agent, as an improvement could also occur when the seller moves along his iso-utility curve. Furthermore, note that the perceived utility improvement could also be negative. To make the concession behavior less chaotic, no negative concessions are made by the customer.

4.3   Results

The seller and the customer in the experiments negotiate in an alternating fashion until an agreement is reached. The efficiency of the agreement is then evaluated based on the distance of the final offer from a Pareto-efficient solution. We measure an offer's distance from a Pareto-efficient solution as the maximum possible utility improvement for the customer if a Pareto-efficient offer was made, all else remaining equal. To evaluate the quality of the results we compare the outcomes using various search strategies and concession strategies of the customer. Table 1 provides an overview of the results. The row labeled *Random* contains the outcomes when both seller and customer use a random search strategy. This strategy selects a random point on the iso-utility curve[4]. The distance of the final offer (from the closest Pareto-efficient solution), when random search is used, lies between 1 and 3 percent of the total costs.

Although the inefficiency with random search is only small compared to the total costs, even better results are obtained when one bargainer (typically the customer) uses orthogonal search and the other (the seller) uses orthogonal-DF (i.e., orthogonal search combined with a derivative follower). The results

---

[4] Only the downward sloping part of the seller's iso-utility curve is used.

Concession strategy	Random search	Orthogonal/DF search	DF/DF search
hardhead	18.92 (±23.56)	**8.03 (±11.44)**	18.63 (±32.81)
fixed ($c = 20$)	26.52 (±34.49)	**10.43 (±17.34)**	28.82 (±46.71)
fixed ($c = 40$)	38.91 (±49.72)	**16.21 (±23.84)**	44.29 (±69.76)
fixed ($c = 80$)	42.12 (±56.88)	**25.61 (±38.72)**	48.84 (±72.12)
fraction ($\gamma = 0.025$)	30.26 (±38.37)	**10.07 (±15.03)**	32.25 (±52.81)
fraction ($\gamma = 0.05$)	31.53 (±40.00)	**11.52 (±16.16)**	28.52 (±52.13)
fraction ($\gamma = 0.1$)	37.81 (±48.82)	**16.91 (±30.80)**	26.28 (±42.20)
tit-for-tat	72.78 (±121.35)	**59.60 (±113.27)**	56.64 (±116.82)

Table 1. Average distance from Pareto-efficient solution for various customer concession strategies (rows) and customer/seller search strategies (columns). Results are averaged over 500 experiments with random parameter settings. Standard deviations are indicated between brackets. Best results (see column *Orthogonal/DF*) are obtained if the customer and seller use orthogonal search, and the seller's search is amplified with a derivative follower.

are shown in the column labeled *Orthogonal/DF* of Table 1. The improvements are considerable. The distance of the final offer as a percentage of total costs lies then, for almost all concession strategies, between 0 and 1. Only for the tit-for-tat strategy the distance lies around 1.8 percent. Notice that the Orthogonal/Orthogonal-DF strategy combination is also robust, as best results are obtained using this strategy, relatively independent of the concession strategy selected by the customer.

Table 1 also shows the results if both customer and seller use orthogonal-DF search (column *DF/DF*). These results are very similar to random, however. The derivative follower relies on a consistent response from the opponent to signal the right direction. If both use a derivative follower, this signal is distorted.

Notice that the average distance depends on the concession strategy used by the customer. Although in individual cases Pareto-efficient agreements (with zero distance) are reached using the orthogonal/DF search, the average distance consistently shows some (usually slight) inefficiencies, even when the customer makes no concessions (i.e., the *hardhead* strategy). The reason for this is twofold. Firstly, the DF accelerates finding the efficient solution by making, at times, large steps on the iso-utility curve. At a certain point the algorithm passed the Pareto-efficient point, and then turns. This way the offers keep oscillating around the optimal point. If the concessions are sufficiently large, an agreement can be reached at a point which is less than optimal.

Secondly, the direction and step-size of the DF are based on changes in the Euclidean distance between the seller and customer offers through time. The distance can be influenced by both concessions and movements along the iso-utility curve. As the opponent's iso-utility curve is unknown, the agents are unable to distinguish between the two. This can mislead the DF whenever concessions are very large. Two possible solutions are to make either small concessions, or have intervals with no concessions allowing the search algorithm to find the best deal.

Particularly *tit-for-tat* results in a relatively high inefficiency, because of the reasons described above. Recall that tit-for-tat uses a subjective measure of the opponent's concessions. In practice, the perceived utility increments are sometimes quite large, resulting in bursts of very large concessions. If this occurs near the agreement point this can result in inefficient outcomes.

To conclude, the orthogonal/DF strategy clearly outperforms other combinations of search strategies in the experiments. Inefficiencies still occur, especially if the concessions are large. A trade-off therefore exists between reaching an agreement fast (by making large concessions) and reaching an efficient agreement.

5   Discussion

5.1   The System Revisited

In the paper, we focus on the problem of selling bundles of news items. Clearly, other types of (information) goods can also be sold through the developed system. A key question for extending the use of the system to other application areas is, however, if customers and (to a lesser degree) sellers are willing to have (autonomous) agents do the actual bargaining for them. A prerequisite would be that the traded goods have a relatively low value and transactions are conducted frequently. Consequently, the risks are low and an agent has a lot of opportunities to learn from past experience and gradually improve performance. Note that the negotiation procedure of the system does not require both seller and customer to use the same level of automation. Depending on the particular application of the system, it may be desirable for the customer to rely more or less on the assistant of the software agent.

An additional important aspect of the relevance to other application areas is the potential benefit of using such a system. The developed system appears particular suitable for selling (bundles) of goods with a high degree of personalization given relatively rapidly changing preferences (as is the case with the news items). More specifically, in the system personalization entails discriminating between customers based on the bundle price and the quality of service. Second-degree price discrimination is the economic term for this type of personalization.

In second-degree price discrimination the price depends on the quantity and/or quality of the purchased good. The distinguishing aspect of second-degree price discrimination is that customers can *self-select* the best purchase. Traditionally, customers are offered a menu of options where a tariff assigns a price to the option in the menu. The work of [8, 9] discusses algorithms which— given a particular tariff structure— learn the best tariffs on-line. They conclude that (especially in a dynamic environment) complex tariffs are generally not the most profitable strategy.

The distinguishing aspect of the developed system is that instead of having explicit tariffs customers can bargain for the most appropriate bundle tariff combination. This can result in a similar (or even higher) degree of discrimination between customers as with explicit complex tariff. In the absence of an explicit tariff structure the seller is, however, more flexible in the degree to which she discriminates. The seller does not have to a priori limit the complexity of the tariff structure. Whenever bundles of (information) goods are being offered, an additional advantage is that, by initiating the negotiation process, customers can explicitly express their interest in a particular bundle of goods. This may facilitate the process of offering customers the appropriate bundles (and consequently it may facilitate the discrimination between customers).

Possibly, bargaining leads to price discrimination based on customers' bargaining skills and not on their preferences. In the developed system this possibility is, however, reduced significantly by the fairness constraint in particular and the fact that bargaining is actually one-to-many in general.

5.2   Bargaining & Pareto Efficiency

In the system the seller agent uses the orthogonal-DF as the Pareto search strategy combined with a concession strategy. The concession strategy determines the next concession relatively independently of the ongoing bargaining process with a particular customer. The idea is that, on the one hand, bargaining with a particular customer should lead to finding the best possible deal for both parties, given the seller's desired utility level. That is, the bargaining outcome should closely approximate a Pareto-efficient solution. On the other hand, the one-to-many aspect of the bargaining process (i.e., bargaining with more than one customer) should guide the updating of the concession strategy. Thus the seller uses the disentanglement of the bargaining strategy (in a concession and Pareto search strategy) to distinguish explicitly between the one-to-many and one-to-one aspects of the bargaining process.

The experiments in Section 4 show that if a customer agent uses an orthogonal strategy as the Pareto-efficient search strategy then the bargaining outcomes will closely approximate a Pareto-efficient solution. The experiments are conducted for a variety of (customer) concession strategies, customer preferences, and seller preferences. Based on the experimental results we can conclude that any other strategy choice of a customer will probably result in less efficient outcomes. Moreover such a strategy will not influence the concession strategy of the seller (due to the independence of the concession strategy). Consequently, any alternative bargaining strategy of the customer is probably at most as good as the orthogonal strategy combined with a concession strategy that mimics the concessions of the alternative strategy. Thus, given the seller's choice of the orthogonal-DF combined with a relatively independent concession strategy, it is in a customer's best interest to choose the orthogonal search strategy combined with a concession strategy. Moreover, this choice results in (a close approximation of) a Pareto-efficient solution.

5.3   Related Work

Related to our work, in [10] a heuristic approach to finding win-win trade-offs between issues is introduced. Contracts which are similar to the opponent's offer are selected based on fuzzy similarity criteria. Their approach, however, is applied to additive utility functions with independent issues. The orthogonal search method, on the other hand, operates on a more general class of utility functions, which is widely accepted in the economic literature as a reasonable representation for ones preferences.[5] Additionally, with an orthogonal search method no (domain-specific) similarity function needs to be specified.

Another approach increasingly used to automate one-to-many negotiations is through auctions. Traditionally, auctions have focused on price as the single dimension of the negotiation. Recently, however, multi-attribute auctions have received increasing attention [11, 12]. Although our system has characteristics similar to those of auctions, bundling and negotiation of information goods have distinct properties which impede the use of current available auction designs. Mainly, a bundle is not sold just once, but can be sold to any number of customers in parallel, with varying contents and configurations. The buyers are also unaware of other buyers in the system and their offers; they perceive the negotiation to be one-on-one. Furthermore, we allow both offers and counter offers, whereas auctions typically have less symmetry.

Rather than via direct negotiation, another way to find (Pareto) efficient solutions for multi-issue problems is through a mediator, see for instance [13, 14, 15, 16]. Both parties need to reveal their preferences to the mediator. With a mediator, however, trust becomes an important issue. Furthermore, additional costs are often involved.

6   Concluding Remarks

We introduce a novel system for selling bundles of news items in this paper. Through the system, customers bargain over the price and quality of the delivered goods with the seller. The advantage of the developed system is that it allows for a high degree of flexibility in the price, quality, and content of the offered bundles. The price, quality, and content of the delivered goods may, for example, differ based on daily dynamics and personal interest of customers.

The system as developed here can take into account business related side-constraints, such as "fairness" of the bargaining outcomes. Partly due to these side-constraints (especially fairness) the actual bargaining process between seller and customers is not really one-to-one bargaining between seller and customer but instead is one-to-many (i.e., between seller and customers).

Autonomous software agents perform (part of) the negotiation on behalf of the users of the system. To enable efficient negotiation through these agents we decompose the bargaining strategies into concession strategies and Pareto search strategies. Moreover, we introduce the orthogonal and orthogonal-DF strategy:

---

[5] More specifically, with convex preferences the approach works particularly well.

two Pareto search strategies. We show through computer experiments that the respective use of these two Pareto search strategies by the two bargainers will result in very efficient bargaining outcomes. Furthermore, the system is set up such that it is actually in the best interest of the customer to have their agent adhere to this approach of decomposing the bargaining strategy into a concession strategy and Pareto search strategy.

References

[1] Amit, R., Zott, C.: Value creation in ebusiness. Strategic Management Journal **22** (2001) 493–520

[2] Bakos, Y., Brynjolfsson, E.: Bundling and competition on the internet: Aggregation strategies for information goods. Marketing Science **19** (2000) 63–82

[3] Mas-Collel, A., Whinston, M.D., Green, J.R.: Mircoeconomic Theory. Oxford University Press (1995)

[4] Webster, R.: Convexity. Oxford Science Publications (1994)

[5] Kephart, J.O., Hanson, J.E., Greenwald, A.R.: Dynamic pricing by software agents. Computer Networks **36** (2000) 731–752

[6] Dasgupta, P., Das, S.: Dynamic pricing with limited competitor information in a multi-agent economy. In Eztion, O., Scheuermann, P., eds.: Cooperative Information Systems: 7th International Conference. Volume 1906 of Lecture Notes in Computer Science., Eilat, Israel, BoopIs, Springer (2000) 291–310

[7] van Bragt, D.D.B., Somefun, D.J.A., Kutschinski, E., La Poutré, H.: An algorithm for on-line price discrimination. technical report SEN-R0213, CWI (2002)

[8] Brooks, C.H., Fay, S., Das, R., MacKie-Mason, J.K., Kephart, J.O., Durfee, E.H.: Automated strategy searches in an electronic goods market: Learning complex price schedules. In: Proceedings of the ACM Conference on Electronic Commerce, ACM Press (1999) 31–41

[9] Kephart, J.O., Brooks, C.H., Das, R.: Pricing information bundles in a dynamic environment. In: Proceedings of the 3rd ACM Conference on Electronic Commerce, ACM Press (2001) 180–190

[10] Faratin, P., Sierra, C., Jennings, N.: Using similarity criteria to make negotiation trade-offs. In: Proc. 4th Int. Conf on Multi-Agent Systems, Boston, USA, IEEE Computer Society Press (2000) 119–126

[11] David, E., Azoulay-Schwartz, R., Kraus, S.: Protocols and strategies for automated multi-attribute auctions. In: Proc. 1st Int. Joint Conference on Autonomous Agents and MultiAgent Systems. (2002)

[12] Parkes, D., Kalagnanam, J.: Iterative multiattribute Vickrey auctions. Technical report, Harvard (2002) Working paper.

[13] Ehtamo, H., Hämäläinen, R.: Interactive multiple-criteria methods for reaching pareto optimal agreements in negotiation. Group Decision and Negotiation **10** (2001) 475–491

[14] Klein, M., Faratin, P., Sayama, H., Bar-Yam, Y.: Negotiating complex contracts. Group Decision and Negotiation **12** (2003) 111–125

[15] Raiffa, H.: The Art and Science of Negotiation. Harvard University Press, Cambridge, MA (1982)

[16] Lin, R.J., cho T. Chou, S.: Bilateral multi-issue negotiations in a dynamic environment. In Faratin, P., Parkes, D., Rodriguez, J., Walsh, W., eds.: Workshop on Agent-Mediated Electronic Commerce V (AMEC V). (2003) 117–123

Two Stock-Trading Agents: Market Making and Technical Analysis

Yi Feng, Ronggang Yu, and Peter Stone

Department of Computer Sciences
The University of Texas at Austin
http://www.cs.utexas.edu/~fengyi, ryu, pstone

Abstract. Evolving information technologies have brought computational power and real-time facilities into the stock market. Automated stock trading draws much interest from both the fields of computer science and of business, since it promises to provide superior ability in a trading market to any individual trader. Trading strategies have been proposed and practiced from the perspectives of Artificial Intelligence, market making, external information feedback, and technical analysis among others. This paper examines two automated stock-trading agents in the context of the Penn-Lehman Automated Trading (PLAT) simulator [1], which is a real-time, real-data market simulator. The first agent devises a *market-making* strategy exploiting market volatility without predicting the exact direction of the stock price movement. The second agent uses technical analysis. It might seem natural to buy when the market is on the rise and sell when it's on the decline, but the second agent does exactly the opposite. As a result, we call it the *reverse* strategy. The strategies used by both agents are adapted for automated trading. Both agents performed well in a PLAT live competition. In this paper, we analyze the performance of these two automated trading strategies. Comparisons between them are also provided.

1 Introduction

With the arrival of the information era, major stock markets such as the NASDAQ are now electronic. The NASDAQ is a distributed trading system completely run through networked computers. It allows customers' best bids and offers to be displayed and represented on the NASDAQ by their brokers or through ECNs (Electronic Crossing Networks), which are electronic trading systems that match buy and sell orders automatically. ECNs such as Island [2], Archipelago [3] and Bloomberg [4] allow customers to display their orders and also allow customer orders to be traded with each other.

ECNs are easy to use, and available to everyone, yet they are not risk-free platforms for customers to test their trading strategies. There are a lot of simulators developed for use without risking money in real markets. The Stock Market Game [5] is a simulator that enables participants to discover the risks and rewards involved in decision-making. Virtual Stock Exchange [6] is another

P. Faratin et al. (Eds.): AMEC 2003, LNAI 3048, pp. 18–36, 2004.

simulator that participants can use to build and manage a virtual portfolio. The Penn-Lehman Automated Trading (PLAT) simulator [1] uses real-world, real-time stock market data available over modern ECNs. It is the first simulator to incorporate complete order book information, thereby allowing it to "match" agent orders with real-world orders and simulate the resulting effects on the market. It also provides APIs so that the participants can program their strategies and trade with other agents and outside markets automatically.

Using these and other simulators, as well as experiments in the real world, many researchers have studied trading strategies from the perspectives of Artificial Intelligence [7,8,12], neural networks [9,10], technical analysis [11], etc., However, experimenting in the real world is expensive and most simulators differ significantly from real markets such that strategies successful in simulation may not be appropriate for real markets. PLAT is among the most realistic simulators because it both includes real-time, real-world data, and realistically models the effects of the agents' own trades on the market. Thus, we think some interesting, potentially applicable conclusions can be reached based on agent experiments in PLAT.

In this paper, we present two successful automated stock-trading strategies that we have implemented and tested in PLAT. The first agent implements a *market-making* strategy which exploit market volatility without considering the directions of price movement at all. The second one uses technical analysis. It might seem natural to buy when the market is on the rise and sell when it's on the decline, but the second agent does exactly the opposite. As a result, we also call it the *reverse* strategy.[1]

The remainder of this paper is organized as follows. In section 2, the PLAT simulator is described. In section 3 and 4, we describe the agent strategies and analyze their performances. In section 5, we present detailed empirical results, including results from a PLAT live competition and from controlled experiments over a 10-day period. Finally, comparison between these two strategies and further work are discussed in section 6.

2   The PLAT Simulator

The PLAT simulator uses real-world, real-time stock market data for automated trading. It frequently queries the Island ECNs web-site to get the most recent stock prices and buy and sell order books. The simulator then matches the buy orders and sell orders. The orders can be from Island or from trading agents. The simulator also computes the profits and losses of each connected trading agent in real time.

PLAT is equipped for testing strategies on historical data and also for running live competitions. The live competition starts and ends at the same time as normal trading sessions of the NASDAQ. The simulator supports limit orders only. A limit order is a request to buy or sell shares of a stock at a specified

---

[1] Similar strategies have been termed "contrarian."

price. In the simulation, the best ask price is the lowest price any seller (either trading agents or outside market customers) has declared that they are willing to accept; the best bid price is the highest price any buyer has declared that they are willing to pay. If a new buy order has bid price equal to the best ask price or a new sell order has ask price equal to the best bid price, the order will be matched in the amount of the maximum available shares and the trade is executed. If a bid price is higher than the ask price, the trading price is the average of these two prices. If orders cannot be matched immediately, they are kept in the queue to wait for possible future matches.

Currently, The PLAT simulator is hardwired to Microsoft Stock (Symbol: MSFT). Trading agents in the simulation can buy or sell MSFT stocks with limit orders. There are two types of sales supported in the simulation: long and short. Long sales are what we normally think of when we think of selling, that is, sales of stocks owned by the seller. Short sales are sales of stocks borrowed by the agents from the simulator. Trading agents can also borrow money from the simulator without any interest, however, the same amount of money will be deducted from the agent's simulated cash account. The cash in the account can be negative or positive. The value that a trading agent has in the simulation is calculated in real time by the formula: *value = cash + holdings * current Price*. The cash and holdings are set to 0 at the beginning of the simulation.

The PLAT simulator differs from real markets in several ways:

- There is some time lag in the simulator either due to the server being overloaded or the lag of the data available from the Island ECNs. Resourceful trading agents could potentially derive some advantage from gaining access to a faster real-time data source, but to our knowledge nobody has done so.
- There are no commission or tax charges in the PLAT simulation. Transactions can be executed without any fees. In the real market, too many transactions will increase the overhead cost.
- The trading in PLAT is fully automated, meaning that once strategies are fixed, participants cannot intervene during the trading day.

Our proposed strategies utilize the fact that there are no commission or tax charges in the simulation, and places orders as frequently as possible. In the following sections, we describe two agent strategies and analyze under what market conditions they can make profits.

3   The Market Making Strategy

In this section, we describe our market making strategy and discuss its performance in detail. Several variations of the original strategy are also suggested.

3.1   Basic Approach

The market making strategy we developed exploits the price volatility of a stock, rather than predicting the direction of its movement. It has some similarity with so called "pairtrade", which buys (goes long) a stronger stock and sells (goes short) a weaker stock by research on individual companies. Instead of trading on two different stocks, our market making strategy will place a pair of buy and sell orders of the same volume on a single stock simultaneously, without predicting the stock's future movement. However, we believe that the price of the stock will have a lot of fluctuations, i.e., going up and down frequently during the trading day. The price of the buy order we place will be likely lower than the the current price, while the price of the sell order will be higher. When the price goes beyond our sell order's price, the sell order matches. Then when the price drops back down below the price at which we sold, we will gain profit from the short position. If the price drops down enough and reaches our buy order, we will then buy back with the same number of shares. At that point, we will establish a neutral market position and obtain a profit according to the trade volume and the price gap between our two orders. Similarly, the idea works equally well if the price drops down first and then goes up.

Here is an intuitive example of how this strategy works. Suppose the current price of stock A is $20.00. We place a buy order of 100 shares at $19.00 and a sell order of 100 shares at $21.00. When the price goes beyond $21.00, our sell order trades and we gain a short position of 100 shares. Obviously, when the price drops back down below $21.00, our short position will gain profit. If the price drops down enough to reach $19.00, our buy order trades and now we have a neutral position. The profit we gain is 100 * ($21.00 - $19.00) = $200.00. We place such pairs of orders at every tick of the simulator throughout the trading day. Although we typically use much smaller margins, we expect that with the abundant micro-variation of the stock price, we will be able to accumulate profits over the trading day. Figure 1 demonstrates how our agent works during the simulation.

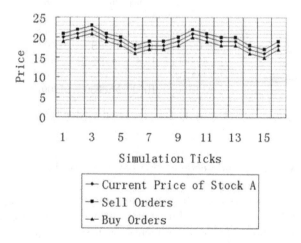

Fig. 1. The Basic Idea of Market Making

A crucial question for this market making strategy is at what price should we place the orders. Note that if we place the order pair far away from the current market price, the orders are unlikely to be executed; on the other hand, if the order pair is too close to the current price, which means they are close to each other, our profit will be compromised. A natural first approach is to use "fixed gaps" related to the current price to set the orders' prices, for example placing the buy order at a price of 0.02 lower than the current price, and the sell order at price of 0.02 higher than the current price. Asymmetric fixed gaps may also be used. But fixed gaps are inflexible and may fail to capture the characteristics of the current market.

After experimenting with a number of fixed gaps, it became apparent that our method is indeed sensitive to the magnitude of the gap. Furthermore, due to the difference in prices and trading patterns for different stocks, it is likely that this value would need to be tuned anew for each different stock. Here we introduce a method for choosing the gaps dynamically based on the current order books. We expect that placing orders with reference to the existent orders in both the buy and sell books will be more robust to a variety of trading scenarios. If and when PLAT expands to include more than one stock we plan to test this hypothesis explicitly. Our strategy currently takes in a parameter n, which varies from 1 to the number of the existent orders. The orders will be placed immediately in front of the nth order in both queues. For example, the buy order we insert will be at $0.0001 higher than the price of the nth buy order, while the sell order will be at $0.0001 lower than that of the nth sell order. Table 1 shows a snapshot of the first five orders in both buy and sell order books where the order book oriented market making strategy is used with $n = 2$. The orders in bold outline are the virtual orders placed in the simulator by our strategy, while the others are the real orders in the market.

Buy Order Book		Sell Order Book	
Price	Volume	Price	Volume
24.0360	500	24.0700	350
24.0061	**1000**	**24.0889**	**1000**
24.0060	1500	24.0890	600
24.0010	800	24.0950	2000
23.9700	1000	24.0950	1200

Table 1. Buy and Sell Order Books

Table 2 gives the pseudo-code of this basic approach. Note that the volume in the order is also an important parameter.

In principle, n is a good candidate for automatic tuning using machine learning techniques. We leave that for future work. Here we use a value of $n = 1$ for the competition and controlled experiments discussed in later sections.

---

while time permits:
buyReferencePrice ← getBuyOrderPrice(n) + 0.0001;
placeOrder(BUY, buyReferencePrice, volume);
sellReferencePrice ← getSellOrderPrice(n) - 0.0001;
placeOrder(SELL, sellReferencePrice, volume);

Table 2. The Order Book Oriented Market Making Strategy

3.2 Performance Analysis

When using the market making strategy, we expect that our agent will accumulate profit when the stock price has a lot of fluctuation over the trading day. If all trades match, our profits are the average differences between prices of the order pairs times the number of the simulation ticks. The ideal situation for our strategy is when the end price of a day is very close to the start price. That means we can have our share position close to neutral, and more pairs of our orders executed. On the contrary, if the stock price moves drastically in one direction (either high or low) and doesn't come back before the end of the day, our strategy will lose money. This becomes clear after some microanalysis. For the simple example we discussed above, when the price drops below $19.00, our buy order will trade and we will have a long position of 100 shares. If the price keeps dropping and never comes back, the value of the 100 shares will be less than $1,900.00 and we will be losing money. Intuitively, such situation will propagate in our strategy, when the price keeps dropping and we keep placing orders. Figure 2 and Figure 3 are the price charts of MSFT on March 21st and March 24th, 2003, which are examples of a "good" day and a "bad" day towards the strategy respectively.

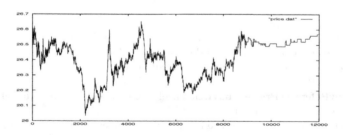

Fig. 2. March 21st 2003, A "Good" Day

Based on the market making strategy we are using, our agent tends to get into a large short position if the price goes up consistently; on the other hand, a large long position if the price goes down stiffly. Either of these situation will lead to a loss in value, according to the discussion above. Furthermore, the value will be at the mercy of the huge position, and the profit accumulated by our strategy will be dominated by it. That is, for instance, if we hold a lot of volume

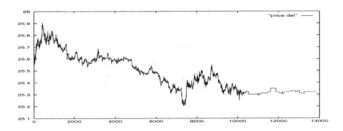

Fig. 3. March 24th 2003, A "Bad" Day

and the stock price goes down, our resulting losses dominate the small profits we get from each matched pair of trades. To mitigate such a problem, we can try to prevent our holdings from going to one extreme or the other. We have designed two methods, which are based on the two most important characters of an order - price and volume, to achieve a better control on our share position.

Our original approach sets the pair of orders at "semi-symmetric" price, placing orders right in front of the nth order in both queues. In order to keep our share position from going to one extreme, we can vary the price of the orders to encourage the opposite trades. For instance, if we now have a large positive holding, we may lower the price of the sell orders calculated by the original method, to encourage sell trades to happen, and vice versa. We name this the *price control method*. A new positive floating point parameter, priceEncouragement, is introduced to accomplish this task. It will encourage the opposite trade according to the current position in a continuous way. The pseudo-code of the price control method is given in Table 3. The currentPosition, which can be a positive or negative integer, records the current holdings of the agent.

```
while time permits:
    buyReferencePrice ← getBuyOrderPrice(n) + 0.0001;
    sellReferencePrice ← getSellOrderPrice(n) - 0.0001;
    currentPosition ← getAgentCurrentPosition()
    if currentPosition < 0
        buyReferencePrice ← buyReferencePrice - currentPosition * priceEncouragement
    elseif currentPosition > 0
        sellReferencePrice ← sellReferencePrice - currentPosition * priceEncouragement
    placeOrder(BUY, buyReferencePrice, volume);
    placeOrder(SELL, sellReferencePrice, volume);
```

Table 3. The Price Control Method

Trade volume is the other perspective from which we can manage our position. In the original method, we have equal trade volumes in every pair of orders we put into the market. However, we can alter the trade volume in both orders with regard to the agent's current share position. For example, if we have positive holdings, we may increase the trade volume of the sell order and decrease that of the buy order for the next pair we insert, and vise versa. This is the *volume control method* we propose to alleviate the huge position problem. We introduce a positive floating point parameter, volumeAlteration, to tune the trade volume of both orders in a continuous way. Table 4 shows the pseudo-code for the volume control method.

```
while time permits:
buyReferencePrice ← getBuyOrderPrice(n) + 0.0001;
sellReferencePrice ← getSellOrderPrice(n) - 0.0001;
currentPosition ← getAgentCurrentPosition()
buyVolume ← volume * (1 - currentPosition * volumeAlteration)
sellVolume ← volume * (1 + currentPosition * volumeAlteration)
placeOrder(BUY, buyReferencePrice, buyVolume);
placeOrder(SELL, sellReferencePrice, sellVolume);
```

Table 4. The Volume Control Method

We also combine the price control and the volume control methods into a new strategy, which will offer more combinations of parameters in the experiments. However, all these control methods may compromise the profit accumulated through the original strategy. This is because they either decrease the price gap between the pair of orders, or decrease the trade volume, or both. They are expected to reduce losses on some "bad days", and can be considered more conservative options of the original market making strategy. But, as demonstrated by numerous experiments, there are also exceptions where the control methods obtain larger profit or lead to bigger losses.

4   The Reverse Strategy

In this section, we first describe the basic and reverse strategies. The reverse strategy is used by the second agent. Then we analyze under what conditions the reverse strategy will make profits using a realistic but simplified price model.

4.1   Strategy Description

Our initial *basic* strategy for the second agent is as follows. At any time during the simulation, if the stock price goes up, it places a buy order; and if the stock price goes down, it places a sell order. The motivation is that a price rise indicates likely further price rises. However, initial testing of this strategy revealed that it lost money more often than it gained. As a result, we decided to flip the buy and sell order conditions. We call the resulting strategy the *reverse* strategy since it does exactly the opposite of the initial strategy. Table 5 and Table 6 show the pseudo-codes for the basic and reverse strategies.

```
while time permits:
lastPrice ← getLastPrice();
currentPrice ← getCurrentPrice();
if currentPrice > lastPrice
    placeOrder(BUY, currentPrice, volume);
elseif currentPrice < lastPrice
    placeOrder(SELL, currentPrice, volume);
```

Table 5. The Basic Strategy

```
while time permits:
lastPrice ← getLastPrice();
currentPrice ← getCurrentPrice();
if currentPrice > lastPrice
    placeOrder(SELL, currentPrice, volume);
elseif currentPrice < lastPrice
    placeOrder(BUY, currentPrice, volume);
```

Table 6. The Reverse Strategy

The reason that the reverse strategy makes profits in many kinds of market is that stock market prices are not constant and in fact undergo frequent changes in direction, rather than moving consistently in one direction. On most trading days, there are a lot of small spikes in the stock price chart. Figure 4 shows such an example. Under these conditions, we expect to make profits with the reverse strategy, as described in the next subsection.

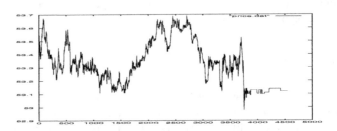

Fig. 4. MSFT Stock Price: Dec. 20, 2002

4.2 Performance Analysis

For any fixed strategy (other than the degenerate do-nothing strategy), there are some market conditions in which it will make money and some under which it will lose money. We analyze the performance of the basic and reverse strategy based on what we think are realistic, though simplified, assumptions about the price trajectories. We assume that the price of MSFT oscillates consistently in a wave pattern around a constant price p. We call the microvariation of the price (the wave's amplitude) during the trading day δ. Figure 5(a) illustrates such a price trend. We also assume that all orders placed in buy queues and sell queues will be matched at some point during the trading day (perhaps immediately). In our analysis, we assume that the start price is $p - \delta$. The start price is not crucial to the analysis since if it's not $p - \delta$, we can ignore the first several ticks until we have the price $p - \delta$. Tables 7 and 8 show the calculations of the changes in holdings, cash and value for the basic and reverse strategy in one cycle. Each time we place a sell order or buy order, the volume size is v.

time	price	action	holding	cash	value
t_0	$p - \delta$	—	0	0	0
t_1	p	buy	v	$-vp$	0
t_2	$p + \delta$	buy	$2v$	$-2vp - v\delta$	$v\delta$
t_3	p	sell	v	$-vp - v\delta$	$-v\delta$
t_4	$p - \delta$	sell	0	$-2v\delta$	$-2v\delta$

Table 7. The Basic Strategy over One Cycle.

time	price	action	holding	cash	value
t_0	$p - \delta$	—	0	0	0
t_1	p	sell	$-v$	vp	0
t_2	$p + \delta$	sell	$-2v$	$2vp + v\delta$	$-v\delta$
t_3	p	buy	$-v$	$vp + v\delta$	$v\delta$
t_4	$p - \delta$	buy	0	$2v\delta$	$2v\delta$

Table 8. The Reverse Strategy over One Cycle

From Tables 7 and 8, we can see that the basic strategy loses $\$2v\delta$ in one cycle. After k cycles, it loses $\$2vk\delta$. On the other hand, the reverse strategy earns $\$2vk\delta$: the value increases linearly over time.

Although the preceding calculation relies on a very restrictive model of market dynamics, it is a pattern that seems to be reasonably representative of reality. Next, we will consider a relaxation to our initial price trajectory assumption: the price of MSFT oscillates around a constant price p.

As is apparent from Figure 4, it is much more common that the price oscillates around a line with a non-zero slope than that it oscillates around a constant price. We define the price trend as a line: $y = ax + b$. a is the slope, while x is the time elapsed from the start of the simulation, which is measured by the number of simulation ticks. If the tick number is odd, price=y. If it is divisible by 4, price $= y - \delta$. If it is even, but not divisible by 4, price $= y + \delta$. Figure 5(b) illustrates such a price trend. Table 9 shows the calculation of the reverse strategy. In the simulation, δ is always positive, while a can be positive or negative. Since the basic strategy does the exact opposite of the reverse strategy, we omit the calculation.

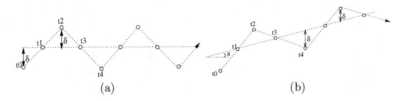

(a)   (b)

Fig. 5. Different price trend models: (a) shows the initial model in which the price oscillates consistently in a wave pattern around a constant price. (b) extends the model to allow for the price to oscillate around a line with non-zero slope.

time	price	action	holding	cash	value
t_0	$b - \delta$	—	0	0	0
t_1	$a + b$	sell	$-v$	$v(a + b)$	0
t_2	$2a + b + \delta$	sell	$-2v$	$v(3a + 2b + \delta)$	$v(-\delta + a)$
t_3	$3a + b$	buy	$-v$	$v(b + \delta)$	$v(\delta - 3a)$
t_4	$4a + b - \delta$	buy	0	$2v(\delta - 2a)$	$2v(\delta - 2a)$

Table 9. The Calculation of the Reverse Strategy: Linear Model

There is one additional assumption in Table 9's calculation: $\delta > |a|$, guaranteeing that the price actually oscillates around the line, rather than moving consistently in one direction. After k cycles, the value of the reverse strategy is $\$2vk(\delta - 2a)$. Combining this formula with the preceding assumption, we see that if $-\delta < a < \delta/2$, the reverse strategy makes a profit in the linear model; otherwise it loses money. Note that If $a = 0$, the result degenerates to that of the constant price model, as expected. Note also that this analysis can be easily extended to the case where the underlying price trajectory is *piece-wise linear*: each line segment can be considered independently.

In general, if the price trend is not biased, i.e. the price goes up and down consistently, the reverse strategy will make profits, otherwise, it will lose money.

5   PLAT Live Competition and Experimental Results

In this section, we present detailed empirical results demonstrating the behavior of our agent strategies under real market conditions. First, we describe their performances in a PLAT live competition that included several agents in addition to our two agents. Then we present several experiments run on historical data with only our own agents participating separately.

The PLAT live competition was held over 15 trading days from February 24th to March 18th 2003. It averaged the performance over many simulations to get more reliable indications of the performances of the trading strategies. The competition was structured as a 3-week, 3-round tournament with one week (5 trading days) for each round. The participants were 25 students with strong interests in the project. In the first round, 13 teams were formed and divided into two pools: the red pool and the blue pool. The total returns for the first round were aggregated and the three top scoring teams from each pool advanced to the second round. In the second round, the 6 remaining teams were run in a single simulation. The top two performing teams in the second round met in the finals. In order to limit the divergence of the simulation from the real market, each agent was restricted to maintain holdings within 100,000 of 0 (positive or negative). Violations were grounds for disqualification from the competition.

The market making strategy used by the first agent included the price control mechanism with priceEncouragement=0.01. For the second agent using the reverse strategy, we set our trade volume to 1000 shares per order in the competition. This volume size was chosen without detailed experimentation on the one hand to be as large as possible, but on the other hand in the hopes that it was small enough that orders would be matched fully. We also introduced a simplified holding control mechanism to avoid violating the 100,000 share limit. When the holdings exceed 85,000 or are lower than -85,000, the reverse strategy stops placing buy orders or sell orders respectively until the holdings are back to a normal level. If the absolute value of holdings exceeds 95,000, the reverse strategy cancels all the orders placed in the buy queue or the sell queue.

In the first round of the PLAT live competition, the market- making strategy was placed in the red pool, and was Team 8. The reverse strategy was placed in the blue pool and was Team 5. Tables 10 and 11 show the results from the first round. Team 11 in the red pool was disqualified after three trading days because of repeated and extreme violation of the share position limit. Team 7 had third-place earnings in the red pool, but was disqualified for its share position limit violations three times in five days. The red pool qualifiers were Teams 12, 8 (our market-making strategy) and 13. The blue pool qualifiers were Teams 4, 5 (our reverse strategy) and 1.

Team	24-Feb	26-Feb	27-Feb	28-Feb	3-Mar	total	Rank
Team 1	-479	3711	17603	1278	-266	21847	3
Team 2	334	2841	-53	-464	338	2996	5
Team 3	1046	3845	1980	379	1644	8894	4
Team 4	100557	-3104	-7314	-1642	-4360	84137	1
Team 5	**12489**	**26357**	**-4304**	**12236**	**-346**	**46432**	**2**
Team 6	-15228	-79442	-2052	4218	-20816	-113370	6

Table 10. PLAT Live-data Competition Round 1, Blue Pool. (Team 5: our reverse strategy)

Team	24-Feb	26-Feb	27-Feb	28-Feb	3-Mar	total	Rank
Team 7	-23935	20338	20791	50949	-28460	39683	3
Team 8	**-9590**	**8200**	**79008**	**21357**	**-20795**	**78180**	**2**
Team 9	2243	4414	6038	2103	3072	17870	6
Team 10	532	-2915	38396	-549	-3088	32376	5
Team 11	-4141632	-3434560	-31561216	N/A	N/A	N/A	7
Team 12	20187	29090	54001	7208	16673	127159	1
Team 13	-15066	8572	42734	25170	-26168	35242	4

Table 11. PLAT Live-data Competition Round 1, Red Pool. (Team 8: our market-making strategy)

The six qualifiers advanced to the second round, facing off in a single pool over a five-day trading period to determine the two finalists to meet in the third round. The second round ran from March 5th to March 11th 2003. Table 12 shows the results of the second round.

Team	5-Mar	6-Mar	7-Mar	10-Mar	11-Mar	total	Rank
Team 8	**22433**	**18640**	**-35475**	**-9826**	**-4156**	**-8384**	**4**
Team 12	-14840	27982	-28438	13257	23120	21081	1
Team 13	-4223	17731	-40912	-18271	21933	-23742	5
Team 1	-563	-395	-967	-776	-486	-3187	3
Team 4	-6700	6	-30608	83	-135	-37354	6
Team 5	**11095**	**12105**	**-21931**	**10399**	**-9979**	**1689**	**2**

Table 12. PLAT Live-data Competition Round 2. (Team 5: our reverse strategy; Team 8: our market-making strategy)

The two top scoring teams (Teams 12 and 5) from the second round advanced to the finals. They were the only two teams in the black after the second round competition. Table 13 shows the result of the third round competition.

Team	12-Mar	13-Mar	14-Mar	17-Mar	18-Mar	total	Rank
Team 12	-54156	-79233	-21896	-18032	-886	-174203	2
Team 5	**-33382**	**-54611**	**6915**	**-71397**	**26304**	**-126171**	**1**

Table 13. PLAT Live-data Competition Round 3. (Team 5: our reverse strategy)

Despite big losses in the third round due in part to some uncommon price patterns, our reverse strategy lost less money than our competitor, and won the competition. The fact that the relative rankings of team 5 and 12 change could be a result of several different factors. For one thing, the economy is different without the other agents participating. In addition, the real market differed during the two runs. In particular, the market was very bullish during the finals, a condition that, ironically, hurt both agents, but agent 12 slightly more.

Figures 6 and 7 show the performance of the reverse strategy on two trading days during the finals. First, on Mar. 17, 2003, Wall Street had its best day since Oct. 2002. However, it was a disaster for our reverse strategy. The MSFT stock price increased consistently on that day, which, as per our analysis, is the worst case scenario for the reverse strategy. As a result, we lost a lot of (simulated!) money. In contrast, on Mar. 18, 2003, The MSFT price roughly oscillated around a constant line, and our reverse strategy finished in the black.

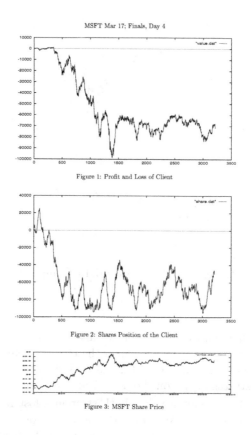

Figure 1: Profit and Loss of Client

Figure 2: Shares Position of the Client

Figure 3: MSFT Share Price

Fig. 6. Reverse Strategy in PLAT Live-data Competition Round 3, Mar. 17, 2003

The market making strategy also did well at the beginning of the Round 2 in the competition. This strategy too favors a trade day with lots of price fluctuation and relatively small difference between starting and ending price. Figures 8 and 9 show the performance of the maket makeing strategy on March 6th and 7th during Round 2.

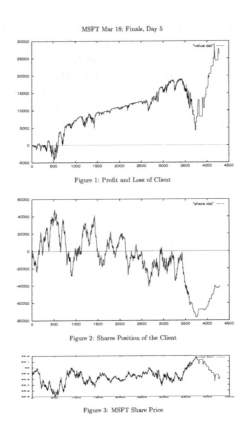

Figure 1: Profit and Loss of Client

Figure 2: Shares Position of the Client

Figure 3: MSFT Share Price

Fig. 7. Reverse Strategy in PLAT Live-data Competition Round 3, Mar. 18, 2003

Besides the live-data competition, we also did some historical experiments with our agent strategies. Table 14 shows the results. Column 2 shows the value of the market-making strategy and Column 3 shows the value of the reverse strategy. Both strategies ran on the historical dates separately.

From Table 14, we can see that both strategies lost money some days and made profits on other days. We did our experiments on dates from Mar 21st to April 3rd 2003. We chose these dates before seeing the results and report all of the results here. The MSFT stock price endured high variability during these days due to the affairs related to the war in Iraq. We expect the performances of our agent strategies to be much better if the MSFT stock price is more stable and consistent. Meanwhile, risk control mechanisms should be emphasized to make the strategies more adaptable and profitable.

The price control, volume control and combined control methods for the market making strategy were also tested during the same period. There are small differences between the implementations of the control parameters and

DATE	Market Making	Reverse
Mar21, 2003	25557	7730
Mar24, 2003	-30845	-21602
Mar25, 2003	-4742	-4504
Mar26, 2003	28453	-5525
Mar27, 2003	5856	-21932
Mar28, 2003	13174	-7146
Mar31, 2003	8520	-3489
Apr01, 2003	31144	6500
Apr02, 2003	-34444	6087
Apr03, 2003	-31938	30929

Table 14. Historical Experiments

those described in the pseudo-codes in Section 3, since we need to cope with the position limit imposed by the PLAT live competition. In the price control method and the combined control method, the price of the buy orders is calculated as follows:

buyReferencePrice ← buyReferencePrice -

currentPosition / positionLimit * priceEncouragement

And the trade volume of the buy orders in the volume control method and the combined control method is calculated as follows:

buyVolume ← volume * (1 - currentPosition / positionLimit * volumeAlteration)

Similar changes are applied to the sell orders in each control method. For all the tests, we used 1000 shares as the volume parameter. 0.01 was used as the priceEncouragement parameter, which implies the largest possible price encouragement will be 0.01 when the share position is at the limit. We picked 0.5 as the volumeAlteration parameter, which implies the largest possible volume alteration will be 500 shares when the share position is at the limit, according to the 1000 shares volume. These parameters were all chosen based on our own informal observations during preliminary testing. They were not tuned extensively. The results are shown in Table 15 with the original strategy.

DATE	Original MM	Price Control	Volume Control	Combined Control
Mar21, 2003	25557	41553	40085	41030
Mar24, 2003	-30845	-23751	-34957	-23139
Mar25, 2003	-4742	-20407	-15353	-20884
Mar26, 2003	28453	12191	28402	9573
Mar27, 2003	5856	-16540	5489	-6504
Mar28, 2003	13174	-1036	1526	-2134
Mar31, 2003	8520	7148	8933	15085
Apr01, 2003	31144	24121	27028	26620
Apr02, 2003	-34444	-15797	-31844	-25801
Apr03, 2003	-31938	-23900	-36376	-34720

Table 15. Experiments on Variations of Market Making Strategy

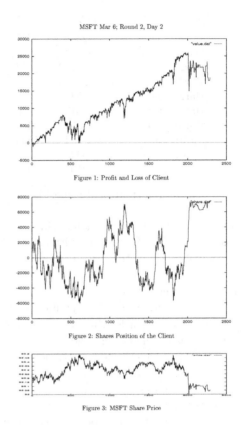

Fig. 8. Market Making Strategy in PLAT Live-data Competition Round 2, Mar. 06, 2003

From Table 15, we can see that normally all the variations of market making strategies behave similarly – either all ending in red or all ending in black. However, exceptions such as Mar 27th and 28th do exist. Overall, no strategy dominates all the others. They offer a good variety when we trade with market making strategies.

6   Discussion and Future Work

The market making strategy and the reverse strategy use different approaches in the PLAT simulator, yet they both performed well in the PLAT live competition. They both utilize the fact there are a lot of small spikes in the MSFT price chart, and make profits little by little when placing each order or pair of orders. The market making strategy is a complicated strategy using order book information which is the unique feature of the PLAT simulator.

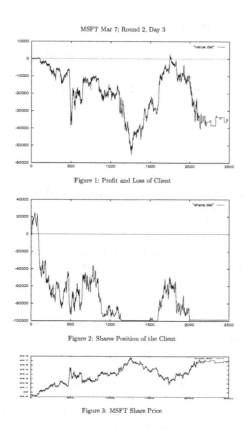

Figure 1: Profit and Loss of Client

Figure 2: Shares Position of the Client

Figure 3: MSFT Share Price

Fig. 9. Market Making Strategy in PLAT Live-data Competition Round 2, Mar. 07, 2003

In the PLAT simulation, there are no tax or commission charges. We utilize this fact and place buy orders and sell orders as frequently as possible. For real markets, there may exist commission or tax charges each time a transaction is executed. Since these charges are entirely predictable in our models, it is a simple matter to compare expected profits of these two strategies against expected charges. When the latter exceeds the former, then these two strategies should not be used.

We have limited information about the strategies used by other agents in the PLAT competition. but some keywords used to describe them on the website [13] are "crossover moving average," "intersecting the geometric trend," "case-based learning," and "Static Order Book Imbalance."

From the historical experiments, we can see that both strategies are less adaptable to external factors like important live news release. We hope that we can use the external data indication as risk control mechanism for both of these two strategies in the future.

7   Acknowledgments

We thank Professor Michael Kearns and his PLAT group at the University of Pennsylvania for their development of the PLAT simulator and for allowing us to participate in the competitions. This research was supported in part by NSF CAREER award IIS-0237699.

References

1. The Penn-Lehman Automated Trading Project. Michael Kearns and Luis Ortiz. *IEEE Intelligent Systems* 18(6):22–31. November/December 2003.
2. Island: http://www.island.com
3. Archipelago: http://www.tradearca.com
4. Bloomberg: http://www.bloomberg.com
5. The 2002 annual report of Securities Industry Foundation for Economic Education, 2001: http://www.sia.com/about_sia/pdf/annual2002.pdf
6. Virtual Stock Exchange: http://www.virtualstockexchange.com
7. R. Freedman et. al., eds., *Artificial Intelligence in Capital Markets*, Chicago, IL: Probus Pub., 1995.
8. A. Skabar and I. Cloete. "Discovery of Financial Trading Rules." In *Proc. Artificial Intelligence and Applications*, pp. 121-125, 2001.
9. J. Kingdon. *Intelligent Systems and Financial Forecasting*. New York, NY: Springer, 1997.
10. R. Donaldson and M. Kamstra, "Forcast Combining With Neural Networks", *Journal of Forecasting*, vol. 15, No. 1, pp.49-61. 1996.
11. M. Sheimo. *Stock Market Rules: 50 of the most widely held investment axioms explained, examined and exposed*, Chicago, IL: Probus Pub., 1991.
12. P. Stone and A. Greenwald, "The First International Trading Agent Competition: Autonomous Bidding Agents". Electronic Commerce Research 5(1), 2005 (To appear).
13. The Penn-Lehman Automated Trading Project: http://www.cis.upenn.edu/~mkearns/projects/pat.html

Acquiring Tradeoff Preferences for Automated Negotiations: A Case Study

Xudong Luo, Nicholas R. Jennings, and Nigel Shadbolt

School of Electronics and Computer Science
University of Southampton
Southampton SO17 1BJ, United Kingdom
{xl,nrj,nrs}@ecs.soton.ac.uk

Abstract. A wide range of algorithms have been developed for various types of automated negotiation. In developing such algorithms the main focus has been on their efficiency and their effectiveness. However, this is only part of the picture. Agents typically negotiate on behalf of their owner and for this to be effective, the agent must be able to adequately represent their owners' preferences. However, the process by which such knowledge is acquired is typically left unspecified. To remove this shortcoming, we present a case study indicating how the knowledge for a particular negotiation algorithm can be acquired. Specifically, we devise new knowledge acquisition techniques for obtaining information about a user's tradeoffs between various negotiation issues and develop knowledge acquisition tools to support this endeavour.

1 Introduction

Negotiation—the process by which a group of agents come to a mutually acceptable agreement on some matter—is a key form of interaction in multi-agent systems. Given its importance, a wide range of models have been developed; these include models for auctions, direct one-to-one negotiations, and argumentation-based encounters (see [20] for an overview). To date, however, research in this field has been almost exclusively concerned with the development of efficient and effective algorithms that enable agents to be successful and obtain acceptable outcomes. While this is clearly important, it is only part of the picture. In most cases, agents negotiate on behalf of their owner (which may be an individual or an organisation). For this to be effective, agents must be able to adequately represent their owners' interests, preferences, and prejudices in the given domain such that they can negotiate faithfully on their behalf. However, at this time, little thought has been given to the problems of exactly what knowledge an owner needs to impart to their agent in order to achieve high fidelity negotiation behaviour, and how such knowledge can be effectively acquired from the owner. These are clearly serious shortcomings of existing research that need to be addressed if negotiating agents are to be widely used.

Against this background, our research seeks to start bridging the knowledge acquisition gap between the negotiating agents' owners and the negotiation algorithms that their agents use. Specifically, in this paper we demonstrate how this

P. Faratin et al. (Eds.): AMEC 2003, LNAI 3048, pp. 37–55, 2004.

can be achieved for a particular negotiation model that we have developed [21]. This model is for bilateral multi-issue negotiations and uses fuzzy constraint satisfaction techniques to achieve Pareto-optimal results in uncertain settings. This particular model is chosen because bilateral encounters are generally among the most difficult classes of negotiations. In addition, the model is representative of the class of heuristic methods that have been applied to automated negotiation problems, and, of course, it is one with which we are familiar. However, we could equally well have chosen any other negotiation model in the literature as our point of departure.

This paper advances the state of the art in a number of ways. Firstly, we highlight importance of tackling the knowledge acquisition problem for negotiating agents. Secondly, we explore how the necessary knowledge for a particular negotiation model can be acquired. This involved devising new knowledge acquisition methods for obtaining information about a user's tradeoffs between negotiation issues (in the previous work [5], we have shown how fuzzy repertory tables can be used to acquire the issues that should be negotiated over). Thirdly, we develop knowledge acquisition tools to obtain this information.

The remainder of this paper is structured as follows. Section 2 outlines the negotiation model, paying particular attention to the preferences that the users need to impart into the agent. Section 3 proposes knowledge acquisition methods to obtain these preferences. Section 4 presents the knowledge acquisition tools we have developed and shows how they were used in an accommodation renting scenario. Section 5 discusses related work. Finally, Section 6 concludes and outlines the avenues of further research.

2   The Negotiation Model

In our model the negotiating agents represent their users' preferences as prioritised fuzzy constraints that are exchanged between the participants with the aim of coming to a mutually acceptable solution. During the course of an encounter, the agents may decide to relax some of their less important constraints in order to find an acceptable deal. The main form of information required from the users in this model is their *requirement model*. This consists of constraints that represent a user's preferences on attribute values and alternative tradeoffs between these negotiation attributes. To this end, we first outline the technical basis of our model (Section 2.1) and then specify the user's preference model (Section 2.2).

2.1   Prioritised Fuzzy Constraints

There are a number of reasons for choosing prioritised fuzzy constraints [22] to express a user's preferences. First, it is a natural representation of the negotiation problem. In many cases, buyers do not know the precise details of the products or services they want to procure, and so their preferences are often expressed by constraints on the various negotiation issues (or attributes). For example, consider the case of an international student who just arrives in the UK for the first time and who has to rent some accommodation. Since he is totally new to the country, he cannot articulate precisely the details and type of accommodation he wants, but he can express his preferences as some constraints. For example, the accommodation must be placed less than 15 minutes walk from the university,[1] the accommodation rental period should be less than one year, and the rental rate should be about £250.

Second, a user often has tradeoffs among various negotiation attributes [8, 9], and these can easily be modelled by fuzzy constraints. For example, in the accommodation renting scenario, the student might be willing to tradeoff rental rate with rental period. That is, if the accommodation is expensive, rent for a shorter period. Specifically, this can be captured by a fuzzy constraint. For example, the following may be possible tradeoffs of the user: (1) accommodation with rental rate £250 and rental period 12 months, (2) accommodation with rental rate £265 and rental period 6 months, and (3) accommodation with rental rate £325 and rental period 0.25 months (one week). Moreover, the user will typically have a preference among these potential tradeoffs and this can be represented by assigning a degree of satisfaction to the alternatives (e.g., tradeoff (1) may have a high degree of satisfaction, whereas tradeoff (3) might be the least preferred and so have a correspondingly lower satisfaction degree).

Third, often there is an ordering over preference constraints [6]. For example, the student may care more about getting a reasonable walking distance than an exact rental period, and may care more about these two constraints than the one expressing the tradeoff between rental rate and rental period. Such orderings can be captured by assigning priorities to the various fuzzy constraints.

In addition, according to human negotiation theory [6, 9], performing negotiation on single point solutions (those are what the negotiating agent wants) can be viewed as *positional bargaining*, while revealing the constraints (that need to be met) to the negotiation partner can be viewed as *interest-based negotiation*. In human negotiations, usually interest-based negotiations are better than positional bargaining (the detailed discussion about the reasons can be found in [6, 9]). Generally speaking, even a small set of constraints can correspond to a large set of possible solutions. Thus, automated negotiation systems that perform over sets of possible solutions are more efficient than ones that perform over single point solutions, one at a time.

We now express these concepts more formally (see [21, 22] for full details).

Definition 1 *A prioritised fuzzy constraint satisfaction problem (PFCSP) is defined as a 4-tuple* (X, D, C^f, ρ), *where:*

(1) $X = \{x_i \mid i = 1, \cdots, n\}$ *is a finite set of* variables.
(2) $D = \{d_i \mid d_i$ *is the domain on which the variable* x_i *takes values,* $i = 1, \cdots, n\}$ *is a finite set of all* domains *associated with each variable in* X.
(3) C^f *is a set of* fuzzy constraints:

---

[1] Notice that crisp constraints are a special case of fuzzy constraints.

$$C^f = \left\{ R_i^f \,|\, \mu_{R_i^f} : \left(\prod_{x_j \in var(R_i^f)} d_j \right) \to [0,1], i = 1, \cdots, m \right\}, \tag{1}$$

where $var(R_i^f)$ denotes the set of variables of fuzzy constraint R_i^f, and $\mu_{R_i^f}$ is R_i^f's satisfaction degree function[2].

(4) $\rho : C^f \to [0, \infty)$ is a priority function. This function puts the constraints into order of importance so that the most important ones have the highest value.

Definition 2 *The assignment of value v to a variable x, denoted as v_x, is said to be a label of the variable. A compound label $v_{X'}$ of all variables in set $X' = \{x_1', \cdots, x_m'\} \subseteq X$ is a simultaneous assignment of values to all variables in set X'. That is:*

$$v_{X'} = (v_{x_1'}, \cdots, v_{x_m'}). \tag{2}$$

For a fuzzy constraint R_i^f and a compound label $v_{var(R_i^f)}$, $\mu_{R_i^f}(v_{var(R_i^f)})$ is the *satisfaction degree* of $v_{var(R_i^f)}$ with respect to R_i^f. Intuitively, this expresses how well a solution covering multiple issues is satisfied by a particular choice of value assignment value of constraint variables.

2.2   User's Preference Model

The model of a user's domain knowledge consists of two main components. Firstly, it has some basic factual information about the user. For example, in the accommodation renting scenario, the user might want the flat to be furnished, to have an Internet connection and to allow pets. This information can be obtained using relative standard knowledge acquisition techniques (as we showed in [5]) and is not explored further in this paper. The second type of information relates to the user's preferences with respect to negotiation alternatives and outcomes. This information is represented as a PFCSP (see Definition 1) and is the main focus of this study.

In more detail, the user's preferences from the accommodation rental scenarios of Section 2.1 can be represented as a PFCSP (X, D, C^f, ρ) where:

(1) X is the set of attributes of the accommodations:

$$X = \{distance, rate, period\}.$$

(2) Domains $d_1, d_2, d_3 \in D$ are the set of possible values of attributes *distance* (minutes), *rate* (pounds) and *period* (months):

$$d_1 = \{0, 3, 6, 9, 12, 15, 18, 21, 24, 27, 30\},$$

---

[2] This function indicates how well a given constraint is satisfied. The bigger its value the more satisfied the value indicates. In particular, 1 indicates completely satisfied and 0 indicates not satisfied at all.

$$d_2 = \{0, (0, 250], (250, 260], (260, 270], (270, 280],$$
$$(280, 290], (290, 300], (300, 310], (310, 320],$$
$$(320, 330], (330, \infty)\},$$
$$d_3 = \{0, 1/4, 1/2, 1, 2, 3, 4, 5, 6, 8, 12, 13\}$$

(3) C^f is the set of fuzzy constraints that express the buyer's preferences on the attributes of the desired accommodation:

$$C^f = \{R_1^f, R_2^f, R_3^f\},$$

where:

- for the distance-from-study constraint (R_1^f), the satisfaction degree function $\mu_{R_1^f} : d_1 \to [0, 1]$ is given by:

$$\mu_{R_1^f}(0) = 1, \mu_{R_1^f}(3) = 1, \mu_{R_1^f}(6) = 1, \mu_{R_1^f}(9) = 1,$$
$$\mu_{R_1^f}(12) = 1, \mu_{R_1^f}(15) = 1, \mu_{R_1^f}(18) = 0, \mu_{R_1^f}(21) = 0,$$
$$\mu_{R_1^f}(24) = 0, \mu_{R_1^f}(27) = 0, \mu_{R_1^f}(30) = 0;$$

- for the rental-period constraint (R_2^f), the satisfaction degree function $\mu_{R_2^f} : d_3 \to [0, 1]$ is given by:

$$\mu_{R_2^f}(0) = 1, \mu_{R_2^f}(1/4) = 1, \mu_{R_2^f}(1/2) = 1, \mu_{R_2^f}(1) = 1,$$
$$\mu_{R_2^f}(2) = 1, \mu_{R_2^f}(3) = 1, \mu_{R_2^f}(4) = 1, \mu_{R_2^f}(6) = 1,$$
$$\mu_{R_2^f}(8) = 1, \mu_{R_2^f}(12) = 1, \mu_{R_2^f}(13) = 0;$$

- for the rental rate-period tradeoff constraint (R_3^f), the satisfaction degree function $\mu_{R_3^f} : d_2 \times d_3 \to [0, 1]$ is given by

$$\mu_{R_3^f}((0, 250], 12) = 1, \mu_{R_3^f}((250, 260], 8) = 0.9,$$
$$\mu_{R_3^f}((260, 270], 6) = 0.8, \mu_{R_3^f}((270, 280], 4) = 0.7,$$
$$\mu_{R_3^f}((280, 290], 3) = 0.6, \mu_{R_3^f}((290, 300], 2) = 0.4,$$
$$\mu_{R_3^f}((300, 310], 1) = 0.3, \mu_{R_3^f}((310, 320], 1/2) = 0.1,$$
$$\mu_{R_3^f}((320, 330], 1/4) = 0.1, \mu_{R_3^f}((330, \infty), 0) = 0.$$

(4) Each constraint $R_i^f \in C^f$ is associated with a *priority* $\rho(R_i^f) \in [0, +\infty)$:

$$\rho(R_1^f) = 0.42, \quad \rho(R_2^f) = 0.35, \quad \rho(R_3^f) = 0.23.$$

This means the user cares most about being an appropriate distance from their study place, then about the period for which the accommodation is rented, and least about the rate-period tradeoff constraint.

Given these constraints, it is clear that a proposal for accommodation with the compound label:

$$(distance, rate, period) = (3, 250, 12)$$

is more acceptable (satisfactory) than one that has the label:

$$(distance, rate, period) = (18, 270, 6).$$

The big problem, however, is to devise acquisition methods that can be used to extract the above information from users. This is the topic of the following sections.

3   The Acquisition Methods

This section presents a straightforward method to acquire, from a human buyer, his preference constraints (*e.g.*, R_1^f, R_2^f and R_3^f) and their relative priorities (*e.g.*, $\rho(R_1^f)$, $\rho(R_2^f)$ and $\rho(R_3^f)$). Each is dealt with in turn.

3.1   Acquiring Preference Constraints

According to standard business negotiation theory [32, 39], the preferences of human negotiators should be extensively explored before the actual negotiation begins. One common technique for doing this is to play simulated negotiation games in which various negotiation scenarios are enacted against various human negotiation partners. Such role playing aims to explore the negotiation space as fully as possible and to tease out the negotiator's real preferences and tradeoffs.

Building upon these intuitions, we view the process of acquiring constraints as a negotiation game in which the knowledge acquisition system plays the role of the negotiation partner. Specifically, the system randomly generates an assignment value for each negotiation attribute (from the domain of the attribute). The system then asks the user whether it is acceptable or not, and further adjusts the assignment until it becomes unacceptable/acceptable. In this way, we acquire some base line data for each negotiation issue (*e.g.*, distance should be less than 15 minutes and rental period should be less than a year). Now, in many cases the negotiation attributes are interlinked and the user needs to make tradeoffs between them. To acquire such information, firstly the system asks the user to assign ideal values to all the attributes. It then makes one of these ideal values worse and asks the user to adjust the other attributes to balance. Moreover, the user is asked to assign a satisfaction degree to each tradeoff alternative. This process is repeated for each of the rest of the negotiation attributes. In this way, the system can acquire the preferences of various tradeoffs that exist between the different attributes. More precisely, the interaction procedure between the system and a user can be described as follows:

Step 1. For each attribute x_i, repeat the following steps:

> **Step 1.1.** The system randomly generates an assignment v_{x_i} to to attribute x_i of the negotiation object and shows this to the user.

> **Step 1.2.** The user tells the system whether the assignment v_{x_i} is acceptable or not.

> **Step 1.3.** In the case that the user regards the assignment v_{x_i} as acceptable, the system gradually decreases[3] the value of attribute x_i from v_{x_i} until it becomes unacceptable. In the case that the user regards the assignment v_{x_i} as unacceptable, the system gradually increases the value of attribute x_i from v_{x_i} until it becomes acceptable. In the case that the user cannot determine whether the assignment v_{x_i} is acceptable or not, the system does nothing.

> **Step 1.4** The system further asks the user whether he prefers enter an intermediate acceptance degree μ for each value of each attribute.[4] If yes, it lets the user to do it; otherwise, the acceptable values are assumed to have 100% as their acceptance degree, and the unacceptable values are assumed to have 0% as their acceptance degree.

Step 2. The system asks the user to give an ideal assignment $(v_{x_1}^{(ideal)}, \cdots, v_{x_n}^{(ideal)})$ to the attributes $(x_1, \cdots, x_n)$.

Step 3. The system changes the ideal assignment $v_{x_i}^{(ideal)}$ of an attribute x_i to a worse assignment v'_{x_i}, and then asks the user to adjust the assignment of some other attributes $x'_1, \cdots, x'_m \in X$ from $(v_{x'_1}^{(ideal)}, \cdots, v_{x'_m}^{(ideal)})$ to $(v'_{x'_1}, \cdots, v'_{x'_m})$ in order to compensate (balance) the change of the assignment to x_i. Furthermore, the user is asked to assign a satisfaction degree μ to the assignment $(v'_{x'_1}, \cdots, v'_{x'_m}, v'_{x_i})$ of attributes $x'_1, \cdots, x'_m, x_i$.

Step 4. The system changes the assignment v'_{x_i} of attribute x_i to an even worse assignment v''_{x_i}, and then asks the user to adjust the assignment of the other attributes $x'_1, \cdots, x'_m$ from $(v'_{x'_1}, \cdots, v'_{x'_m})$ to $(v''_{x'_1}, \cdots, v''_{x'_m})$ in order to compensate (balance) the change of attribute x_i. Again the user is asked to indicate an associated satisfaction degree μ to the assignment $(v''_{x'_1}, \cdots, v''_{x'_m}, v''_{x_i})$ of attributes $x'_1, \cdots, x'_m, x_i$.

Step 5. Repeat step 4 until the system cannot change any attribute's value to a worse one or the user can no longer specify any tradeoffs.

---

[3] We assume the set of all possible values for each attribute are ordered linearly.

[4] When estimating uncertainties, people are often reluctant to provide real numbers chosen from a predefined range. Instead they feel more comfortable with a qualitative estimate [23, 30, 44] (*i.e.*, a linguistic term). So, this is what our system offers. A linguistic term usually corresponds to a fuzzy set [43]. However, for simplicity and consistency with the negotiation model (where the regular framework of fuzzy constraints, instead of the linguistic framework of fuzzy constraints [19], is employed), the system automatically maps these linguistic terms to numbers in [0, 1]. That is, *completely satisfactory* to 100%, *very satisfactory* to 90%, *highly satisfactory* to 80%, *generally satisfactory* to 70%, *satisfactory* to 60%, *neutral* to 50%, *unsatisfactory* to 40%, *generally unsatisfactory* to 30%, *highly unsatisfactory* to 20%, *very unsatisfactory* to 10%, and *completely unsatisfactory* to 0%.

Step 6. For the remaining attributes, the system repeats steps 3-5 until no more attributes are left or the user cannot specify any more such preferences on tradeoffs between attributes.

Although the workload of the above method for users is heavy if all possible combinations of many attributes[5] need to be explored, it is significant for the following reasons:

- The method is feasible in many situations of practical applications. This is because in the practice tradeoffs do not exist among an arbitrary combination of attributes and so human users need not explore all possible combination of negotiation attributes. In fact, human negotiation theory [38, 39, 41] have identified which attributes tradeoffs usually exist between for a specific type of negotiations. For example, in business negotiations, usually tradeoffs exist between *price* and *quality*, between *price* and *quantity*, and so on. Moreover, human negotiations often focus on such pairwise exchanges [38] and so our method that acquires tradeoffs via changing assignment of a single attribute is simple and good. In addition, in human negotiations a tradeoff among more than two attributes are often realised by two tradeoffs between two attributes.[6] For example, a tradeoff among *price*, *quality*, and *quantity* can be realised by two tradeoffs: (1) one between *price* and *quality* and (2) another between *price* and *quantity*. That is, for instance, first make *quality* worse to get *price* down, and then increase *quantity* to get *price* down further when the *quality* cannot be made any more worse.
- This can motivate the further work that aims at reducing the workload (the work in the coming sections is motivated by this). A lot of heuristic methods for eliciting user preferences [13, 15, 14, 11, 35, 16, 7] has been motivated by reducing high cost of elicitation. Thus, like that used in heuristic elicitation of user preferences, neural networks, case based reasoning and inductive learning methods are alternative techniques for reducing elicitation workload of user tradeoff preference. This is similar to that although the first solving algorithms of Bayesian networks [31] and constraint satisfaction problems [24] are NP-hard, they motivate and serve as baseline of further work.

3.2   Acquiring Constraint Priorities

Having acquired constraints of tradeoff preferences, the next step is to assign them a relative priority (see Definition 1). The most common method to elicit priorities of items is the fuzzy pairwise comparison method [40] (it is based on the intuitions that a common way for people to grasp a group of items is to compare them in a pairwise fashion). For our case, the items are constraints. Thus, the method of pairwise comparison is as follows. Firstly, ask the user to

---

[5] For n attributes the number of all combination among which tradeoffs could exist is $2^n - n - 2$.

[6] Of course, it is not always the case. We will seek to remove this limitation in subsequent work.

compare each pair of constraints and tell the system how much more important one constraint is than the other. Then the priority of the constraint can be determined by aggregating the levels of relative importance of that constraint when compared with those of all the other constraints.

There are a number of methods (each with their relative advantages and disadvantages) for aggregating the level of relative importance of an item when compared with those of all the other items. For example, the eigenvalue method [36], the geometric mean [42], the arithmetic mean [37], the fuzzy programming method [25], and the α-cuts decomposition method [26]. Here, however, we chose the arithmetic mean because it is easy for human users to understand: (1) the sum of all the individual relative importance levels for a constraint against all the others is indicative of the total importance level of the constraint when compared with the others; and (2) the importance levels of all the constraints can then be normalised so that the user can easily fine tune the allocation of importance levels of constraints. This method for aggregating offers the simpleness and consistency with intuitions that are very important for a system's success in the real world (since deviations from these aspects lead to loss of potential users).

The procedure is defined more precisely in the following:

Step 1. The user compares constraints one by one. For each pair of constraints R_i^f and R_j^f, the user is required to determine the degree, $r_{ij} \in [0, 1]$,[7] to which R_i^f is: (1) more important than R_j^f if $r_{ij} > 0.5$; (2) equally important as R_j^f if $r_{ij} = 0.5$, and (3) less important than R_j^f if $r_{ij} < 0.5$. Then, the degree, r_{ji}, to which R_j^f is more or less important than R_i^f is given by:

$$r_{ji} = 1 - r_{ij}. \tag{3}$$

In particular, when i=j, the system sets:

$$r_{ij} = 0.5 \tag{4}$$

(since the same constraint should be equally important). Then the following matrix is obtained:

$$R = (r_{ij})_{n \times n}, \tag{5}$$

where n is the number of the constraints.

Step 2. The system calculates the relative priorities of all constraints:

$$\rho(R_i^f) = \frac{\sum_{j=1}^{n} r_{ij}}{\sum_{s=1}^{n} \sum_{t=1}^{n} r_{st}}, \tag{6}$$

where $i = 1, \cdots, n$, and r_{ij} and r_{st} are elements of the comparison matrix R.

---

[7] Similar to the handling of assessing constraint satisfaction degrees, our system can also provide its users with a set of linguistic terms to do this, and then internally map these terms to numbers in $[0, 1]$. That is, the system automatically maps, for example, *very much less important* to 0, *less important* to $\frac{1}{6}$, *slightly less important* to $\frac{1}{3}$, *equally important* to $\frac{1}{2}$, *slightly more important* to $\frac{2}{3}$, *more important* to $\frac{5}{6}$, and *very much more important* to 1.

4   Knowledge Acquisition Tools

To show the correctness and effectiveness of our methods in practical applications, we have implemented a prototype knowledge acquisition system. The basic
idea of the system is to visualise the alternatives since this has been shown to
be effective when there are many multi-variate options [1, 33]. Specifically, we
applied the tools to an accommodation renting scenario in which the student
seeking accommodation instructs a software agent to negotiate on his behalf
with a real estate agent. These two agents negotiate with one another (using our
algorithm [21]) to try and find a suitable accommodation for the student. In what
follows, we show how the system operates during the course of the acquisition
of the student's preferences and tradeoffs. Firstly, we deal with the acquisition
of preference constraints (Step 1 in Section 3.1).

Step 1. As shown in Fig. 1, the system randomly generates an assignment:

$$distance = 21(minute\text{-}walk)$$

and then shows it to the student.

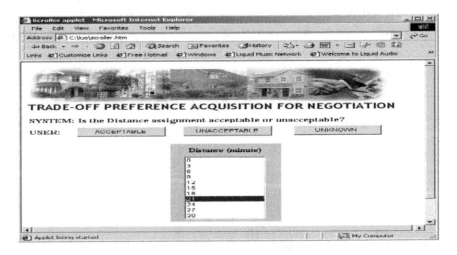

Fig. 1. Screen shot of the preference acquisition system.

Step 2. The student (user) tells the system that this assignment is unacceptable.

Step 3. The system then gradually decreases the distance value until it finds
a value that the student regards as acceptable. In this case, the value is
15 minutes. Thus, the system acquires the following distance-from-study
constraint:

$$distance \leq 15(minute\text{-}walk).$$

Step 4. The system then randomly generates an assignment for the rental rate attribute:

$$rate = (250, 260]$$

and shows it to the student.

Step 5. The student replies "unknown" to the system (since he does not want to discuss this attribute at this moment).

Step 6. The system then randomly generates an assignment for the rental period attribute:

$$period = 8(months)$$

and then shows it to the student.

Step 7. The user tells the system that this assignment is acceptable.

Step 8. The system then gradually increases the value of the rental period from 8 months until it finds the value that the user regards as unacceptable (in this case 13 months). Thus, the system obtained the following rental period constraint:

$$period \leq 12(months).$$

Having identified the individual constraints, the system now seeks to uncover the tradeoffs between the different negotiation attributes (Steps 2 to 6 in Section 3.1).

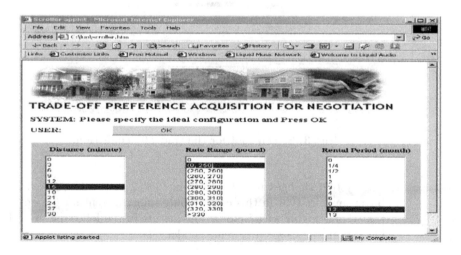

Fig. 2. Screen shot for specifying the ideal values.

Step 1. As shown in Fig. 2, the system asks the user to give an ideal assignment to all the attributes, and then the student answers:

$$(distance, rate, period) = (15, (0, 250], 12).$$

Step 2. The system changes the ideal value of distance to a worse value (*i.e.*, 18 minute walk), and then asks the student to adjust some other attributes' values to compensate for the change. However, the buyer answers that no changes can compensate. Thus, the attribute *distance* cannot be traded off.

Step 3. The system changes the ideal value of rental rate to a worse value, then asks the student to adjust some of the other attributes' values to compensate.

1. As shown in Fig. 3, the system changes the rental rate from $(0, 250]$ to $(250, 260]$. Then the buyer answers that in this case he just wants to rent for 8 months, and that this is very satisfactory. This results in the following value being inserted into his preference model:

$$((rate, period), satisfaction\text{-}degree) = (((250,260],8), very\text{-}satisfactory).$$

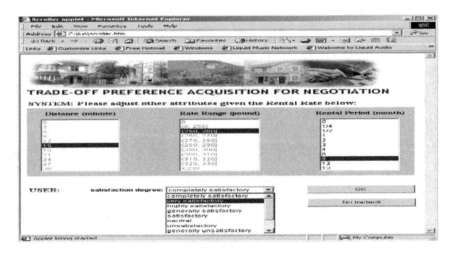

Fig. 3. Screen shot for the tradeoff acquisition.

2. The system changes rental rate from $(250, 260]$ to $(260, 270]$, then the buyer answers that in this case he only wants to rent for 6 months and that this is highly satisfactory. This results in the following value being inserted in the user's preference model:

$$((rate, period), satisfaction\text{-}degree) = (((260,270],6), highly\text{-}satisfactory).$$

This process continues for each of the other rental rate ranges until the user can no longer make any tradeoffs. The information acquired in these steps is shown in Fig. 4.

Now having acquired the constraints of the user's preferences and tradeoffs, we turn to capturing their relative priorities (as per Section 3.2).

Rate range (£)	Rental period (months)	Satisfaction degree
(0, 250]	12	100%
(250, 260]	8	90%
(260, 270]	6	80%
(270, 280]	4	70%
(280, 290]	3	60%
(290, 300]	2	40%
(300, 310]	1	30%
(310, 320]	1/2	20%
(320, 330]	1/4	10%
>330	0	0%

Fig. 4. Fuzzy tradeoffs between rate and period.

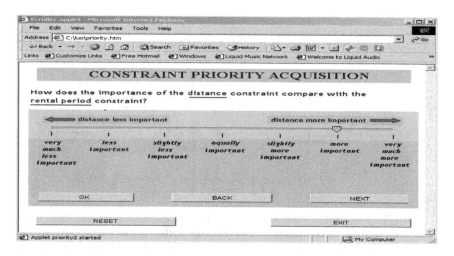

Fig. 5. Screen shot of constraint priority acquisition tool. Underlining indicates hyperlink to page where the constraint is displayed.

Step 1. As shown in Fig. 5, the user compares two randomly chosen constraints (as per step 1 in Section 3.2). This process is repeated for each pairwise combination of constraints. Then by formulas (3), (4) and (5), the system obtains the following comparison matrix:

$$R = \begin{pmatrix} \frac{1}{2} & \frac{5}{6} & \frac{1}{3} \\ \frac{1}{6} & \frac{1}{2} & \frac{5}{6} \\ \frac{1}{3} & \frac{1}{6} & \frac{1}{2} \end{pmatrix}$$

Step 2. The system then calculates the normalised priorities of these constraints (as per step 2 in Section 3.2). First, by (6) the normalised priorities of the three constraints are:

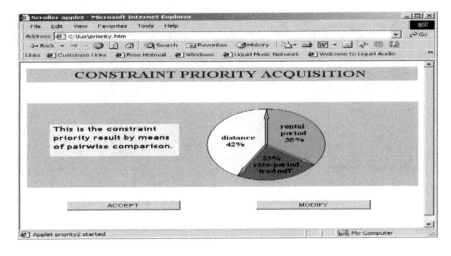

Fig. 6. Screen shot of result of constraint priority acquisition stage.

$$\rho(R_1^f) = \frac{\frac{1}{2} + \frac{5}{6} + \frac{1}{3}}{\frac{1}{2} + \frac{5}{6} + \frac{1}{3} + \frac{1}{6} + \frac{1}{2} + \frac{5}{6} + \frac{1}{3} + \frac{1}{6} + \frac{1}{2}} = 0.42,$$

$$\rho(R_2^f) = \frac{\frac{1}{6} + \frac{1}{2} + \frac{5}{6}}{\frac{1}{2} + \frac{5}{6} + \frac{1}{3} + \frac{1}{6} + \frac{1}{2} + \frac{5}{6} + \frac{1}{3} + \frac{1}{6} + \frac{1}{2}} = 0.35,$$

$$\rho(R_3^f) = \frac{\frac{1}{3} + \frac{1}{6} + \frac{1}{2}}{\frac{1}{2} + \frac{5}{6} + \frac{1}{3} + \frac{1}{6} + \frac{1}{2} + \frac{5}{6} + \frac{1}{3} + \frac{1}{6} + \frac{1}{2}} = 0.23.$$

Step 3. The user is then shown a visual representation of the relative priorities of the different constraints (see Fig. 6). If the user is happy with this outcome the acquisition phase is complete. If the user feels the outcome does not reflect their true priorities then they can modify their priority allocation until they are satisfied.

5   Related Work

The background of our work is knowledge acquisition and preference elicitation. There are many methods for acquiring knowledge from humans for knowledge-based system in general (see [17] for an overview). However, usually they do not aim at eliciting user preferences for decision making. Fortunately, there are also some methods for user preference elicitation for decision making problems. The most common ones elicit a user's preferences by means of utility functions. For instance, (1) gambling elicitation techniques [28] in which the utility of one outcome is ascertained by comparing it to a lottery involving two others; and (2) visual exploration and incremental utility elicitation [3] in which suggestions are made visually to a human user based on an incomplete model of their utility function and the model is updated based on the feedback from the user. However, the workload that users use these methods to elicit preferences can be very high. In order to address the limitation, a number of heuristic ways of acquiring preferences from users have been proposed. For example, (1) case based preference elicitation [13, 15, 14] that requires a user to provide partial information about their preference and then the system constructs the whole preference structure by choosing the most similar one in the case base of preference structure; and (2) preference elicitation via theory refinement [11, 35, 16] that starts with approximate and incomplete domain knowledge and then corrects inaccuracies and incompleteness by training on examples (*i.e.*, knowledge-based artificial neural networks are used to learn user preferences).

While a procedure of negotiation can be viewed as one of dynamic decision making over time, our tradeoff preference elicitation for negotiation is different from preference elicitation for decision making in general. In the area of preference elicitation for decision making problems, the term *preference* refers to *ordering* on a set of *alternatives* and its focus is on eliciting the *orderings* and little work is on eliciting *alternatives*. In this paper, our focus is on eliciting *tradeoff alternatives*. As to the problem of eliciting *ordering* on a set of *tradeoff alternatives* (*i.e.*, the preference on tradeoff alternative), we just use a direct rating method. In future work, we believe it is worth merging more elaborate methods for preference elicitation into our method for eliciting tradeoff alternatives.

While existing techniques for constraint elicitation have shown some success in particular contexts, they are not easily able to handle our tradeoff acquisition problem.[8] *Firstly*, a number of methods have been proposed to acquire crisp constraints. For example, [29] presents an approach to interactive constraint acquisition based on the techniques of Mitchell's *List-Then-Eliminate* method [27]. In this approach, there is a "hypothesis space" of constraints over which a general-to-specific ordering is known (or is implicit in the hypothesis space representation). Then the user's examples (where a constraint should be satisfied or violated) are used to eliminate hypotheses that are inconsistent with the examples. In this procedure, a strategy is also employed to minimise the dialog length between the user and the computer. However, this method is only applicable to crisp constraints. *Secondly*, Biso *et al.* used neural networks to tackle the problem of soft constraint acquisition [2] (fuzzy constraints are a special case of soft constraints). However, their method is used to learn the solution rating function given a fixed constraint graph and some examples of solution ratings. Thus, their method assumes the constraints are already available, and what their method learns is how to rate a solution according to the available constraints. It does not resolve the problem of how to acquire soft constraints themselves.

Perhaps the most related work to ours is that of [10] that aims to acquire tradeoffs. However, there are a number of important differences. *First*, [10] uses heuristic strategies to generate various tradeoffs and then asks the user to confirm whether they are acceptable (their aim is to improve the efficiency of the acquisition process). This approach may cause some tradeoffs to be missed in

---

[8] This is true even though in our model the users' tradeoff preferences are represented by fuzzy constraints.

complex multi-dimensional spaces and so we focus on a more systematic exploration of the whole space of possible tradeoff relations. *Second*, the method in [10] is not designed for negotiation problems, and their example scenario, the N-Queens problem, is much more objective than that typically used in negotiations. *Third*, in [10] each tradeoff is assumed to be an equal alternative (*i.e.*, users have no preference on these alternatives); whereas in this paper for different alternative tradeoffs the user has different satisfaction degrees (*i.e.*, the user has a preference on tradeoff alternatives).

Finally, in the research area of agent-based automated negotiation little work has addressed the problem of preference acquisition from human users.

- In [18, 34], different methods have been developed for one agent to elicit preferences from another agent in combinatorial auction and bilateral negotiation settings, respectively. However, they both assume that the users of agents have already imparted their preferences into the negotiating agents (the aim of our work presented in this paper). Thus, the aim of the elicitation process in [18] is to prune the auctioneer agent's search space; and in [34] the opponent's preference models are used to predict its behaviour during the course of negotiation.

- In [4], negotiation and preference elicitation are linked. However, this work is different from ours in the following aspects: (1) Its preference elicitation does not refer to user preference elicitation. Actually, it refers to a program (an automated resource manager) that elicits the preferences on resources from other programs (workload managers). Rather, the aim of our work in this paper is to elicit tradeoff preferences from users. (2) The process of its preference elicitation is viewed as a cooperative negotiation between an automated resource manager and workload managers. In other words, the motivation of its elicitation is not for a program to negotiate faithfully on behalf of its human owner (the motivation of our work in this paper). In fact, its motivation is to find near-optimal allocations of resources to distinct computing elements in large, distributed computing systems.

- In our work [5], the most valuable contribution is that it can acquire seller's rewards and restrictions to products, but user tradeoff preference elicitation is involved little there. Acquiring buyer's tradeoffs between negotiation issues is the focus of this paper. So, they are complementary to each other.

- The work [12] employs an evolutionary algorithm to address the problem of preference elicitation in form of utility functions. However, there term *preference* is general rather than tradeoff preference. As a result, it cannot easily be distinguished from the general research area of user preference elicitation.

6   Conclusions and Future Work

This paper adds the dimension of user knowledge acquisition to the research area of automated negotiation. To our best knowledge, it is the first attempt to formally investigate methods for eliciting user tradeoff preferences in order for an autonomous agent to negotiate faithfully on their behalf. This is fundamental to this and other negotiation models but has been addressed little in area of general knowledge acquisition and user preference elicitation. In particular, we developed appropriate knowledge acquisition methods and tools to get at the information. Our preliminary (and informal) evaluation of the methods and the tools indicate that they are effective in their task, but for the future a more systematic evaluation is needed. This evaluation needs to address two facets of the knowledge acquisition problem for negotiating agents. Firstly, can the base data on which negotiation objects operate be successfully obtained from users? Secondly, once this base line has been established, is the user happy with the outcomes that the negotiating agent prefers and the tradeoffs that were made on their behalf? Further work is also needed to see whether the knowledge acquisition system can proactively suggest different attributes to tradeoff. For example, based on knowledge about inter-relationships between negotiation attributes (which may be obtained via data mining techniques), the tool may automatically suggest that a product's price can be traded off against its quality, quantity or way to pay (e.g., installment, cash, and credit card). Finally, work is needed to determine if there are knowledge requirements that are common to many negotiation algorithms and, if so, what knowledge acquisition methods can be applied to these broad classes of requirements.

Acknowledgements

The work is supported by Hewlett Packard Research Labs. Authors are also obliged to Partha S. Dutta for his proof-reading an earlier version of this paper.

References

[1] C. Ahlberg and B. Shneiderman. Visual information seeking: Tight coupling of dynamic query filters with starfield display. In *Human Factors in Computing Systems: Conference Proceedings CHI'94*, pages 313–317, 1994.

[2] A. Biso, F. Rossi, and A. Sperduti. Experimental results on learning soft constraints. In Anthony G. Cohn, F. Giunchiglia, and B. Selman, editors, *KR2000: Principles of Knowledge Representation and Reasoning*, pages 435–444, San Francisco, 2000. Morgan Kaufmann.

[3] J. Blythe. Visual exploration and incremental utility elicitation. In *Proceedings of the Eighteenth National Conference on Artificial Intelligence*, pages 526–532, 2002.

[4] C. Boutilier, R. Das, J.O. Kephart, G. Tesauro, and W.E. Walsh. Cooperative negotiation in autonomic systems using incremental utility elicitation. In *Proceedings of the Nineteenth International Conference on Uncertainty in Artificial Intelligence*, pages 89–97, Acapulco, Mexico, August 2003.

[5] J.J. Castro-Schez, N.R. Jennings, X. Luo, and N.R. Shadbolt. Acquiring domain knowledge for negotiating agents: A case of study. *International Journal of Human Computer Studies*, 2004. To Appear.

[6] S.P. Cohen. *Negotiating Skills for Managers*. McGraw-Hill, 2002.

[7] M. Dastani, N. Jacobs, C.M. Jonker, and J. Treur. Modeling user preferences and mediating agents in electronic commerce. In F. Dignum and C. Sierra, editors, *Agent Mediated Electronic Commerce: The European AgentLink Perspective*, volume 1991 of *Lecture Notes in Artificial Intelligence*, pages 163–193. Springer, 2001.

[8] P. Faratin, C. Sierra, and N.R. Jennings. Using similarity criteria to make issue tradeoffs in automated negotiations. *Artificial Intelligence*, 142(2):205–237, 2002.

[9] R. Fisher and W. Ury. *Getting to yes: Negotiating an agreement without giving in*. Random House Business Books, 1981.

[10] E.C. Freuder and B. O'Sullivan. Generating tradeoffs for constraint-based configuration. In *Proceedings of the Seventh International Conference on Principles and Practice of Constraint Programming*, pages 590–594, 2001.

[11] B. Geisler, V. Ha, and P. Haddawy. User modeling via theory refinement. In *Proceedings of the International Conference on Intelligent User Interface*, pages 87–90, 2001.

[12] Y. Guo, J.P. Muller, and C. Weinhardt. Learning user preferences for multi-attribute negotiation: An evolutionary approach. In J. Muller, V. Marik, and M. Pechoucek, editors, *Multi-Agent Systems and Applications III*, volume 2691 of *Lecture Notes in Artificial Intelligence*, pages 303–313. Springer, 2003.

[13] V. Ha and P. Haddawy. Toward case-based preference elicitation: Similarity measures on preference structures. In *Proceedings of the Fourteenth International Conference on Uncertainty in Artificial Intelligence*, pages 193–201, 1998.

[14] V. Ha and P. Haddawy. Similarity of personal preferences: Theoretical foundations and empirical analysis. *Artificial Intelligence*, 146(2):149–173, 2003.

[15] V. Ha, P. Haddawy, and J. Miyamoto. Similarity measures on preference structure, Part II: Utility functions. In *Proceedings of the Seventeenth International Conference on Uncertainty in Artificial Intelligence*, pages 186–193, 2001.

[16] P. Haddawy, V. Hu, B. Geisler, and J. Miyamoto. Preference elicitation via theory refinement. *Journal of Machine Learning Research*, 4:317–337, 2003. Special Issue on Fusion of Domain Knowledge with Data for Decision Support.

[17] R.R. Hoffman and N.R. Shadbolt. Eliciting knowledge from experts: A methodological analysis. *Organizational and Human Decision Process*, 62(2):129–158, 1995.

[18] B. Hudson and T. Sandholm. Effectiveness of preference elicitation in combinatorial auctions. In J. Padget, O. Shehory, D. Parkes, N. Sadeh, and W.E. Walsh, editors, *Agent-Mediated Electronic Commerce IV: Designing Mechanisms and Systems*, volume 2531 of *Lecture Notes in Computer Science*, pages 69–86, 2002.

[19] R. Kowalczyk. On linguistic fuzzy constraint satisfaction problems. In L.A. Zadeh and J. Kacprzyk, editors, *Computing with Words in Intelligent Information Systems*, pages 305–321. Physica-Verlag, 1999.

[20] A.R. Lomuscio, M. Wooldridge, and N.R. Jennings. A classification scheme for negotiation in electronic commerce. *International Journal of Decision and Negotiation*, 12(1):31–56, 2003.

[21] X. Luo, N.R. Jennings, N. Shadbolt, H.F. Leung, and J.H.M. Lee. A fuzzy constraint based model for bilateral, multi-issue negotiation in semi-competitive environments. *Artificial Intelligence*, 148(1-2):53–102, 2003.

[22] X. Luo, H.F. Leung, J.H.M. Lee, and N.R. Jennings. Prioritised fuzzy constraint satisfaction problems: Axioms, instantiation and validation. *Fuzzy Sets and Systems*, 136(2):155–188, 2003.

[23] X. Luo, C. Zhang, and N.R. Jennings. A hybrid model for sharing information between fuzzy, uncertain and default reasoning models in multi-agent systems. *International Journal of Uncertainty, Fuzziness and Knowledge-Based Systems*, 10(4):401–450, 2002.

[24] A.K. Mackworth. Consistency in networks of relations. *Artificial Intelligence*, 8(1):99–118, 1977.

[25] L. Mikhailov. A fuzzy programming method for deriving priorities in the analytic hierarchy process. *Journal of the Operation Research Society*, 51(3):341–349, 2000.

[26] L. Mikhailov. Deriving priorities from fuzzy pairwise comparison judgements. *Fuzzy Sets and Systems*, 134(3):365–385, 2003.

[27] T. Mitchell. Concept learning and the general-to-specific ordering. In *Machine Learning*, chapter 2, pages 20–51. McGraw Hill, 1997.

[28] J. Von Neumann and O. Morgenstern. *Theory of Games and Economic Behaviour*. Princeton University Press, 1944.

[29] S. O'Connell, B. O'Sullivan, and E.C. Freuder. Strategies for interactive constraint acquisition. In *Proceedings of CP-02 Workshop on User-Interaction in Constraint Satisfaction*, New York, 2002.

[30] S. Parsons. *Qualitative Methods for Reasoning under Uncertainty*. MIT Press, 2001.

[31] J. Pearl. *Probabilistic Reasoning in Intelligent Systems: Networks of Plausible Inference*. Morgan Kaufmann, 1988.

[32] D. Pruitt. *Negotiation Behavior*. Academic Press, 1981.

[33] P. Pu and B. Faltings. Enriching buyers' experiences: The smartclient approach. In *ACM CHI Conference on Human Factors in Computing Systems*, pages 289–296, 2000.

[34] A. Reistificar and P. Haddawy. Constructing utility models from observed negotiation actions. In *Proceedings of the Eighteenth Joint International Conference on Artificial Intelligence*, pages 1404–1405, 2003.

[35] A. Reistificar, P. Haddawy, V. Ha, and J. Miyamoto. Eliciting utilities by refining theories of monotonicity and risk. In *Working Notes of the AAAI'2002 Workshop on Preferences in AI and CP: Symbolic Approach*, 2002.

[36] T.L. Saaty. *The Analytic Hierarchy Process*. McGraw-Hill, 1980.

[37] T.L. Saaty. *Multicriteria Decision Making: The Analytic Hierarchy Process*. RWS Publications, 1988.

[38] P.T. Steel and T. Beasor. *Business negotiation: A practical workbook*. Gower Publishing Limited, 1999.

[39] I. Unt. *Negotiation Without A Loser*. Copenhagen Business School, 1999.

[40] G.C. van Kooten, R.A. Schoney, and K.A. Hayward. An alternative approach to the evaluation of goal hierarchies among farmers. *Western Journal of Agricultural Economics*, 11(1):40–49, 1986.

[41] R.J. Volkema. *The negotiation toolkit: How to get exactly what you want in any business or personal situation*. Amacom, 1999.

[42] M. Wagenknecht and K. Hartmann. On fuzzy rank ordering in polyoptimisation. *Fuzzy Sets and Systems*, 11:253–264, 1983.

[43] L. Zadeh. The calculus of fuzzy restrictions. In L.A. Zadeh et. al., editor, *Fuzzy Sets and Applications to Cognitive and Decision Making Processes*, pages 1–39. Academic Press, 1975.

[44] L.A. Zadeh. The concept of a linguistic variable and its application to approximate reasoning. Part I. *Inf. Sci.*, 8:199-249, 1975; Part II. *Inf. Sci.,*, 8:301-357, 1975; Part III. *Inf. Sci.*, 9:43-80, 1975.

A Decommitment Strategy in a Competitive Multi-agent Transportation Setting

P.J. 't Hoen[1] and J.A. La Poutré[2]

[1] Center for Mathematics and Computer Science (CWI)
P.O. Box 94079, 1090 GB Amsterdam, The Netherlands
[2] TU Eindhoven,
De Lismortel 2, 5600 MB Eindhoven, The Netherlands

Abstract. Decommitment is the action of foregoing of a contract for another (superior) offer. It has been shown that, using decommitment, agents can reach higher utility levels in case of negotiations with uncertainty about future prospects. In this paper, we study the decommitment concept for the novel setting of a large-scale logistics setting with multiple, competing companies. Orders for transportation of loads are acquired by agents of the (competing) companies by bidding in online auctions. We find significant increases in profit when the agents can decommit and postpone the transportation of a load to a more suitable time. Furthermore, we analyze the circumstances for which decommitment has a positive impact if agents are capable of handling multiple contracts simultaneously.

1 Introduction

A recent development is the investigation of application of multi-agent systems (MASs) [7, 12, 25] in the logistics of the transportation sector, a challenging area of application. The transportation sector is very competitive and profit margins are typically low. Furthermore, planning of operations is a computationally intensive task which is classically centrally organized. Such centralized solutions can however quickly become a bottleneck and do not lend themselves well to changing situations, for example incidence management, or exploiting new profitable opportunities. MASs can overcome these challenging difficulties and offer new opportunities for profit by the development of robust, distributed market mechanisms [4, 23, 14]. In this paper, we use as a model online, decentralized auctions where agents bid for cargo in a MAS logistics setting. We study a bidding strategy which is novel for such a large scale setting.

In [20, 1, 21], a leveled commitment protocol for negotiations between agents is presented. Agents have the opportunity to unilaterally *decommit* contracts. That is, they can forgo a previous contract for another (superior) offer. Sandholm *et al.* have shown formally that by incorporating this decommitment option the degree of Pareto efficiency of the reached agreements can increase as agents can escape from premature local minima by adjusting their contracts. In this paper,

P. Faratin et al. (Eds.): AMEC 2003, LNAI 3048, pp. 56–72, 2004.
© Springer-Verlag Berlin Heidelberg 2004

decommitment is the possibility of an agent to forgo a previously won contract for a transport in favor of a more profitable load.

We show in a series of computer experiments that significant increase in performance (profit) can be realized by a company with agents who can decommit loads, as opposed to a company with agents that only employ the option of regular, binding bidding. As a necessary precondition for this gain, the experiments show that decommitment is only a clearly superior strategy for an agent close to the limit of its capacity. This is a new, general result for agents capable of handling simultaneous tasks. Furthermore, the increase in performance for our (abstract) model can be seen as a lower bound for expected increased performance in practice. We substantiate this claim through experiments that show that the relative impact of a decommitment strategy increases with the complexity of the world.

The remainder of this paper is organized as follows. Section 2 presents the transportation model that we use in this paper. The market mechanism is described in Section 3. Section 4 details our application of decommitment in a market setting. Section 5 discusses a required precondition for a successful decommitment strategy by an agent capable of handling multiple tasks concurrently. The computer experiments are presented in Section 6. Section 7 contains concluding remarks.

2   The Transportation Model

In this section, we present the transportation model that is used in this paper.[3] We have kept the transportation model, the market mechanism, and the structure of the bidding agents relatively simple to keep the analysis as transparent as possible. Some extensions of the basic model are further discussed in Section 6, where we show that performance can increase significantly when a decommitment strategy is used. We expect the (positive) effect of decommitment to increase when the complexity of the transportation model increases as the uncertainty of possible future events consequently increases. In Section 6.6 we investigate some venues to substantiate this claim.

2.1   Outline

The world is a simple n by n grid. This world is populated by trucks, depots with cargo, and competing companies. The trucks move over the grid and transport cargo picked up at the depots to destinations on the grid. Each truck is coupled with an agent that bids for cargo for its "own" truck.[4] The trucks are each owned by one of the companies. The performance of a company is measured by the total profits made by its fleet of owned trucks. We consider (for simplicity and to facilitate the analysis of the model's results) that all companies consist of the same number of (identical) trucks.

---

[3] The computer model has been programmed in the Java programming language (version 1.4). We thank Stefan Blom for allowing us to use the STW cluster at CWI.

[4] In the text, we sometimes blur the line between the agent and its truck.

2.2   Profits

Poot *et al.* [15] give an extensive list of performance measures for the transportation of cargo found in literature. The indicative performance measures from this list that we consider are (i) the profit made as a function of the total number of transported loads, (ii) the profit as a function of the bulk of the transported loads, and (iii) the costs as a function of the distance traveled for the made deliveries.

2.3   Loads

Loads for pickup prior to delivery by the trucks are locally aggregated at depots. Such an aggregation procedure is for example used by UPS,[5] where cargo is first delivered to one of the nearby distribution centers. Warehousing, where goods from multiple companies are collected for bundled transport, is another, growing example. This aggregation can take place over relatively short distances or over more substantial distances (e.g., in case of international transport). In general, the origin of loads will not be randomly distributed but clustered, depending on population centers and business locations [11]. We thus also consider depots as abstractions of important population or business centers. Section 6 presents such a model.

Like most regular mail services (e.g., UPS) and many wholesale suppliers, we employ a model of "next day delivery". In the simulations, each depot has a number of loads available for transport at the start of the day. Furthermore, new orders can also arrive for transport in the course of the day.

According to [27], transportation is dominantly limited in one dimension for roughly 80% of the loads. In Europe, this dimension is volume; in the United States this dimension is weight.[17] We hence use a model where we characterize the cargo (and the carrying capacity of the trucks) in only one dimension, which we, without loss of generality, call weight.

2.4   The Trucks

The trucks drive round trips in the course of a day. Each individual truck starts from the same initial location each day, to return to this location at the end of the day. Multiple round trips on the same day are allowed as long as sufficient time remains to complete each trip the same day.

Alternative distributions of the trucks (e.g., dynamically changing over time) can of course occur in practice. Such distributions, however, significantly complicate the analysis of the model's results, especially over multiple days. Furthermore, a repeating pattern is common as population and business centers do not change dramatically overnight. In our simulations, the truck start their trips at the depots. This is in line with the tendency of companies to base their trucks close to the sources of cargo (to maximize operational profits).

---

[5] See www.ups.com.

Legal restrictions typically limit the number of hours that truck drivers can work per day. There may also be a maximum distance which can be driven in one day. In addition, speed limits need to be taken into account. We set the length of a typical working day of eight hours. We also assume (for simplicity) that the trucks travel with a constant "average" speed.

3   The Market Mechanism

Each piece of cargo is sold in a separate auction. Auctions for loads are held in parallel and can continue over several rounds. The auctions continue until all cargo is sold or until no further bids are placed by the agents in a round. After a load is sold, it awaits pickup at its depot and is no longer available for bidding.

Agents are not allowed to bid for bundles of cargo. Such a combinatorial auction type is as yet beyond the scope of our research because the number of different bidding options is huge (around 300 pieces of cargo are sometimes offered in the experiments, yielding an intractable number of bundles for each of which traveling salesman problems have to be solved.).[6] We also do not allow agents to participate simultaneously in multiple auctions with all implied complications [16, 3, 26]. An agent's valuation for a load is typically strongly dependent on which other loads are won, and at what cost.[7] For this reason, and for the sake of computational feasibility, we allow each agent to place a bid for at most one load in each round of auctions. Our agents can thus be seen as computationally and rationally bounded (in the sense of [20, 30, 22]), although they repair (some of) their non-optimal local decisions through a decommitment strategy (see Section 4).

Each piece of cargo is sold in a separate Vickrey auction. In this auction type, the highest bidder wins the contract but pays the second-highest price.[8] In our model, neither the number of participants nor the submitted bids are revealed by the auctioneer.[9] An attractive property of the one-shot (private-value) Vickrey auction is that it is a (weakly) dominating strategy to bid the true valuation for the good [29, 8].[10] Another attractive property of the Vickrey auction is that

---

[6] Determining the winners of a combinatorial auction is NP-complete. There has recently been a surge of research in this area, however. A fast algorithm for winner determination has for instance been proposed in [24].

[7] Schillo *et al.* analyzed the risk of over-bidding when participating in simultaneous auctions and propose a strategy with a constrained number of decommitments (and associated penalties).

[8] Ties are broken at random.

[9] We do not use or reveal sensitive business information in our market mechanism. When extensions of the model are considered (e.g., models where companies receive information about their competitors' actions and behavior) privacy issues should be taken into account.

[10] It is important to note here that the Vickrey auction has some known deficiencies. Furthermore, limitations of the protocol may arise when the Vickrey protocol is used for automated auctions and bidding is done by computational agents [19]. These aspects deserve further attention for future implementations.

a limited amount of communication between the auctioneer and the bidders is required (as opposed to, for example, the "open-cry" English auction).

The agents use the following strategy in each bidding round. First, they determine the valuation of each piece of cargo which is offered in an auction. The valuation of an added load is equal to added profit for this load (the amount of money which the truck receives when the load is delivered minus the additional costs associated with the new path). The application of more elaborate valuation functions can also be useful. For example, the value of a load can increase when the truck, by transporting the extra load, can move cheaply to an area of the grid with a high density of depots. Another venue of research is in the line of COIN [28, 13], where the aim would be to modify the agents' valuation function to let them more efficiently cooperate as one company. Such refinements of the agent's valuation function form an interesting topic for further studies.

There is however obviously an incentive for a company to avoid competition between its own trucks. As part of its strategy, each company therefore makes a pre-selection that determines which agents are allowed to bid for the company in each auction. In this pre-selection phase, the company compares the valuations of the company's agents for the available cargo. The agent with the highest valuation (overall) then bids (its valuation) in the proper auction. This auction is then closed for other agents of the same firm. In this manner, we eliminate the possibility that the no. 2 in the auction, who determines the price, is an agent from the same company. The company then repeats this procedure to select a second agent, which is allowed to bid in another auction, etc. Using this strategy, the agents of a company distribute themselves over a larger set of auctions than would otherwise be the case. This, in general, also increases the competition between the trucks of different companies.

4   The Decommitment Option

Contracts are typically binding in traditional multi-agent negotiation protocols with self interested agents. In [20, 23, 1], a more general protocol with continuous levels of commitment is proposed and analyzed. The key ingredient of this protocol is the option to break an agreement, in favor of, hopefully, a better deal, at the possible cost of a prenegotiated penalty. In our the experiments, an agent with a decommitment strategy can improve its immediate profits by bidding for a new load with the additional possibility to discard a load to which it committed earlier. The agent is hence more flexible in the choice of loads to choose to bid on, at the cost of discarding a previously won bid.

Trust and reputation are however of importance in the world of (electronic) contract negotiation [10, 5]. A bad track-record can, for example, lead to the shunning of a party in negotiations. How an auctioneer or a client will change its attitude towards a party which in the past has decommitted from a negotiated contract has to be quantified for specific areas of application. For example, for many bulk transports, a delayed delivery is not too detrimental as another transporter can easily be found and the transport does not have a tight delivery schedule. This is however not the case for expensive, quickly perishable goods.

In our market mechanism, we circumvent the above quantification issue. We achieve this by delivering decommitted cargo by a truck of the same company as the truck that decommitted the load (with consideration of delivery constraints). We thus "hide" the process of rejecting deals from the customer who offered the load at auction: a truck only postpones the transport of decommitted cargo until another truck of the same company becomes available. A company that uses a decommitment strategy in this fashion retains its reputation and performs according to the contract. For more complex scenario's (not considered here) where there is no "hiding" the decommitment and where a good cost function is available to quantify the impact of decommitment on trust, we however expect the benefits of a decommitment strategy to increase. The agents then have more options available to optimize their choice of loads.

The "hiding" of the decommitment strategy is achieved by internal reauctioning of loads. Decommitted cargo is once again offered in a Vickrey auction. This auction is, however, only accessible for agents of the company which should deliver the load. The auctions for decommitted cargo thus serve as internal re-sale markets for companies. Effectively, through a "hidden" decommitment strategy, tasks are redistributed between the agents of one company. Implicitly, the agents renegotiate their concurrent plans.

The bids for decommitted cargo are made in terms of "blue" (i.e., fake) money as the contract for transportation has already been won by the company. We however require that new bids for decommitted cargo (in terms of blue money) exceed the original bid costs (in terms of real or "green" money). This rule is used to ensure that the original bidding costs for winning the decommitted load in the original auction are covered. As an alternative, a decommitted load could be offered in a public auction to other companies, i.e. outsourcing, a common practice in the transportation world. The internal resale auctions of decommitted loads are held in parallel with the public auctions as experiments showed that this as a good approach to maintain a sufficient degree of competition with the other companies on the auctions for publicly available loads.

For simplicity and from a computational viewpoint, we allow agents to discard only one load in each round of bidding. Furthermore, only loads which have been won but are not yet picked up can be discarded, to avoid the possible extra cost of unloading. Decommitment is hence an administrative action.

Furthermore, we do not allow agents to decommit cargo which must be delivered today (see Section 2.1) to minimize the chance of a too-late delivery. Additionally, we have constrained the possible backlog of decommitted loads by only allowing a decommitment by an individual truck if the total number of currently unassigned, decommitted loads does not exceed the number of trucks in the company.[11] This approach leads to good results: In the computational experiments less than 0.2% of the decommitted loads were delivered too late.

---

[11] Alternative, more sophisticated heuristics are a topic of research.

Penalties for too-late delivery will hence have to be exorbitant in order to offset the benefits of decommitment presented in Section 6.

5   Conditions for Decommitment

We observe in the computational experiments that decommitment of a load occurs predominantly when trucks are close to filling their maximum capacity. To understand this result, it is useful to first consider two extreme situations: (i) an extreme shortage of available cargo and (ii) an extreme excess of available cargo (relative to the carrying capacity of the trucks).

In case of an extreme shortage of loads, a truck will not decommit a load as it has a large excess capacity: it is more profitable to add a load to a relatively empty truck than to replace one load by another one. In the other case of a large selection of loads to choose from, a new load, which (closely) fills the remaining capacity of the truck is mostly available. Again, decommitment does not occur as adding a load which fits is more profitable than fine tuning profits at the cost of another load which is dropped.

Figure 1 illustrates the impact of decommitment for a range of offered loads for a single truck to bid on. We plot the number of transported loads as a function of the number of loads presented. On the far left, the number of available loads is low. As a consequence, the available loads are almost all picked up and transported. If the production rate increases, we move to the right in Figure 1. The (positive) effect of decommitment then increases, until the trucks reach their capacity limits. On the far right in Figure 1, the number of offered loads is very high. In this case (an excess of cargo), the added value of decommitment also decreases as the maximum number of tasks that the truck is able to handle can be achieved. Note that for specific scenario's a slightly higher performance can be reached than without the use of a decommitment strategy, but in the limit of available loads (tasks) the added benefit of decommitment will disappear.

Hence, we hypothesize a decommitment strategy is most beneficial when a truck is close to reaching its maximum capacity and has a limited number of extra tasks to choose from. We believe this is a general result for an agent capable of doing multiple tasks in parallel. This hypothesis must be kept in mind when evaluating whether to apply a decommitment strategy.

In our experiments, we observe for a company with multiple trucks, the use of a decommitment strategy only has a strongly positive effect when a significant fraction of its trucks actually decommit loads. When the supply of loads during one day approximately matches the carrying capacity of the trucks, the above condition is met. We note in real-life situations that there are often economic incentives which drive the market to such a balanced situation, if supply and demand do not match. Hence, a decommitment strategy can be expected to have an impact in real markets.

In our simulations, we keep the number of companies and trucks constant when observing the performance of the companies over a number of days. In case of a balanced market, this implies that the amount of cargo which is transported

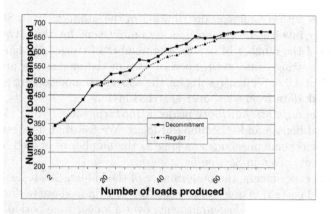

Fig. 1. The added value of decommitment for a wide range of number of offered loads for one truck. The decommitment strategy only has a strong impact for a subset of the range of number of offered loads.

per day is relatively constant. To this end, we search for an equilibrium "production" of new cargo. In a sense, this is a reversion of the normal market operation. The addition or removal of a truck is however an operation with a large impact. It is not straightforward to formulate criteria in terms of profits which make the addition/removal of a truck an issue, especially over a short time period. Furthermore, differentiation between the various companies in composition makes evaluation of the experiments non trivial. We hence set the production level at a good initial estimate and adapt towards the equilibrium for the strategy used.

We in our experiments achieve this equilibrium in supply and demand by setting the production level of loads to match the approximate carrying capacity of the trucks, while as yet not using a decommitment strategy. An initial number of loads is generated and new loads are produced in the course of the day. The level of production is chosen so as to arrive at a constant number of loads available for transport the next day (within 5% of the initial number of loads available). When this constraint is met, the number of loads and the carrying capacity of the trucks on the grid are in equilibrium over the days of the simulation. With the derived production schedules, we rerun the experiments, but with the additional possibility of a truck to decommit an earlier won bid. The performance of the regular bidding strategy versus the decommitment strategy can then be calculated.

6   Results

In this section, we study the performance of a companies who uses a decommitment strategy relative to companies which do not. Section 6.1 contains results for a Sugarscape-like model. In this model, the edges of the transportation grid are connected (to suppress boundary effects). In Section 6.2 we consider a finite-

size model with a Gaussian distribution of the production. In Sections 6.1–6.4, we further investigate the effect of decommitment for these two models (as a function of the number of depots, the number of trucks per depot, the number of decommitting firms, etc.). Special cases of the models are presented in Sections 6.5 and 6.6. Similar results for the above two models were also found using benchmark data from www.opsresearch.com and
www.sintef.no/static/am/opti/projects/top/vrp/ for
location of depots and scheduling of loads. We feel that our results hence hold for a wide scheme of settings as long as the number of offered loads meets the requirements given in Section 5.

In the experiments, the performance of the bidding strategies is tested over a period of days (15) in order to measure not only immediate performance but also the effect of a bid (or decommitment) over a longer time period. All companies place an equal number of trucks at each depot for fair competition. Unless stated otherwise, we use one truck per depot per company. See also Appendix A for settings of the experiments.

6.1   The Sugarscape Model

We first consider a "Sugarscape-like" grid [6]. Like in Sugarscape, we connect the edges of the grid (to suppress boundary effects). In addition, trucks can only move along the grid lines (i.e., they cannot move diagonally). We place the depots with equal spacing on the grid (the distance is 2 nodes); each depot also has the same production rate. With these assumptions, we obtain a highly symmetric "transportation world".

The performance of the Sugarscape model for one company without and with a decommitment strategy is summarized in Table 1 for respectively 4, 9, and 25 depots. We consider two companies in these experiments of which only one can use a decommitment strategy. In Table 1, we report the number of transported loads and the profit that is generated (in 1000 monetary units), with and without use of a decommitment strategy. Note that the grid is already filled densely in case of 25 depots (out of 100 possible locations). Competition between the two companies then becomes intense and profit margins drop as competition in the auctions increases.

6.2   A Gaussian Distribution Model

The Sugarscape transportation model of Section 6.1 is highly stylized. For example, boundary effects are suppressed by using a toroidal grid, depots are equally spaced, production is uniform, and trucks can only move along the grid lines. We investigate in this section whether the decommitment strategy also works for a transportation model which does not make these limiting assumptions.

This alternative model consists of a plain square grid. The trucks can move in arbitrary directions on the grid, as long as they do not exceed the grid's boundaries. The depots are placed at random locations on the grid. Furthermore, we do no longer assume that production is uniform. Instead, we assume that

Table 1. Results for a Sugarscape model.

depots	decommitment?	loads	profit
4	no	940	91
4	yes	987	99
increase		5%	8.7%
9	no	1826	420
9	yes	1920	446
increase		5.1%	10.6%
25	no	3704	585
25	yes	4197	627
increase		10.6%	7.1%

the spatial production rate follows a Gaussian distribution (with its peak in the center of the grid) and then assign each new load to the nearest depot for transportation[12]. Such a model is representative of a large city or a major business center which is surrounded by smaller cities or businesses [11]. The remainder of this paper discusses results obtained for this model.

Figure 2 shows the profits made by a company (with and without the use of a decommitment strategy) as a function of the number of depots on the grid. Note

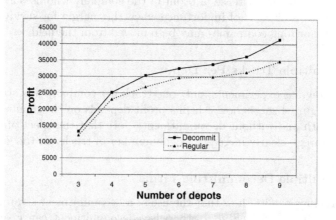

Fig. 2. Profits made by a company (with and without decommitment) as a function of the number of depots on the grid.

the positive effect of decommitment on a company's profit. This effect becomes especially large in case of a densely filled grid. In the experiments, we observed on average one decommitment per truck per day, increasing to a maximum of three per day for a densely filled grid. Results for more than two companies show similar trends for the decommitting company. Figure 3 shows that the number of transported loads also increases when a company uses a decommitment strategy.

---

[12] Production is maximized by maximizing the standard deviation of the Gaussian.

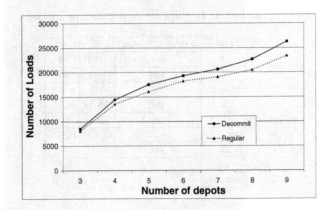

Fig. 3. Number of transported loads as a function of the number of depots on the grid. Decommitment has a clear positive effect: the number of carried loads increases significantly.

It is also important to note that the use of decommitment by one company can decrease the performance of the non-decommitting companies. This loss can amount to half the increase in profit of the company who uses a decommitment strategy. This effect is of importance when the margin for survival is small and under-performing companies may be removed from the field.

6.3   Multiple Trucks Per Depot

In the previous experiments, only one truck per company was stationed at each depot. Figure 4 shows how a firm's profit depends on the number of trucks per depot, with and without decommitment. Note that the effect of the decommitment strategy clearly increases as the number of trucks on the grid increases.

6.4   Multiple Decommitting Firms

The previous results show that the use of a decommitment strategy can be beneficial for a company. Stated otherwise, decommitment can give a company a competitive edge in an otherwise symmetric market. Intelligent opponents are, however, not static and counter measures can be expected if a firm uses a superior strategy [9, 18]. For instance, competitors can also adopt a decommitment strategy once this strategy has proven its usefulness.

We have studied what happens if multiple companies use a decommitment strategy. Experimental results show improvements for each decommitting company, as in Figs. 2 and 3. In general, it is thus attractive for a company to use a decommitment strategy. The absolute performance of the decommitment strategy increases slightly as more companies adopt this tactic. However, as can be expected, the relative increase in performance with respect to the competing companies drops with a growing number of decommitters.

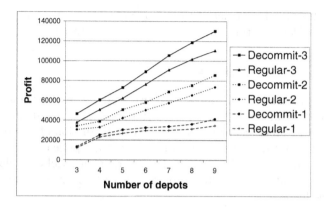

Fig. 4. Influence of the number of trucks per depot on the profit made by a company, with and without decommitment. The number of trucks per depot is indicated in the figure's key.

6.5 Depot-to-Depot Routing

An interesting modification of the transportation model is to restrict the destination of loads to depots. This is a typical scenario in a factory setting where produced items are inputs for other production processes, similar to supply chain management. Such a scenario can also be relevant in case of international transport e.g., a layered, holistic setting as discussed in [2] and [25].

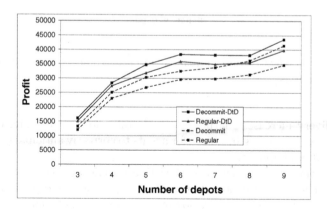

Fig. 5. The effect of decommitment in case of depot-to-depot (DtD) routing.

In Figure 5, we show results with and without depot-to-depot routing. Note that the profits increase in case of depot-to-depot routing as there is a stronger bundling in the destinations of the goods. Consequently, more efficient routes can be driven. The impact of the decommitment strategy also increases, as the shuffling of loads within an existing route is facilitated.

6.6   Alternative Settings

In this final section, we investigate two changes in the transportation model which further increase the impact of the decommitment strategy. We first consider a price function for which the correct prediction of future loads becomes more important due to a greater difference in the price of individual loads. Secondly, we investigate the impact of restricting the available information to the agents by limiting the distance over which an agent can sample the grid for available loads.

In Figure 6, we show the strong relative increase in profits when a quadratic price function is used.[13] A similar effect as visible in Figure 6 occurs if the price

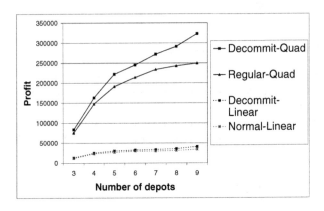

Fig. 6. The effect of decommitment in case of linear and nonlinear (quadratic) price functions.

for delivery increases sharply as the deadline for delivery approaches. In both cases there is a strong incentive for agents to correctly anticipate which profitable loads will still appear.

Additional experiments also show that the effect of decommitment increases if the truck's agents are more "myopic". Truck agents can decide to limit their bidding range due to communication overhead or a lack of computational resources. In Figure 7, we show the impact of decommitment when an agent only considers loads for pickup which are not too far away from its current location.[14] This figure shows that the absolute and relative impact of decommitment increases in

---

[13] The price for a load l is $40 + weight(l)^2 + distance(l)$, instead of the linear price function given in Appendix A.

[14] We use an operating range of one quarter of the size of the grid.

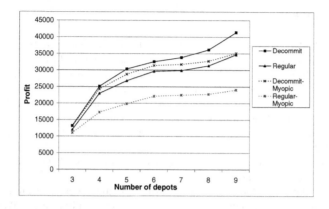

Fig. 7. The role of decommitment in case of "myopic" bidding agents.

this case, as an agent is less able to observe the available loads and thus makes less optimal choices in the course of time, which need to be repaired.

7   Conclusions and Discussion

We study the use of a decommitment strategy in case of on-line bidding for cargo by agents in a multi-company, multi-depot transportation setting. In our model, an agent bidding for a truck can decommit a load in lieu of a more favorable item of cargo. We observe significant increases in profit that scale with the size of operations and uncertainty of future prospects. The observed profit margins are significant in the competitive market of transport where a 4% profit is considered exceptional. For example, the average profit margin before taxes for the Dutch road transport sector (from 1989 to 1999) was only 1.6% [27]. Adoption of a decommitment strategy can thus give a company a significant edge.

For specific applications beyond that of our model and for novel areas, the added value of decommitment, and the circumstances where it can be applied successfully should be studied further. However, based upon our computational experiments, we hypothesize that the positive impact of a decommitment strategy increases with the complexity of the operating domain, as it then becomes of greater importance to have the opportunity to roll-back a previous sub optimal decision [21].

We also observe that decommitment has the highest impact when an agent is close to its maximum capacity for handling multiple contracts in parallel. With sufficient capacity, it is often more beneficial to add an extra contract than to replace a won contract in favor of a superior offer. Hence, for multi-agent systems where agents are capable of handling several tasks simultaneously, a decommitment strategy can be expected to have its largest impact when the agents are operated at (almost) full capacity.

References

[1] M. Andersson and T. Sandholm. Leveled commitment contracts with myopic and strategic agents. *Journal of Economic Dynamics and Control*, 25:615–640, 2001.

[2] H.-J. Bürckert, K. Fischer, and G. Vierke. Transportation scheduling with holonic MAS - the TELETRUCK approach. In *Third International Conference on Practical Applications of Intelligent Agents and Multiagents (PAAM 98)*, 1998.

[3] A. Byde, C. Preist, and N. R. Jennings. Decision procedures for multiple auctions. In *Autonomous Agents & Multiagent Systems*, pages 613–622, part 2. ACM press, 2002.

[4] S. Clearwater, editor. *Market based Control of Distributed Systems*. World Scientific Press, Singapore., 1995.

[5] C. Dellarocas. Goodwill hunting: An economically efficient online feedback mechanism in environments with variable product quality. In W. Walsh, editor, *Proceedings of the 4th Workshop on Agent Mediated Electronic Commerce at AAMAS 2002. Lecture Notes in Artificial Intelligence from Springer-Verlag volume 2531*, pages 238–252. Springer, 2002.

[6] J. Epstein and R. Axtell. *Growing Artificial Societies: Social Science From The Bottom Up*. Brookings Institution, 1996.

[7] K. Fischer, J. P. Müller, and M. Pischel. Cooperative transportation scheduling, an application domain for DAI. *Journal of Applied Artificial Intelligence, special issue on intelligent agents*, 10(1), 1996.

[8] P. Klemperer. Auction theory: a guide to the literature. *Journal of economic surveys*, pages 227–286, 1999.

[9] E. N. Luttwak. *Strategy, The Logic of War and Peace*. The Belknap Press of Harvard University Press, 1987.

[10] L. Mui, A. Halberstadt, and M. Mojdeh. Notions of reputation in multi-agents systems: A review. In *Autonomous Agents & Multiagent Systems*. ACM press, 2002.

[11] H. S. Otter, A. van der Veen, and H. J. de Vriend. ABLOoM: Location behaviour, spatial patterns, and agent-based modelling. *Journal of Artificial Societies and Social Simulation*, 4(4), 2001.

[12] D. C. Parkes and L. H. Ungar. An auction-based method for decentralized train scheduling. In *Proceedings 5th International Conference on Autonomous Agents (Agents'01)*, 2001.

[13] P.J. 't Hoen and S. Bohte. COllective INtelligence with sequences of actions. In *14th European Conference on Machine Learning*, Lecture Notes in Artificial Intelligence, LNAI 2837. Springer, 2003.

[14] P.J. 't Hoen, S. Bohte, E. Gerding, and H. La Poutré. Implementation of a competitive market-based allocation of consumer attention space. In W. Walsh, editor, *Proceedings of the 4th Workshop on Agent Mediated Electronic Commerce at AAMAS 2002. Lecture Notes in Artificial Intelligence from Springer-Verlag volume 2531*, pages 273–288. Springer, 2002.

[15] A. Poot, G. Kant, and A. Wagelmans. A savings based method for real-life vehicle routing problems. Technical Report EI 9938/A, Erasmus University Rotterdam, Econometric Institute in its series Econometric Institute Reports, 1999.

[16] C. Preist, C. Bartolini, and I. Phillips. Algorithm design for agents which participate in multiple simultaneous auctions. In *Proceedings of Agent Mediated E-Commerce, LNAI 2003*, page 139 ff, 2001.

[17] Private communication with E. Tempelman, author of [26].

[18] J. S. Rosenschein and G. Zlotkin. *Rules of Encounter*. MIT Press, Cambridge, MA, USA, 1994.

[19] T. Sandholm. Limitations of the vickrey auction in computational multiagent systems. In *2nd International Conference on Multiagent Systems (ICMAS-96)*, pages 299–306. AAAI Press, 1996.

[20] T. Sandholm and V. Lesser. Issues in automated negotiation and electronic commerce: Extending the contract net framework. In *Proceedings of the First International Conference on Multiagent Systems.*, pages 328–335, Menlo park, California, 1995. AAAI Press / MIT Press.

[21] T. Sandholm and V. Lesser. Leveled-commitment contracting, a backtracking instrument for multiagent systems. *AI Magazine*, Fall 2002:89–100, 2002.

[22] T. Sandholm and V. R. Lesser. Coalitions among computationally bounded agents. *Artificial Intelligence*, 94(1-2):99–137, 1997.

[23] T. Sandholm and V. R. Lesser. Leveled commitment contracts and strategic breach. *Games and Economic Behavior*, 35:212–270, 2001. Special issue on AI and Economics. Early version: *Advantages of a Leveled Commitment Contracting Protocol* in the proceedings of the National Conference on Artificial Intelligence (AAAI), pp. 126–133, Portland, OR, 1996.

[24] T. Sandholm, T. Suri, S. Gilpin, and A. Levine. CABOB: A fast optimal algorithm for combinatorial auctions. In *International Joint Conference on Artificial Intelligence (IJCAI)*, 2001.

[25] J. Sauer, T. Freese, and T. Teschke. Towards agent-based multi-site scheduling. In *ECAI 2000 European Conference on Artificial Intelligence 14th Workshop, New Results in Planning, Scheduling and Design (PUK2000)*, 2000.

[26] P. Stone, R. Schapire, J. Csirik, M. Littman, and D. McAllester. ATTac-2001: A learning, autonomous bidding agent. In W. Walsh, editor, *Proceedings of the 4th Workshop on Agent Mediated Electronic Commerce at AAMAS 2002. Lecture Notes in Artificial Intelligence from Springer-Verlag volume 2531*, pages 143–160. Springer, 2002.

[27] E. Tempelman. Daf-trucks- where materials make money. In *Second Workshop on Cold and Hot Forging of Light-Weight Materials, Delft, from the ICFG (International Cold Forging Group)*, 2002.

[28] K. Tumer, A. Agogino, and D. Wolpert. Learning sequences of actions in collectives of autonomous agents. In *Autonomous Agents & Multiagent Systems*, pages 378–385, part 1. ACM press, 2002.

[29] W. Vickrey. Counterspeculation, auctions and competitive sealed tenders. *Journal of Finance*, 16:8–37, 1961.

[30] T. Wagner and V. Lesser. Toward ubiquitous satisficing agent control. In *1998 AAAI Symposium on Satisficing Models*, 1998.

A   Experimental Settings

For each experiment, we averaged the results over 60 runs and 15 consecutive days. We applied the Wilcoxon test to verify that the reported effects of decommitment are statistically significant.

We set the distance between two adjacent nodes of the grid equal to 20 km. By default, the grid size is equal to $10 * 10$. In the Sugarscape-like model studied in Section 6.1, the grid size is depending on the number of depots (to ensure a uniform spacing between them).

The (average) speed of all trucks is equal to 70 km/hour. The carrying capacity of the trucks is set at 350 units of weight. The weight of the loads is in the range of 10 to 70.

The *price* for a load l is set equal to $40 + 2 * weight(l) + distance(l)$ where the transportation *distance* for a load l is the distance from the origin of the load to its destination, and where *weight* denotes the size of the load. This cost function is derived from UPS (see www.ups.nl). UPS uses a constant fee plus a weight-proportional term for its standard packages. We also added a cost per distance. This improved performance (with and without decommitment) as distance then became a stronger issue in bidding. The cost for movement per km is one currency unit.

It is important to note that we set the price for delivery independent of the moment that a load is offered for transport. The price does therefore not increase as the time window for delivery shrinks. This ensures that the results of our experiments are not biased to show good results for decommitment. With increasing prices (close to the delivery time) there is otherwise an incentive for trucks to favor new loads with tight deadlines due to higher profits.

Sequences of Take-It-or-Leave-It Offers: Near-Optimal Auctions Without Full Valuation Revelation*

Tuomas Sandholm and Andrew Gilpin

Computer Science Department
Carnegie Mellon University
Pittsburgh, PA 15213
{sandholm,gilpin}@cs.cmu.edu

Abstract. We introduce *take-it-or-leave-it auctions (TLAs)* as an allocation mechanism that allows buyers to retain much of their private valuation information as do the most common auction mechanisms (English and Dutch auctions), yet, unlike them, generates close-to-optimal expected utility for the seller. We show that if each buyer receives at most one offer, each buyer's dominant strategy is to act truthfully. In more general TLAs, the buyers' optimal strategies are more intricate, and we derive the perfect Bayesian equilibrium for the game. We develop algorithms for finding the equilibrium and also for optimizing the offers in both types of TLAs so as to maximize the seller's expected utility. We prove that optimal TLAs have many desirable features. In several example settings we show that the seller's expected utility already is close to optimal for a small number of offers. As the number of buyers increases, the seller's expected utility increases, and becomes increasingly (but not monotonically) more competitive with Myerson's expected utility maximizing auction. Myerson's uses full valuation revelation and is arguably impractical because its rules are unintuitive, unlike ours.

1 Introduction

Auctions have emerged as a key mechanism for task and resource allocation in multiagent systems. We focus on the problem of allocating an indivisible good to one of a group of interested buyers, while maximizing the seller's expected utility. (All of our results apply to reverse auctions as well, in which a single buyer, facing many sellers, wants to minimize her procurement cost.) This is the canonical auction setting (e.g., [1, 2, 3, 4]).

In this setting, the *Myerson auction* (see Definition 1) yields the highest expected utility to the seller, compared to *any* other allocation mechanism [5]. Despite being the optimal allocation mechanism, the Myerson auction has several

---

* This material is based upon work supported by the National Science Foundation under CAREER Award IRI-9703122, Grant IIS-9800994, ITR IIS-0081246, and ITR IIS-0121678.

P. Faratin et al. (Eds.): AMEC 2003, LNAI 3048, pp. 73–91, 2004.

undesirable features. First, buyers must fully reveal their true valuations for the good.[1] Buyers may be unwilling to reveal private information because such information is proprietary or its revelation would have a negative strategic long-term impact. For example, after such an auction the buyers will be at a disadvantage in future negotiations with the seller (who may be able to extract more surplus in the future using information about the buyers' valuations). Similar long-term adverse effects have been observed in other truthful full-revelation auction mechanisms when it comes to future negotiation between a bidder and the bidder's subcontractors [7]. Second, buyers may not understand the complex, unintuitive rules of the Myerson auction, and therefore choose to not participate. Third, for a layman, it is unintuitive to submit true valuations because bid shading is rational in many commonly used auction mechanisms. Buyers are thus likely to shade bids even in Myerson auctions, with unpredictable and suboptimal results. For these reasons and potentially others, to our knowledge, the theoretically elegant Myerson auction is not being used anywhere.

In the most commonly used auction mechanisms—the *English auction* (a.k.a. ascending open-cry auction) and the *Dutch auction* (a.k.a. descending auction)[2] —bidders do not reveal their valuations completely [1]. Unfortunately, in these auctions, the seller's expected utility is not optimal and in fact can be arbitrarily far from optimal (for example when one bidder's valuation for the good is arbitrarily much higher than the other bidders', and each bidder's valuation is common knowledge). The *Vickrey auction* [2] suffers from both full valuation revelation and seller's expected utility being arbitrarily far from optimal.

In this paper we present a mechanism that achieves close-to-optimal expected utility for the seller while allowing each buyer to retain much of her private valuation information. Our *take-it-or-leave-it auction (TLA)* mechanism consists of a sequence of take-it-or-leave-it offers made by the seller to the buyers, each buyer in turn. Before the auction is held, the seller publicizes the order in which the buyers receive offers and the amount of each offer. During a fixed time after receiving an offer, the buyer has to accept ("take") the offer, at which point the auction ends, or reject ("leave") the offer, in which case the seller may proceed to make other offers. After rejecting an offer, the buyer never has the option of accepting that offer. We show how rational buyers should act in such an auction and how the seller can optimize the sequence of offers given her knowledge about the buyers. In this sense, our approach is *automated mechanism design* [8].

In many applications the seller may be aware of some statistical information about the buyers. (For example, in the reverse auction setting, the buyer may know that a particular seller's cost of production is much less than the other sellers' due to geographic location or through some other means.) By taking this

---

[1] Recently, cryptographic techniques have also been proposed to address this drawback [6].

[2] At first glance, it appears that the Dutch auction and TLAs are equivalent. This is not true. The Dutch auction is more powerful in the sense that the seller can make an infinite number of offers, and less powerful in the sense that the seller has to make the offers symmetrically to the buyers.

information into account, the seller can design mechanisms so as to maximize her expected utility. In our setting, this is done by making the assumption that every buyer's valuation is drawn from some known probability distribution. This assumption violates the *Wilson doctrine* which states that mechanisms should be designed without the use of any priors. Some examples of auctions that follow the Wilson doctrine include Vickrey, English, Dutch, and first-price sealed bid auctions. These types of auctions are not optimal, and in fact can be arbitrarily far from optimal. Further, it is generally not possible to design utility maximizing auctions (or even approximately optimal auctions) without using priors. The Myerson auction, on the other hand, does not adhere to the Wilson doctrine, and as a result is able to extract more surplus from the buyers. Just as is done in the Myerson auction, we use priors in our mechanism.

2   The Setting and Background

We study the usual auction setting in which a seller has an indivisible good that she can allocate to any one (or none) of a set of buyers $B = \{1, \ldots, n\}$. Each buyer i has a valuation v_i for the good that is drawn from a distribution f_i with cumulative density F_i. The buyers' valuations are drawn independently.[3] The distributions f_i are common knowledge, but the valuation v_i is only known by the buyer i herself. The setting is *symmetric* if each buyer draws her valuation from the same distribution (i.e., $f_i = f_j$ for all buyers i and j). Otherwise the setting is *asymmetric*. Finally, we make the standard auction theory assumption that there is no aftermarket (i.e., no trade occurs after the auction is over).

By designing the rules of the auction, the seller tries to maximize her expected utility. The seller has a valuation v_0 (potentially zero) for the good. By the standard quasilinearity assumption about the seller, the seller's utility is v_0 if she keeps the item, and if she allocates the item to a buyer, her utility is the revenue that she receives from the buyers.

To motivate the buyers to participate in the auction, the rules of the auction have to guarantee that each buyer receives no less utility by participating than by not participating. Such *ex post* participation constraints imply that 1) a buyer who does not get the good cannot be charged, and 2) the buyer who receives the good cannot be charged more than her valuation.

We review the optimal auction for this setting [5] below. It is the benchmark against which we will compare our TLA mechanism.[4]

Definition 1. (Myerson auction [5])

- *Every buyer i reveals a valuation $\hat{v}_i$. (A buyer's dominant strategy is to reveal her true valuation: $\hat{v}_i = v_i$.)*

---

[3] If the valuations can have arbitrary correlations, then even designing an approximately optimal auction is hard computationally [9].

[4] The proof of optimality of the Myerson auction assumes that the setting is *regular*, i.e., the hazard rate $f_i/(1 - F_i)$ is increasing for each buyer i [5]. This assumption is satisfied in all cases where we benchmark against the Myerson auction (in Section 7), so we are benchmarking against the real optimum.

– *For each buyer i, compute that buyer's* virtual valuation:

$$\psi_i = \hat{v}_i - \frac{1 - F_i(\hat{v}_i)}{f_i(\hat{v}_i)} \ .$$

– *Select the buyer i^* with the highest virtual valuation ψ_{i^*}.*
– *If $\psi_{i^*} > v_0$, buyer i^* receives the item and pays the smallest valuation, $\underline{\hat{v}}_i$, that would still have made her win.*
– *If $\psi_{i^*} \leq v_0$, the seller keeps the good and no payments are made.*

In the symmetric setting, the Myerson auction is a second-price auction[5] with an appropriately tailored reserve price. However, this is not the case in the asymmetric setting.

3   Take-It-or-Leave-It Auction

In this section we define our idea of using a sequence of take-it-or-leave-it offers as an auction mechanism.

Definition 2. (Take-it-or-leave-it auction (TLA))
Let $\mathcal{A} = \langle b_1, a_1 \rangle, \langle b_2, a_2 \rangle, \ldots, \langle b_k, a_k \rangle$ be a sequence of k offers. Let an offer $\mathcal{A}_j$ be a tuple $\langle b_j, a_j \rangle$, where a_j is the amount of the offer and $b_j \in B$ is the buyer to whom the offer is made. The entire sequence of offers $\mathcal{A}$ is revealed by the seller to the buyers before the auction. The auction proceeds as follows:

– *For j from 1 to k*
  • *Let $\langle b, a \rangle = \mathcal{A}_j$.*
  • *The seller offers the good to buyer b for amount a.*
  • *If buyer b accepts, she gets the good and pays a to the seller. The auction ends.*
  • *If buyer b rejects offer a, the auction continues.*
– *If the auction has reached this point, the seller keeps the good and collects no payments.*

The following auction mechanism turns out to be an interesting special case:

Definition 3. (Single-offer TLA)
A TLA is a single-offer TLA if each buyer gets at most one offer, i.e., $b_q \neq b_r$ for all $q, r \in \{1, 2, \ldots, k\}$, $q \neq r$.

When we need to differentiate between a single-offer TLA and a TLA in which a buyer may receive multiple offers, we will refer to the latter as a *multiple-offer TLA*.

Note that in a TLA it is entirely possible for the seller to allocate the good to a buyer who does not have the highest valuation, thus making the mechanism *inefficient*. This is also the case in the Myerson auction. It is well-known that among asymmetric bidders, there is no mechanism that maximizes both seller's expected utility and efficiency.

---

[5] A second-price auction is a sealed-bid auction in which the winner pays the price of the second-highest bid [2].

3.1 Strategies and Utility

A formal notation for strategies in a TLA is useful. Strategies for TLAs are slightly different than for other auctions since a single buyer may need to make many decisions during the course of an auction.

Definition 4. (Strategy for a TLA)
A buyer's strategy for a TLA is a function from the buyer's valuation and the number of the offer (made to that buyer), to one of two possible actions: accept *or* reject*:*

$$s_i : \mathbb{R} \times \{j \mid j \in \{1, 2, \ldots, k\}, b_j = i\} \to \{accept, reject\} .$$

A strategy profile is $s = (s_1, \ldots, s_n)$*. A strategy profile excluding* s_i *is* $s_{-i} = \{s_1, \ldots, s_{i-1}, s_{i+1}, \ldots, s_n\}$*, and a strategy profile* s *with* s_i *replaced with* s_i' *is* (s_{-i}, s_i')*.*

We make the standard assumption of quasilinearity, that is, a buyer's utility u_i is zero if she does not get the good (and does not pay anything), and $v_i - a$ if she gets the good and pays amount a. Given a strategy profile s and the valuation v_i, the expected utility $u_i(v_i, s)$ of buyer i in a TLA $\mathcal{A}$ is

$$u_i(v_i, s) = \sum_{\{j \mid b_j = i\}} \left(\prod_{l=1}^{j-1} R_l \right) u_i^j(v_i, s_i) , \tag{1}$$

where

$$u_i^j(v_i, s_i) = \begin{cases} v_i - a_j & \text{if } s_i(v_i, j) = accept \\ 0 & \text{if } s_i(v_i, j) = reject . \end{cases} \tag{2}$$

Here, R_l is the probability that offer l is rejected by buyer b_l if that offer is made. These probabilities depend on the buyers' strategy profile s, as discussed next.[6]

4 Equilibrium Analysis

We use definitions from game theory to help us understand how rational buyers will behave in a TLA. We use the two most prevalent solution concepts for sequential games [10]: dominant strategies and perfect Bayesian equilibrium.[7]

4.1 Single-Offer TLAs

A strategy s_i^* for a buyer with valuation v_i is called a *dominant strategy* if for all other strategies s_i' and all strategies s_{-i}, we have $u_i(v_i, (s_i^*, s_{-i})) \geq$

---

[6] When buyer i computes the utility, $R_l \in \{0, 1\}$ when $b_l = i$, because the buyer knows her own strategy.

[7] In game theory there are notions of *pure* and *mixed* strategies. Playing a mixed strategy requires a buyer to perform some randomization among different possible strategies. We only study pure strategy equilibria in this paper.

$u_i(v_i, (s'_i, s_{-i}))$. As the following proposition illustrates, the strategies employed by rational buyers in a single-offer TLA are straightforward and truthful. They are dominant strategies, so a buyer is best off playing that way regardless of what the other buyers' preferences are and even if others play irrationally. Also, a buyer does not have to know much about her own valuation (the determination of which can be a complex optimization problem itself, see e.g. [11, 12, 13, 14]), merely whether it is greater or less than the offer, making a single-offer TLA easy to play.

Proposition 1. *In a single-offer TLA, a buyer's dominant strategy is*

$$s_i^*(v_i, j) = \begin{cases} accept \ if \ v_i > a_j \\ reject \ if \ v_i \le a_j \ . \end{cases}$$

Proof. Consider buyer i with valuation v_i facing offer a_j. Suppose $v_i > a_j$, but buyer i rejects. Then she gets payoff 0, whereas she would have gotten payoff $v_i - a_j > 0$ by accepting the offer. Now suppose $v_i \le a_j$, but buyer i accepts. Then she gets payoff $v_i - a_j \le 0$, whereas she would have gotten payoff 0 by rejecting the offer. □

Note that in a single-offer TLA, buyers don't even need to know their own valuations exactly. They only need to know if it is above or below a certain value. This is also true, but to a lesser extent, for multiple-offer TLAs.

4.2   Multiple-Offer TLAs

If the sequence of take-it-or-leave-it offers includes potentially multiple offers per buyer, the buyers' equilibrium strategies become significantly more intricate. The reason is that *a rational buyer will be reluctant to accept an offer at—or somewhat below—her valuation, because there is a chance that the auction will make her a significantly lower offer later on.* The analysis is further complicated by the fact that a buyer's passing on an offer gives a signal to the other buyers and the seller about the buyer's valuation.

Perfect Bayesian equilibrium (PBE) [15] is the most common solution concept for sequential games with observed actions and private valuations (types). In such a game, with independently drawn valuations, each buyer i has a strategy s_i and beliefs (for each step j of the game, the buyer has, for each other buyer k, a cumulative probability density function F_k^j about the type of k). A strategy profile s^* is a PBE if the following conditions hold: 1) Each buyer updates her beliefs using Bayes rule whenever possible; 2) Whenever it is buyer i's turn to move, s_i prescribes an action that maximizes i's expected utility from then on, given i's beliefs; and the three technical conditions: 3a) At every step of the game, buyer i's beliefs about other buyers are independent of i's valuation, 3b) the beliefs about buyer i can only be changed when i acts, and 3c) at every step of the game, for every triple of buyers i, k, and l ($i \ne l$, $k \ne l$), i and k have the same beliefs about l.

We illustrate the PBE analysis through a 5-offer 2-buyer auction and present the general method after that. For readability, we refer to buyer 1 in the feminine and buyer 2 in the masculine. Suppose that the seller's chosen TLA prescribes that the first offer goes to buyer 1 and the remaining four offers alternate between the buyers.

Buyer 1, when facing the first offer, must decide whether or not she should accept it. If her valuation, v_1, is less than the first offer, a_1, then clearly she must reject. However, the converse is not as simple. *Even though she might stand to gain positive utility by accepting the first offer, she might expect to gain even more utility by rejecting the first offer and accepting a later offer.* For each offer made to a buyer, we would like to compute a *threshold* value above which the buyer will accept and below which she will reject. (If the buyer's valuation is equal to the threshold, she is indifferent between rejecting and accepting.) We will refer to buyer i's threshold at offer j as t_i^j.

At the last offer made to each buyer, both buyers have dominant strategies. They simply accept if the offer is below their valuation and reject otherwise. This is analogous to the strategies employed by buyers in a single-offer TLA.

Now, consider the third offer (the second offer made to buyer 1). Buyer 1 knows what her utility is if she accepts this offer. She wishes to determine what her *expected* utility is if she rejects the third offer (in a gamble to face the fifth offer). To compute this she needs to compute the probability that buyer 2 rejects the fourth offer. At this point in the game, buyer 1 knows that buyer 2 has rejected the second offer. Assuming buyer 2 is playing in equilibrium, his valuation must be less than t_2^2, his threshold when facing the second offer. Buyer 1 must take this into account when computing the probability that buyer 2 will reject the fourth offer. *That is, buyer 1 updates her belief about the distribution from which buyer 2's valuation is drawn.* Buyer 1 is able to perform these computations using her knowledge about buyer 2's prior distribution, which is common knowledge. After buyer 2 has rejected the second offer, by Bayes rule, the right tail of his valuation distribution (probability density function) above t_2^2 can be cut, and the remaining distribution needs to be rescaled to make its integral one. Thus the new cumulative distribution is

$$F_2^4(x) = \frac{F_2(x)}{F_2(t_2^2)} . \tag{3}$$

(In general, we will write F_i^j to denote the world's belief about buyer i's distribution when facing offer j. If a buyer i is facing her first offer j, then $F_i^j = F_i$.) With this new notation, we can write equations describing the thresholds for buyers 2 and 1 when facing offers 2 and 3, respectively:

$$\begin{aligned}
t_2^2 - a_2 &= F_1^3(t_1^3)(t_2^2 - a_4) \\
t_1^3 - a_3 &= F_2^4(a_4)(t_1^3 - a_5) .
\end{aligned} \tag{4}$$

We evaluate F_1^3 at t_1^3 since we know that buyer 1 will only reject if her valuation is below t_1^3.

Determining the strategy that buyer 1 should use at the first offer is slightly more complicated since buyer 1 could reject the first offer in a hope to accept the third offer or the fifth offer. The following equation describes buyer 1's threshold at the first offer:

$$t_1^1 - a_1 = F_2^2\left(t_2^2\right) \cdot \max\left\{t_1^1 - a_3, F_2^4\left(a_4\right)\left(t_1^1 - a_5\right)\right\} . \tag{5}$$

A Simplifying Observation At this point we have completely *characterized* the strategies that the buyers will use, but we have said nothing about how to compute these strategies. Computing the strategies is complicated by the max operation in the above equation. The determination of the strategies could be split into cases, with each case corresponding to a particular term within the max operation being greatest. However, as we move beyond 5 offers, this becomes complex. As the number of offers increases by one, the number of max operations in the system increases by one, thus doubling the number of cases to analyze. Therefore, the number of cases is exponential in the number of offers.[8]

This computation would be easier if we could assume that the thresholds only depend on the next offer. In the above equation, this would mean that $t_1^1 - a_3 \geq F_2^4\left(a_4\right)\left(t_1^1 - a_5\right)$. We observe that if this inequality does not hold, the third offer would in effect be wasted because it certainly would be rejected. Since this paper is concerned with optimal TLAs, we can assume that such offers will never be made.[9] Therefore, we need to focus on only one of the exponentially many cases.

Equilibrium for Any Number of Buyers and Offers Algorithm 1 is a general procedure for generating the system of equations that determines buyers' thresholds. First, we need an expression for evaluating updated distributions:

$$F_i^j(x) = \begin{cases} F_i(x) & \text{if } b_j \notin \{1,\ldots,b_{j-1}\} \\ \dfrac{F_i(x)}{F_i\left(t_i^{j'}\right)} & \text{if } b_j \in \{1,\ldots,b_{j-1}\} \end{cases} \tag{6}$$

where j' is the most recent offer made to buyer i.

Second, we need an expression for the probability that a buyer will reject a given offer j:

$$R_j = \begin{cases} F_{b_j}^j\left(a_j\right) & \text{if } b_j \notin \{b_{j+1},\ldots,b_k\} \\ F_{b_j}^j\left(t_{b_j}^j\right) & \text{if } b_j \in \{b_{j+1},\ldots,b_k\} . \end{cases} \tag{7}$$

---

[8] Actually, the number of cases is further increased by the fact that as an offer is added, the number of terms in the existing max operations of that buyer's threshold equations increases by one (a max operations with 2 terms is added in the equation where there was no max operation before).

[9] This assumes that the order in which buyers receive offers is not fixed. If this order is fixed (for example, due to external constraints), then making a surely rejected offer can be beneficial in order to *in effect* change the order without actually changing it.

The above value depends on whether or not the buyer faces another offer or not. If the buyer does face another offer, then the expression involves a threshold value. Otherwise, the expression only involves the offer. The algorithm below makes a pass through the offers. If an offer is not the last one offered to a buyer, then an equation is output containing an expression for the threshold. The output of this algorithm can then be used as input to a software package that can solve systems of equations in order to determine the equilibrium thresholds (in our implementation, we used Matlab).

Algorithm 1. Output system of threshold equations

1. For j from 1 to k
   (a) If buyer b_j faces another offer after offer j
       − Then denote the index of the next offer as j' and output the equation

$$t_{b_j}^j - a_j = R_{j+1} R_{j+2} \cdots R_{j'-1} \left(t_{b_j}^j - a_{j'} \right)$$

The product of R_j's that is output for each equation is the expression describing the probability that the auction will go from offer $j+1$ to offer j' without a buyer accepting an offer.

With the above discussion in mind, we can now present our main equilibrium result.

Theorem 1. *Suppose we have a multiple-offer TLA $\mathcal{A} = \langle b_1, a_1 \rangle, \langle b_2, a_2 \rangle, \ldots,$ $\langle b_k, a_k \rangle$ that is optimal in the sense of maximizing the seller's utility, subject to the constraint that only k offers are made. Consider the following strategy for buyer i with valuation v_i facing offer a_j:*

$$s_i^*(v_i, a_j) = \begin{cases} accept \ if \ v_i > a_j, i \notin \{b_{j+1}, \ldots, b_k\} \\ reject \ if \ v_i \le a_j, i \notin \{b_{j+1}, \ldots, b_k\} \\ accept \ if \ v_i > t_i^j, i \in \{b_{j+1}, \ldots, b_k\} \\ reject \ if \ v_i \le t_i^j, i \in \{b_{j+1}, \ldots, b_k\} \end{cases}$$

where the t_i^j values solve the system of equations generated by Algorithm 1. The strategy profile $s^* = (s_1^*, s_2^*, \ldots, s_n^*)$ is a perfect Bayesian equilibrium.

Proof. It is easy to see that the technical Conditions 3a-3c of PBE are satisfied. As described above, the buyers update their beliefs using Bayes rule whenever possible, so Condition 1 is satisfied. What remains to be shown is that Condition 2 is satisfied, i.e., that it is never profitable to deviate from the above strategy (in any of the four scenarios). For the first two scenarios, the proof is analogous to the proof of Proposition 1. For the other two scenarios, in which the buyers face another offer later in the auction, we need to make use of the thresholds. Consider buyer i with valuation v_i, facing offer a_j. Let $a_{j'}$ be the next offer that buyer i faces. Suppose $v_i > t_i^j$, but buyer i rejects. The highest expected utility she can expect to get later in the auction is $R_{j+1} \cdots R_{j'-1} (v_i - a_{j'})$. But, by the construction of the thresholds, this is less than $v_i - a_j$. So buyer i is better off accepting the offer. The scenario where $v_i \le t_i^j$ is proven similarly.   □

5 Optimizing the Offers

So far we have described how we would expect buyers to behave in a TLA. Now we turn to the problem faced by the seller: how to maximize expected utility? The seller can choose the order in which the offers are made as well as the offer values. Before describing the optimization problem, we formalize the seller's objective.

Definition 5. (Seller's expected utility)
Given an instance $\mathcal{A}$ of a TLA, the seller's expected utility from step j onward is defined recursively as

$$\pi_j = \begin{cases} (1 - R_j)\, a_j + R_j v_0 & \text{if } j = k \\ (1 - R_j)\, a_j + R_j \pi_{j+1} & \text{if } j < k \ . \end{cases}$$

The seller's expected utility *is given by π_1, and we denote it by $\pi(\mathcal{A})$. (Recall that v_0 is the seller's valuation.)*

We can now formally define the design problem faced by the seller.

Definition 6. (TLA design problem)
Given a limit k_{max} on the number of offers made, the seller's TLA design problem is

$$\mathcal{A}^* = \operatorname{argmax}_{\{\mathcal{A} \mid |\mathcal{A}| \le k_{max}\}} \pi(\mathcal{A}) \ .$$

We say that $\mathcal{A}^*$ is an optimal TLA.

Note that in Definition 6 the k_{max} parameter is exogenous. It is a constraint imposed on the optimization problem that comes from some external source, for example a limit on the amount of time or resources the seller is able to commit to the auction.

We now discuss some characteristic properties of optimal TLAs.

Proposition 2. *For any given TLA design problem, an optimal TLA exists in which no buyer receives consecutive offers.*

Proof. If a buyer receives consecutive offers, she will never accept any of them except possibly the lowest. Thus, the other ones of those offers can be removed from $\mathcal{A}$. □

In an optimal TLA, the offers might not decrease over time:

Example 1. Consider the 2-buyer, 3-offer setting where buyer 1's valuation is uniformly distributed on the interval $[0, 1]$ and buyer 2's valuation is uniformly distributed on the interval $[1, 4]$. The only optimal sequence of offers is $\mathcal{A} = \langle 2, 2.125 \rangle, \langle 1, 0.5275 \rangle, \langle 2, 2.0 \rangle$.

However, decreasing offers can be made to each buyer:

Proposition 3. *For any given TLA design problem, an optimal TLA exists in which each buyer individually receives strictly decreasing offers.*

Proof. If, in equilibrium, all the rejection probabilities R_j of the other buyers that get offers in between two offers of buyer i are zero, that is equivalent to buyer i receiving consecutive offers, which is unnecessary by Proposition 2. We can therefore restrict attention, without loss in the seller's expected utility, to TLAs where this never occurs.

We now show that a buyer will never accept an offer that is equal to or higher than her previous offer. The main idea is that since the buyer knows the sequence of offers at the start of the auction, she knows she can get more utility by accepting an earlier, lower offer, rather than accepting the later, higher offer. Suppose that in an optimal TLA, buyer i is offered a_j at some point in the auction, and the next offer to buyer i is $a_{j'}$, where $a_j \leq a_{j'}$. Without loss of generality, say buyer i's valuation v_i is at least $a_{j'}$. (If it is less than, then buyer i will clearly never accept the offer.) Then the expected utility from accepting offer a_j is $v_i - a_j$, while the expected utility from rejecting offer a_j and later accepting offer $a_{j'}$ is strictly less than $v_i - a_{j'}$ since the utility must be multiplied by the probability that the auction will continue to offer $a_{j'}$ without another buyer accepting an offer and thus ending the auction. Let r denote the probability that no other buyer accepts in between. Since $a_j \leq a_{j'}$ and $r < 1$ (by the argument in the paragraph above), we have $v_i - a_j > r\,(v_i - a_{j'})$, so buyer i will never accept offer $a_{j'}$. Thus, the wasted offer a'_j can be removed from the auction and the auction remains optimal.   □

6   Computational Results

In this section we develop the computational methodology for solving for an optimal TLA (which involves as a subproblem solving for how the buyers will behave). Designing a TLA involves finding an order (the b_j values) in which the buyers receive the offers, and determining the value of each offer (the a_j values).

6.1   Multiple-Offer TLAs

In computing the optimal multiple-offer TLA, we assume that the order of the offers is fixed (e.g., one can include an outer loop to try all orders)[10] and then optimize the TLA for that order as follows.

We run Algorithm 1 to generate the equations for the thresholds t_i^j. Because the shorthand values R_j are expanded in each of those equations, each equation has on the right hand side the offer levels $a_1, a_2, \ldots, a_k$, the specific functional forms of the prior distributions on the types $F_1, F_2, \ldots, F_n$, and the thresholds t_i^j. We then solve this group of nonlinear equations (we used Matlab to do this) to obtain the perfect Bayesian equilibrium as a function of the offers. In other words, we have each t_i^j equal to a nonlinear function of the offer levels $a_1, a_2, \ldots, a_k$.

---

[10] We also set $k = k_{max}$. This is without loss of generality because the optimizer simply can make some of the offers so high that they surely will be rejected (in practice this never occurred for any of the valuation distributions that we tried).

Finally, we run a nonlinear optimizer (Matlab in our case[11]) with these equations as constraints and the expanded recursion for $\pi(\mathcal{A})$ from Definition 6 as the objective, which is now just a function of the offer levels $a_1, a_2, \ldots, a_k$. The output of the optimizer is the values of the optimal offer levels $a_1^*, a_2^*, \ldots, a_k^*$.

The computational complexity of computing the optimal offers in a multiple-offer TLA is an open problem. The analysis is complicated by the system of equations that describe the buyer's thresholds. Solving for the threshold variables directly produces large algebraic expressions, and the complexity of these expressions depends heavily on the underlying distribution.

A Tractable Case Although the question of complexity remains open for the general case, we have developed a linear-time algorithm for the special case of two buyers with uniform distributions on the interval $[0, 1]$. This algorithm relies heavily on results obtained recently by Blumrosen and Nisan [16]. They examine auctions in which the amount of information a buyer can transmit to the seller is severely limited. One of the main results is that when a buyer is limited to choosing from among k possible messages, the buyer's valuation range is partitioned into k continuous intervals (the intervals are, in general, asymmetric among the bidders). The buyer signals which interval her valuation happens to fall in. It turns out that the thresholds that separate the intervals are the same as the equilibrium thresholds in an optimal TLA. (Note that these are the equilibrium thresholds, not the offer levels.) This is easily seen by considering a TLA where each buyer receives k offers, and thus has k threshold values. The TLA could be converted to a direct mechanism where the buyer simply states the first offer that she is willing to accept. Then the problem of computing the thresholds in a TLA becomes the same as computing the thresholds in a communication-bounded auction. The following theorem from [16] (stated using our threshold notation) motivates Algorithm 2.

Theorem 2. *([16]) When there are two buyers with valuations drawn uniformly from the interval $[0, 1]$ the thresholds in an optimal $2k$-offer TLA, $k \geq 2$, are:*

$$t_i^j = \begin{cases} t + \frac{(2k-j-1)\cdot(1-t)}{2k-3} & \text{if } j \in \{1, 2, \ldots, 2k-1\} \\ \frac{1}{2} & \text{if } j = 2k \ . \end{cases}$$

The first offer in the TLA goes to buyer 1, and the offers alternate after that.

Algorithm 2 computes the offer levels for a multiple-offer TLA with two buyers having uniform distributions on the interval $[0, 1]$.

Algorithm 2. Let $k_{max} \geq 4$ be an even number denoting the total number of offers made.

1. $k \leftarrow \frac{k_{max}}{2} + 1$
2. $\alpha \leftarrow \frac{1}{(2k-3)^2}, t \leftarrow \frac{-2\alpha + \sqrt{1+3\alpha}}{2(1-\alpha)}$

---

[11] Matlab uses a numeric algorithm for finding the global maximum. This method is not guaranteed to converge at the global optimum.

3. For j from 1 to $k_{max} - 1$
   (a) If j is odd, then $i \leftarrow 1$, else $i \leftarrow 2$
   (b) $t_i^j \leftarrow t + \frac{(k_{max}-j-1)(1-t)}{2k-3}$
4. $t_2^{k_{max}} \leftarrow \frac{1}{2}$
5. $a_{k_{max}} \leftarrow t_2^{k_{max}}$, $R_{k_{max}} \leftarrow \frac{a_{k_{max}}}{t_2^{k_{max}-2}}$
6. $a_{k_{max}-1} \leftarrow t_1^{k_{max}-1}$, $R_{k_{max}-1} \leftarrow \frac{a_{k_{max}-1}}{t_1^{k_{max}-3}}$
7. For j from $k_{max} - 2$ down to 1
   (a) If j is odd, then $i \leftarrow 1$, else $i \leftarrow 2$
   (b) $a_j = t_i^j - R_{j+1}\left(t_i^j - a_{j+2}\right)$
   (c) If $j > 2$, then $R_j \leftarrow \frac{t_i^j}{t_i^{j-2}}$, else $R_j \leftarrow t_i^j$

Theorem 3. *Algorithm 2 computes an optimal TLA for the setting with two buyers having uniform distributions on the interval $[0, 1]$.*

Proof. Immediate from Theorems 1 and 2 and from the algorithm. □

6.2 Single-Offer TLAs

Now we are considering single-offer TLAs, so we have $k_{max} \leq n$ by definition. Since making at least some offer to every buyer cannot hurt the seller's expected utility, we always have an optimal single-offer TLA with $k = k_{max}$. So, we set $k = k_{max}$.

For convenience, we will think of the optimization problem as two separate problems. The first problem is to determine the order in which the buyers receive the offers. The second problem is to compute the actual offer values.

First, consider symmetric settings, i.e., $F_i = F_j$ for all buyers i, j. In this case the order does not matter, so we set them arbitrarily. The offer values can be determined by first making an offer to the last bidder equal to the inverse virtual valuation of the reserve price and computing the expected profit from this offer as the new reserve price. Formally:

Algorithm 3. Compute offer levels for single-offer TLA

1. $\pi \leftarrow v_0$
2. For i from k_{max} down to 1
   (a) $a_i \leftarrow \text{argmax}_a (1 - F_i(a)) a + F_i(a)\pi$
   (b) $\pi \leftarrow (1 - F_i(a_i))a_i + F_i(a_i)\pi$

Proposition 4. *In the symmetric setting, the single-offer TLA design problem is solved optimally by Algorithm 3.*

Proof. Consider the last offer made in a TLA. The result of the last offer does not affect the result of any of the other offers. Thus, the seller should make an optimal offer, which is computed in step 2(a) during the first iteration. Now consider the next to last offer. Again, the result of this offer does not affect any of the previous offers. Also, the expected utility the seller earns if this offer is rejected has already been computed and is stored in π. Thus, the offer computed in step 2(a) is the optimal offer. Continuing with this "backward induction," it is easy to see that Algorithm 3 correctly computes the optimal offer levels.   □

If we assume that F_i can be evaluated in constant time and that the "argmax" computation can also be done in constant time, then Algorithm 3 runs in time linear in the number of offers k_{max}. For a wide range of common distributions, including uniform and exponential distributions, these assumptions hold.

Now, consider asymmetric settings. Clearly the order of offers now can make a difference to the seller's expected utility. For general asymmetric preferences, we do not know of an efficient algorithm for ordering the offers. (For example, always greedily making an offer to the remaining buyer from whom the seller can myopically expect the greatest utility is not generally optimal.) One could try all possible orderings, running Algorithm 3 to evaluate each ordering. However, for a large number of buyers this would be infeasible since the number of orderings is $k_{max}!$. Fortunately, we have been able to show that in some commonly used special cases one can order the buyers in polynomial time. We denote a uniform distribution over the interval $[a, b]$ as $U[a, b]$ and an exponential distribution having mean $1/\mu$ as $Exp[\mu]$ (its cumulative density is $F(x) = 1 - e^{-\mu x}$).

Theorem 4. *With $v_i \sim U[0, w_i]$, an optimal single-offer TLA can be determined in $O(n \log n)$ time by sorting the buyers in decreasing order of w_i and passing the sequence to Algorithm 3.*

Proof. See Appendix A.

Theorem 5. *With $v_i \sim Exp[\mu_i]$, an optimal single-offer TLA can be determined in $O(n \log n)$ time by sorting the buyers in increasing order of μ_i and passing the sequence to Algorithm 3.*

Proof. See Appendix A.

7   Economic Performance of TLAs

In this section we present experiments and theoretical results to give an indication of how one can expect our TLAs, optimized as explained above, to perform in practice. (Throughout these experiments, we set the seller's valuation v_0 to zero.)

First we studied the performance of our optimal single-offer TLA as the number of buyers increases. Naturally, as the number of buyers increases, the expected utility of the single-offer TLA increases. Table 1 shows how well an optimal single-offer TLA fares relative to Myerson's utility-maximizing auction as the number of buyers increases (and each buyer is made exactly one offer). The single-offer TLA is close to optimal. Interestingly, the relative performance does not improve monotonically, but does improve when the number of buyers is large.[12] The advantage of our single-offer TLA over the English auction is greatest when the number of buyers is not very large. Also, it tends to be greatest in the asymmetric settings. (Naturally, our multiple-offer TLAs would yield even greater expected utility for the seller.) In the case of 1 buyer, a TLA performs exactly as the Myerson auction, and the English auction does not generate any expected utility for the seller.

Table 1. The left (right) number in each cell is the expected utility of an optimal single-offer TLA (English auction) divided by the expected utility of the Myerson auction. Values of 1 indicate that the auction was within 0.0005 of optimal

Num buyers:	2	4	6	8	10	20	100
$v_i \sim U[0,1]$	.938 / .800	.981 / .978	.894 / .997	.900 / 1	.907 / 1	.937 / 1	.992 / 1
$v_i \sim U[0,i]$	.980 / .646	.959 / .844	.953 / .898	.952 / .922	.952 / .936	.958 / .963	.979 / .987
$v_i \sim U[i,i+1]$	.979 / .735	.990 / .866	.993 / .910	.995 / .933	.996 / .946	.998 / .973	1 / .995
$v_i \sim \mathrm{Exp}[2]$	.932 / .749	.994 / .961	.847 / .991	.837 / .997	.833 / .999	.836 / 1	.872 / 1
$v_i \sim \mathrm{Exp}[i]$	.509 / .657	.917 / .813	.900 / .824	.918 / .822	.927 / .819	.942 / .813	.948 / .810

Figure 1 shows how the seller's expected utility in an optimal multiple-offer TLA increases as the number of offers increases. As can be seen, the TLA performs extremely well after a small number of offers. The following result, which follows immediately from a result in [16] and the correspondence between communication-bounded auctions and TLAs, shows that we can expect a TLA to perform well for a wide variety of distributions.

Theorem 6. *([16]) The revenue loss in an optimal k-offer TLA with 2 symmetric buyers having regular distributions*[13] *is* $O\left(\frac{1}{k^2}\right)$.

For some distributions, including the uniform distribution, the above bound is tight. This result is asymptotic, but in practice TLAs yield close to optimal expected utility for the seller, as exemplified in Table 2 where we considered several 2-buyer settings, showing how close a TLA gets to the expected utility generated by Myerson's utility-maximizing auction as the number of offers increases. Even with a small number of offers, the expected utility of a TLA is close to optimal, and increases monotonically with the number of offers.

---

[12] In the third row, the optimal single-offer TLA deterministically allocates the good to the highest buyer, thus making the allocation *efficient* in this case, where the Myerson auction is inefficient.

[13] Recall that a distribution F_i is said to be regular if $f_i/(1 - F_i)$ is increasing.

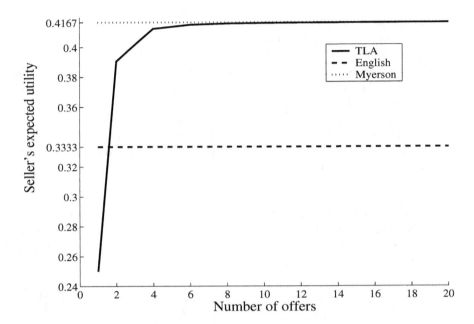

Fig. 1. Seller's expected utility as the number of offers increases. The two buyers' valuations have uniform distributions on the interval $[0, 1]$

Table 2. Seller's expected utility of an optimal 2-buyer TLA and the English auction divided by the expected utility of the Myerson auction. The number of offers for the TLA is varied from 1 to 3. In each case, it is optimal to give the first offer to buyer 1

Total number of offers:	1	2	3	English
$v_1 \sim U[0, 1]$, $v_2 \sim U[0, 1]$	.600	.938	.979	.800
$v_1 \sim U[0.5, 2]$, $v_2 \sim U[0, 1]$	.857	.977	.992	.625
$v_1 \sim U[1, 4]$, $v_2 \sim U[0, 1]$	.932	.994	.997	.350
$v_1 \sim \text{Exp}[2]$, $v_2 \sim \text{Exp}[2]$	.551	.932	.977	.749
$v_1 \sim \text{Exp}[2]$, $v_2 \sim \text{Exp}[4]$	.726	.968	.986	.658

8   Mechanisms Similar to TLAs

In the economics literature, we know of one paper that discusses sequential take-it-or-leave-it offers [17]. The authors propose sequential offers for holding an *optimal* auction. However, the authors assume that the seller can decide the accuracy to which the buyers learn their own valuations. One way they can achieve this is by withholding information. In our model, the seller has no control of the buyers' information. Furthermore, the authors do not address any computational issues.

We are aware of one fielded mechanism that is similar to a TLA. Amazon.com has recently introduced the "Gold Box" on their web site [18]. Each day, registered users are given up to ten take-it-or-leave-it offers for ten different goods. The offers expire after one hour, and after an offer is rejected, it is no longer available to the user. The offer levels appear to be below the normal retail price, but we do not know what pricing strategy is in use. The techniques developed in this paper could be used to compute optimal values for these prices so as to maximize Amazon's expected utility (under certain reasonable assumptions).

A piece of closely related research concerns online auctions [19] and online exchanges [20]. In those papers the authors examine how bids should be treated in an online setting where the auctioneer (or exchange administrator) has to make accept/reject decisions about expiring bids before all potential future bids are received. The authors have developed online algorithms and analyzed how well their algorithms do compared to an omniscient algorithm that knows all future bids in advance. Many of those algorithms end up choosing bid acceptance thresholds, so in that sense they use (implicit) take-it-or-leave-it offers.

Finally, most retail is of the form of making take-it-or-leave-it offers. In the typical retail setting the seller posts price for each item she wishes to sell. The seller generally does not have specific information about a given buyer, and so all buyers face the same prices (i.e. the prices are *non-discriminatory*). This distinguishes the typical retail setting from single-offer TLAs where the prices are *discriminatory*.

9   Conclusions and Future Work

We introduced TLAs as a selling (or buying) mechanism that has low valuation revelation as do the most commonly used auction mechanisms (English and Dutch auctions), yet, unlike them, generates close-to-optimal expected utility for the seller. We showed that in single-offer TLAs, each buyer's dominant strategy is to act truthfully. In multiple-offer TLAs, the buyers' optimal strategies are more intricate, and we derived the perfect Bayesian equilibrium for the game. We developed algorithms for finding the equilibrium and for optimizing the offers in single-offer and multiple-offer TLAs so as to maximize the seller's expected utility (subject to an exogenous constraint on the number of offers), and proved that optimal TLAs have many desirable features. We applied a recent result by Blumrosen and Nisan to TLAs to show that the seller's expected utility is close to optimal already for a small number of offers. We also showed in several examples that as the number of buyers increases, the seller's expected utility increases and becomes increasingly (but not monotonically) more competitive with Myerson's expected utility maximizing auction. Myerson's uses full valuation revelation and is arguably impractical because the rules are unintuitive, unlike ours in which the mechanism is simply a sequence of take-it-or-leave-it offers. Even our single-offer TLA tends to yield significantly greater utility to the seller than the English auction when the setting is asymmetric or the number of buyers is not very large.

Future research includes developing fast offer-ordering algorithms for asymmetric single-offer TLAs for arbitrary valuation distributions, as well as fast special-purpose algorithms for PBE finding, offer ordering, and offer value optimization in multiple-offer TLAs. We also plan to extend this work to auctions of multiple identical units and to auctions of multiple distinguishable items. We think it would be interesting to perform laboratory experiments to see how humans respond to TLAs. Finally, we are interested in examining how sensitive TLAs are to the various assumptions that are made, especially concerning the assumption that the prior distributions are common knowledge.

References

[1] Krishna, V.: Auction Theory. Academic Press (2002)
[2] Vickrey, W.: Counterspeculation, auctions, and competitive sealed tenders. Journal of Finance **16** (1961) 8–37
[3] Monderer, D., Tennenholtz, M.: Optimal auctions revisited. In: Proceedings of the National Conference on Artificial Intelligence (AAAI), Madison, WI (1998) 32–37
[4] Ronen, A.: On approximating optimal auctions. In: Proceedings of the ACM Conference on Electronic Commerce (ACM-EC), Tampa, FL (2001) 11–17
[5] Myerson, R.: Optimal auction design. Mathematics of Operation Research **6** (1981) 58–73
[6] Naor, M., Pinkas, B., Sumner, R.: Privacy preserving auctions and mechanism design. In: Proceedings of the ACM Conference on Electronic Commerce (ACM-EC), Denver, CO (1999)
[7] Rothkopf, M.H., Teisberg, T.J., Kahn, E.P.: Why are Vickrey auctions rare? Journal of Political Economy **98** (1990) 94–109
[8] Conitzer, V., Sandholm, T.: Complexity of mechanism design. In: Proceedings of the 18th Annual Conference on Uncertainty in Artificial Intelligence (UAI-02), Edmonton, Canada (2002) 103–110
[9] Ronen, A., Saberi, A.: Optimal auctions are hard. In: FOCS. (2002) 396–405
[10] Fudenberg, D., Tirole, J.: Game Theory. MIT Press (1991)
[11] Sandholm, T.: An implementation of the contract net protocol based on marginal cost calculations. In: Proceedings of the National Conference on Artificial Intelligence (AAAI), Washington, D.C. (1993) 256–262
[12] Sandholm, T.: Issues in computational Vickrey auctions. International Journal of Electronic Commerce **4** (2000) 107–129 Special Issue on Applying Intelligent Agents for Electronic Commerce. A short, early version appeared at the Second International Conference on Multi–Agent Systems (ICMAS), pages 299–306, 1996.
[13] Parkes, D.C.: Optimal auction design for agents with hard valuation problems. In: Agent-Mediated Electronic Commerce Workshop at the International Joint Conference on Artificial Intelligence, Stockholm, Sweden (1999)
[14] Larson, K., Sandholm, T.: Costly valuation computation in auctions. In: Theoretical Aspects of Rationality and Knowledge (TARK VIII), Sienna, Italy (2001) 169–182
[15] Fudenberg, D., Tirole, J.: Perfect bayesian equilibrium and sequential equilibrium. Journal of Economic Theory **53** (1991) 236–260
[16] Blumrosen, L., Nisan, N.: Auctions with severely bounded communication. In: FOCS. (2002) 406–415

[17] Bergemann, D., Pesendorfer, M.: Information structures in optimal auctions. Discussion Paper 1323, Cowles Foundation for Research in Economics, Yale University, New Haven, CT (2001)

[18] Amazon.com: Gold box offers. http://www.amazon.com/gold-box (2003)

[19] Lavi, R., Nisan, N.: Competitive analysis of incentive compatible on-line auctions. In: Proceedings of the ACM Conference on Electronic Commerce (ACM-EC), Minneapolis, MN (2000) 233–241

[20] Blum, A., Sandholm, T., Zinkevich, M.: Online algorithms for market clearing. In: Annual ACM-SIAM Symposium on Discrete Algorithms (SODA), San Francisco (2002) 971–980

A   Proof Sketch of Theorems 4 and 5

In this appendix we sketch the proof of Theorem 4. A proof of Theorem 5 can be given similarly.

The main idea of the proof is to take a sequence of offers that is not made in descending order of w_i and modify the sequence so that it yields a higher expected utility for the seller. Assume, by way of contradiction, that the optimal TLA $\mathcal{A}$ has a sequence of offers in which the offers are not made to the buyers in decreasing order of w_i. Then for some offer $\langle b_j, a_j \rangle$ we have $w_{b_j} < w_{b_{j+1}}$. Consider another TLA $\mathcal{A}'$ which makes the offers in the same order as $\mathcal{A}$ but switches the order of b_j and b_{j+1}. We will show that the new auction, with appropriately chosen offers $\langle b'_j, a'_j \rangle$ and $\langle b'_{j+1}, a'_{j+1} \rangle$, achieves a strictly better expected utility for the seller.

By assumption, we have $\pi(\mathcal{A}) \geq \pi(\mathcal{A}')$. The goal is to show that $\pi(\mathcal{A}') > \pi(\mathcal{A})$. We simply need to show that $\pi'_j > \pi_j$ where π'_j and π_j are the seller's expected utility from step j onward in TLAs $\mathcal{A}'$ and $\mathcal{A}$, respectively. Note that in both TLAs the offers $j + 2$ to k are the same.

So we just need to show the following inequality holds:

$$(1 - F_{b_{j+1}}(a'_j))a'_j + F_{b_{j+1}}(a'_j) \left[(1 - F_{b_j}(a'_{j+1}))a'_{j+1} + F_{b_j}(a'_{j+1})\pi_{j+2} \right] >$$
$$(1 - F_{b_j}(a_j))a_j + F_{b_j}(a_j) \left[(1 - F_{b_{j+1}}(a_{j+1}))a_{j+1} + F_{b_{j+1}}(a_{j+1})\pi_{j+2} \right] \quad (8)$$

We have $F_{b_j}(a) = \frac{a}{w_{b_j}}$ and $F_{b_{j+1}}(a) = \frac{a}{w_{b_{j+1}}}$ so we can rewrite (8) as:

$$\left(1 - \frac{a'_j}{w_{b_{j+1}}} \right) a'_j + \frac{a'_j}{w_{b_{j+1}}} \left[\left(1 - \frac{a'_{j+1}}{w_{b_j}} \right) a'_{j+1} + \frac{a'_{j+1}}{w_{b_j}} \pi_{j+2} \right] >$$
$$\left(1 - \frac{a_j}{w_{b_j}} \right) a_j + \frac{a_j}{w_{b_j}} \left[\left(1 - \frac{a_{j+1}}{w_{b_{j+1}}} \right) a_{j+1} + \frac{a_{j+1}}{w_{b_{j+1}}} \pi_{j+2} \right] \quad (9)$$

Using a similar argument as in the proof of Proposition 4, we can compute the following offers:

$$a_j = \frac{w_{b_j} + \pi_{j+1}}{2}, a_{j+1} = \frac{w_{b_{j+1}} + \pi_{j+2}}{2}, a'_j = \frac{w_{b_{j+1}} + \pi'_{j+1}}{2}, a'_{j+1} = \frac{w_{b_j} + \pi_{j+2}}{2}$$

Plugging these values into (9) and simplifying the expression completes the result. $\qquad\square$

Mechanism for Optimally Trading Off Revenue and Efficiency in Multi-unit Auctions

Anton Likhodedov and Tuomas Sandholm

Carnegie Mellon University
Computer Science Department
5000 Forbes Avenue, Pittsburgh, PA 15213
{likh, sandholm}@cs.cmu.edu

Abstract. We study auctioning multiple units of the same good to potential buyers with single unit demand (i.e. every buyer wants only one unit of the good). Depending on the objective of the seller, different selling mechanisms are desirable. The Vickrey auction with a truthful reserve price is optimal when the objective is efficiency - allocating the units to the parties who values them the most. The Myerson auction is optimal when the objective is the seller's expected utility. These two objectives are generally in conflict, and cannot be maximized with one mechanism. In many real-world settings—such as privatization and competing electronic marketplaces—it is not clear that the objective should be either efficiency or seller's expected utility. Typically, one of these objectives should weigh more than the other, but both are important. We account for both objectives by designing a new *deterministic* dominant strategy auction mechanism that maximizes expected social welfare subject to a minimum constraint on the seller's expected utility. This way the seller can maximize social welfare subject to doing well enough for himself.

1 Introduction

Electronic commerce has spawned the use of increasingly sophisticated auction mechanisms. There are several possible reasons for this. First, in many ecommerce settings the bidders are automated agents that are programmed to act rationally even in complex situations. Also human users of ecommerce systems are typically quite savvy and able to recognize attractive properties of sophisticated mechanisms. This motivates the analysis of unintuitive auction mechanisms, which are capable of meeting complicated design objectives.

One example is the Vickrey auction [11]. In this auction with q_0 units of the same good on sale, q_0 highest bidders win, but only pay the price of the first *unsuccessful* bid. The Vickrey auction maximizes economic *efficiency*, aka. *social welfare* (assuming the reserve price is set to equal the seller's valuation for a unit of good being sold), that is, the units end in the hands of the party who values it the most.

Another example is the Myerson auction [9], which maximizes the *seller's expected utility* (expected *revenue* in case the seller does not value the object).[1] The unintuitive

---
[1] The formal characterization of the seller's optimal multi-unit mechanism was given by E.Maskin and J.Riley in [7]. However in the single-unit demand case, which is considered

P. Faratin et al. (Eds.): AMEC 2003, LNAI 3048, pp. 92–108, 2004.

aspect of the Myerson auction is that it sometimes allocates the goods to bidders other than the q_0 highest bidders.

Expected social welfare and the seller's expected utility cannot be maximized with the same auction mechanism in general because these objectives conflict. Furthermore, in many real-world settings it is not clear that the objective should be either of the two.

For example, most privatization auctions are motivated by the belief that private companies can make more efficient use of an asset than the government can. It seems thus reasonable to allocate the asset to the party who can make the most effective use of it, that is, to use efficiency as the auction objective. At the same time, the government would like to raise as much money from the sale as possible (maximize the seller's expected utility) because the asset is owned by the tax payers who prefer to pay for government expenditures out of the auction revenue rather than taxes.

As another example, consider electronic auction houses that compete with each other. To attract sellers, an auction house would use an auction mechanism that maximizes the seller's expected utility. On the other hand, this would not be desirable from the perspective of attracting buyers. Clearly, an auction house needs both buyers and sellers to operate. Therefore, including some element of social welfare measurement in the objective may be desirable.

We account for both objectives by designing a new deterministic auction mechanism that maximizes expected social welfare subject to a minimum constraint on the seller's expected utility. This way the seller can maximize social welfare subject to subject to doing well enough for himself. We show that this auction mechanism belongs to a family of mechanisms, maximizing a linear combination of the seller's expected utility and expected social welfare, controlled by one free parameter λ.[2] We then present an algorithm for determining the optimal value for this parameter and constructing an auction with desired characteristics. This approach is different from the traditional mechanism design - the mechanism is not completely specified upfront - rather we compute the particular mechanism for every instance of the problem (that is, given the constraint on the revenue and the distributions of buyers' valuations). In a way this is similar in spirit to automated mechanism design [2].

We also present a family of much simpler randomized mechanisms that *under some assumptions*, which we state later in the paper achieve the same expected revenue and efficiency. However, in Section 4 we argue, that randomization is inappropriate for the settings, which motivate the present work. This discourages the use of the randomized mechanisms even in the cases, when they yield similar expected revenue and social welfare.

Although most of the results in this paper are derived under the independent private values model, which assumes that the distributions of valuations (types) of buyers are common knowledge, it is possible to relax this assumption. In Section 5 we describe a

---

in this paper, the seller's optimal multi-unit mechanism can be derived similarly to the seller's optimal single-unit mechanism from [9]. Therefore we will refer to the seller's-optimal mechanism as Myerson auction.

[2] Note that we *do not* assume in advance that the tradeoff is attained with a linear combination of seller's expected utility and expected social welfare - instead the linearity of the tradeoff is proved explicitly

prior-free mechanism, which utilizes the idea of sampling from [1]. When the number of buyers tends to infinity this mechanism approaches expected efficiency and expected seller's utility of the auction, designed with distributions known upfront. This way we meet the principle, known as Robert Wilson doctrine.[3]

2   Framework and Notation

We focus on settings with one seller, multiple buyers, and multiple units of the same good on sale. For convenience buyers are indexed with numbers from 1 to n and the set of all buyers is denoted by $N = \{1\ldots n\}$. Index 0 always refers to the seller. We analyze the case of the single unit demand: each buyer wants to buy just one unit of the good.[4]

The seller's valuation for each item is v_0. The number of items on sale is denoted by q_0. We also make the following usual assumptions about valuations, known as the *independent private values (IPV) model*:

1. The valuation of buyer i, v_i, is a realization of the random variable X_i with the cumulative distribution F_i and the density $f_i : [a_i, b_i] \rightarrow \mathbb{R}$. Each density function f_i is continuous and positive on $[a_i, b_i]$, and zero elsewhere.
2. All densities f_i are common knowledge.[5]
3. All random variables X_i are independent of each other.

We use the following notation. V denotes the set of all possible combinations of valuations of buyers:

$$V = \times_{i \in N}[a_i, b_i] \quad \text{and} \quad V_{-i} = \times_{j \in \{N \setminus i\}}[a_j, b_j]$$

We also need a special notation for vectors of valuations:

$$v = (v_1, \ldots, v_n)$$
$$v_{-i} = (v_1, \ldots, v_{i-1}, v_{i+1}, \ldots v_n)$$
$$(v_{-i}, w_i) = (v_1, \ldots, v_{i-1}, w_i, v_{i+1}, \ldots v_n)$$

The joint distribution of the valuations is denoted by $f(v)$. By the independence assumption we have

$$f(v) = \prod_{j=1}^{n} f_j(v_j) \quad \text{and} \quad f_{-i}(v) = \prod_{j \neq i}^{n} f_j(v_j)$$

Utilities of buyers are assumed to be quasi linear: The utility of buyer i is $u_i = p_i \cdot v_i - t_i$, where p_i is the probability that she gets an item, v_i is her valuation, and t_i is the

---

[3] Robert Wilson doctrine of mechanism design states that the mechanism should be independent of the prior distribution of the bidder's valuations
[4] The case when buyers want to buy more then one good can be handled by the same model as long as buyers' demand functions are constant (i.e. a buyer's valuation for each additional unit of the good is the same as her valuation for the first unit).
[5] We relax this assumption in Section 5.

amount that she has to pay. The utility of the seller is $u_0 = (q_0 - \sum_{i=1}^{n} p_i)v_0 + \sum_{i=1}^{n} t_i$ (the first term in the expected number of items kept by the seller).

We try to design a *mechanism* in order to meet some objective, described later, when each buyer plays the game so as to maximize his own expected utility. By the *revelation principle* we can now, without loss in the objective, restrict our attention to mechanisms where each buyer *truthfully* bids for a unit of good on sale in a sealed-bid format.

Definition 1 (sealed-bid mechanism) *Each buyer i submits a bid b_i for a unit of the good on sale. Upon obtaining the bids, the seller computes the allocation and the payment of each buyer. The allocation is the probability vector $p(b) = (p_1(b_1), \ldots p_n(b_n))$, where $p_i(b_i)$ is the probability that buyer i gets a unit of good, when bidding b_i. These probabilities do not have to sum to q_0: the seller may keep some units. The payments are specified by the vector $t(b) = (t_1(b_1), \ldots, t_n(b_n))$, where $t_i(b_i)$ is the payment of buyer i. The allocation rule $p(b)$ and the payment rule $t(b)$ are common knowledge.*

The bid of buyer i depends on his valuation v_i for a unit of good on sale. If each buyer is motivated to submit a bid that equals that buyers valuation, the mechanism is *incentive compatible*. As is standard in the literature on optimal auction design, throughout this paper we focus on *Bayes-Nash* incentive compatibility, that is, each buyer expects to get highest utility by bidding truthfully rather than insincerely—given that the other buyers bid truthfully. However, the mechanisms, which we derive in this paper turn to be also *(ex post) incentive compatible*.

When all participant are truthful, the expected utility of buyer i can be expressed as follows:

$$U_i(p, t, v_i) = E_{v_{-i}}\left[p_i(v_i)v_i - t_i(v)\right] = \int_{V_{-i}} (p_i(v_i)v_i - t_i(v))f_{-i}(v_{-i})dv_{-i} \quad (1)$$

When a buyer chooses to bid differently from his true type and given that other bidders bid vector is v_{-i}, her utility is

$$p_i(v_{-i}, w_i)v_i - t_i(v_{-i}, w_i)$$

Now, the buyers' incentive compatibility constraints can be stated formally:

Definition 2 (incentive compatibility (IC))

$$U_i(p, t, v_i) \geq E_{v_{-i}}\left[p_i(v_{-i}, w_i)v_i - t_i(v_{-i}, w_i)\right] \forall v_i, w_i \in [a_i, b_i], \quad \forall i \in N$$

The expression on the right side of the inequality is the expected utility of bidding w_i when the true valuation is v_i.

Another important property of auction mechanisms is individual rationality. An auction mechanism is *ex ante* individually rational if each buyer is no worse off participating than not—on an expected utility basis:

Definition 3 (individual rationality (IR))

$$U_i(p, t, v_i) \geq 0 \quad \forall v_i \in [a_i, b_i], \quad \forall i \in N$$

Same as with incentive compatibility constraint, the optimal mechanism turns to be (ex post) individually rational.

Different (individually rational, incentive compatible) auctions are usually evaluated either according to the expected utility of the seller or *efficiency* (aka *social welfare* in this setting where parties have quasi linear utility functions):

Definition 4 *The* expected utility of the seller *is*

$$U_0(p,t) = E_v\left[(q_0 - \sum_{i=1}^n p_i(v_i)) \cdot v_0 + \sum_{i=1}^n t_i(v)\right] \tag{2}$$

$$= \int_V \left((q_0 - \sum_{i=1}^n p_i(v_i)) \cdot v_0 + \sum_{i=1}^n t_i(v)\right) f(v)dv$$

In the important special case where the seller's valuation for a unit of the good on sale is zero, then the seller's expected utility is the seller's expected revenue.

Definition 5 *Given the allocation rule $p(v)$, the* expected social welfare *is*

$$SW(p) = E_v\left[\sum_{i=1}^n p_i(v_i) \cdot v_i + \left(q_0 - \sum_{i=1}^n p_i(v_i)\right) \cdot v_0\right] \tag{3}$$

$$= \int_V \left(\sum_{i=1}^n p_i(v_i) \cdot v_i + \left(q_0 - \sum_{i=1}^n p_i(v_i)\right) \cdot v_0\right) f(v)dv$$

When the objective of the auctioneer is efficiency (i.e., allocating the items to the parties who values them the most), the optimal mechanism is given by the Vickrey auction [11]. The Myerson auction is optimal when the objective is the seller's expected utility (see [9] for a single-unit case and [7] for a multi-unit case). These two objectives are generally in conflict, and cannot be maximized with one mechanism. In many real-world settings—such as privatization and competing electronic marketplaces—it is not clear that the objective should be either efficiency or expected utility of the seller.

One way to account for importance of both objectives is to set up a constrained optimization problem: optimize one of the objectives, subject to a constraint on the other. In this paper we derive a new auction mechanism that maximizes expected social welfare *subject to a minimum constraint on the seller's expected utility*. We now give the formal statement of this auction design problem:

Problem 1. Maximize $SW(p)$ subject to the following constraints:

1. Constraint on the seller's expected utility:

$$U_0(p,t) \geq R_0 \tag{4}$$

2. The usual probability normalization (PN) constraints:

$$\begin{cases} 1 \geq p_i(v_i) \geq 0, & \forall i \in N, \quad \forall v \in V \\ \sum_{i=1}^n p_i(v_i) \leq q_0 \end{cases} \tag{5}$$

3. Incentive compatibility (IC) constraints:

$$U_i(p, t, v_i) \geq E_{v_{-i}} \left[p_i(v_{-i}, w_i)v_i - t_i(v_{-i}, w_i) \right]$$
$$\forall v_i, w_i \in [a_i, b_i], \quad \forall i \in N \tag{6}$$

4. Individual rationality (IR) constraints:

$$U_i(p, t, v_i) \geq 0 \quad \forall v_i \in [a_i, b_i], \quad \forall i \in N \tag{7}$$

We call a solution (mechanism) to this problem a *welfare maximizing R_0-seller's expected utility (WM-R_0) auction*. Constraints IC, IR and PN are referred to as *feasibility constraints* [9].

The main difference between this problem and Myerson's seller's expected utility maximization is the choice of the objective function. In Problem 1 the objective is efficiency and the seller's expected utility appears as an additional constraint, while in [9] and [7] the objective is the seller's expected utility.

The problem is easier in the symmetric case where the valuations of different buyers come from the same probability distribution ($f_i = f_j, \forall i, j \in N$). In that setting, both social welfare and seller's expected utility are maximized by second-price auctions with reserve prices.[6] The two auctions differ by the value of the reserve price: in the welfare maximizing auction the reserve price equals the seller's valuation for a unit of good. In the auction that maximizes seller's expected utility, the reserve price is generally greater than that. However, the set of buyers, receiving items in the seller's utility maximizing auction is a subset of the set of buyers, receiving items in the welfare maximizing auction.

In the asymmetric case where the densities f_i are not the same, the mechanism that maximizes welfare and the one that maximizes seller's expected utility differ fundamentally. Myerson showed that the latter sometimes allocates the items on sale to bidders other than the highest bidders (we discuss Myerson's auction in Section 3.2). With respect to our problem, the Myerson auction introduces the following complication: mechanisms optimizing seller's expected utility and those optimizing welfare might yield different allocations.

---

[6] The second-price auction with a reserve price is defined by the following allocation and payment rules:

- Each of the q_0 highest bidders gets one unit of the good, provided that his bid exceeds the reserve price.
- Every bidder getting a unit of good, pays the maximum of the first unsuccessful bid and the reserve price. The other bidders pay 0.

Since we only consider feasible auctions, the bid of the buyer is equal to her private valuation for the good. The reserve price is a threshold value, such that all the bids below it are ignored.

3 Designing the Optimal Mechanism

It can be shown that due to the particular form of the functionals $SW(p)$ and $U_0(p,t)$ the problem has a solution with one free parameter, whose optimal value can be easily found numerically.

Before deriving the mechanism in detail, we present the high-level ideas of the derivation, in order:

1. We show that the optimal payment rule t is the same as in the Myerson auction. We also demonstrate that the problem of designing the optimal mechanism (p,t) can be reduced to an optimization problem in p only. The optimal allocation rule is computed by maximizing $SW(p)$ subject to the constraint

$$\hat{U}_0(p) \geq R_0 \tag{8}$$

where $p(t)$ are valid probability distributions such that the mechanism (p,t) is incentive compatible and individually rational. Here $\hat{U}_0(p)$ is a linear functional that depends only on the allocation rule $p(t)$, and not on the payment rule t. (The expression is given in Sec. 3.1.)
2. Constraint 8 is either inactive (i.e. the unconstrained global maximum satisfies it) or is satisfied with equality at the maximum.[7]
   (a) If Constraint 8 is inactive, the optimal auction is the standard Vickrey auction with the reserve price set to equal the seller's valuation for a unit of the good on sale.
   (b) If Constraint 8 is active, we do the following:
      i. We solve the problem using Lagrangian relaxation. The optimal allocation rule $p^{opt}(v)$ is found as the maximum of

$$\hat{L}(p,\lambda) = SW(p) + \lambda \cdot (\hat{U}_0(p) - R_0) \tag{9}$$

with respect to (p,λ) on the convex set of feasible allocation rules $p(v)$. In Sec. 3.2 we argue that this indeed yields a solution to the original optimization problem. We derive the allocation rule $p^\lambda(v)$ that, for given λ, maximizes $\hat{L}(p,\lambda)$.
      ii. This way the problem reduces to finding a value λ so that p^λ maximizes the objective $SW(p)$ subject to Constraint 8. Since Constraint 8 is active, the maximum can be found by solving the following integral equation:

$$\hat{U}_0(p^\lambda) = R_0$$

We prove that $\hat{U}_0(p^\lambda)$ is non-decreasing and continuous in λ. This allows us to find the optimal λ with a simple numerical algorithm, as we explain in Section 3.3.

The following subsections present the derivation of the optimal mechanism in detail.

---

[7] The feasibility constraints PN, IC, IR and Constraint 8 are linear in p, so the feasible region is convex. Since the objective $SW(p)$ is a linear functional, the maximum is attained on the boundary of the region, and if a constraint is active, it must be satisfied with equality in extremum. While this is analogous to linear programming, the problem is more complex because the optimization is over functions rather than variables.

3.1   New Formulation of the Optimization Problem

In this subsection we reduce the problem of designing the optimal mechanism (p, t) to an optimization problem in p only. The derivation relies on the following lemma from [9] and [7], which we state without proof.

Lemma 1. (Myerson and Maskin, Riley) *The expected utility of the seller in any feasible multi-unit auction is given by*

$$U_0(p, t) = \sum_{i=1}^{n} E_v \left[(v_i - v_0 - \frac{1 - F_i(v_i)}{f_i(v_i)}) p_i(v_i) \right] + q_0 \cdot v_0 - \sum_{i=1}^{n} U_i(p, t, a_i) \quad (10)$$

[7] proves a more general result about multi-unit auctions with general (not necessarily unit) demand. Restricting the buyers' demand functions to single-unit demand yields Lemma 1. The special case of the above lemma (with one item on sale) is stated as Lemma 3 in [9].

Lemma 1 and the revenue equivalence theorem(see [9] and [6] for generalized version) imply that the expected utility of the seller in a feasible WM-R_0 auction is given by

$$\hat{U}_0(p^{opt}) = \sum_{i=1}^{n} E_v \left[(v_i - v_0 - \frac{1 - F_i(v_i)}{f_i(v_i)}) p_i(v_i) \right] + q_0 v_0 \quad (11)$$

where p^{opt} is a solution to Problem 1. The payment of buyer i in a feasible WM-R_0 auction is given by

$$t_i(v) = p_i(v_i) v_i - \int_{a_i}^{v_i} p_i(v_{-i}, w_i) ds_i \quad (12)$$

We call $\hat{U}_0(p)$ the *pseudo-utility* of the seller. Trivially, $\hat{U}_0(p)$ and $U_0(p, t)$ are not equal for arbitrary t and p. However, by revenue equivalence

$$\hat{U}_0(p^{opt}) = U_0(p^{opt}, t)$$

Note that the expression for the seller's utility in the constrained optimum that is given by (11) does not involve t.

We now can restate the original optimization problem in terms of the allocation rule p only.

Problem 2. Maximize $SW(p)$ subject to

1. Pseudo-utility (PU) constraint

$$\hat{U}_0(p) = \sum_{i=1}^{n} E_v \left[(v_i - v_0 - \frac{1 - F_i(v_i)}{f_i(v_i)}) p_i(v_i) \right] + q_0 v_0 \geq R_0 \quad (13)$$

2. Monotonicity condition - the expected probability of buyer i getting an item -

$$E_{v_{-i}} p_i(v_i, v_{-i}) = \int_{V_{-i}} p_i(v_i) f_i(v_{-i}) dv_{-i} \tag{14}$$

is non-decreasing in v_i.
3. Probability normalization constraints (PN).

Again, correctness of this approach can be justified by revenue equivalence theorem.

We now solve the auction design problem using a form of Lagrangian relaxation. We find a solution to Problem 2 by computing the saddle point of the following functional:

$$\hat{L}(p, \lambda) = SW(p) + \lambda \cdot (\hat{U}_0(p) - R_0) \tag{15}$$

in (p, λ), where p is restricted to the convex set of valid feasible allocation rules.

This approach of moving just one of the constraints into the objective is not the standard way of using Lagrangian relaxation, but is nevertheless valid for the following reason. The full Lagrangian corresponding to Problem 2 (and containing the terms corresponding to the feasibility constraints and the PU constraint (13)) is exactly the same as the Lagrangian corresponding to maximizing the objective (15) subject to the feasibility constraints only. And by the Kuhn-Tucker Theorem, the saddle point of the Lagrangian is a solution to Problem 2.

Problem 2 can be solved with the following algorithm:

1. For all λ, find the allocation rule $p^\lambda(v)$ that maximizes (15).
2. Find the optimal λ.[8]

The next two subsections explain the implementation of the two steps of this algorithm, respectively.

3.2   Finding the Optimal Allocation Rule p^λ

We now present the mechanism for maximizing $\hat{L}(p, \lambda)$ with respect to p, for given λ. We first transform $\hat{L}$ into a more convenient form:

$$\hat{L}(p, \lambda) = E_v \left[\sum_{i=1}^{n} p_i(v_i) \cdot v_i + \left(q_0 - \sum_{i=1}^{n} p_i(v_i) \right) \cdot v_0 \right]$$

$$+ \lambda \left(\sum_{i=1}^{n} E_v \left[\left(v_i - v_0 - \frac{1 - F_i(v_i)}{f_i(v_i)} \right) p_i(v_i) \right] + q_0 v_0 - R_0 \right)$$

$$= \int_V \sum_{i=1}^{n} \left((c_i^\lambda(v) - (1 + \lambda) v_0) p_i(v_i) \right) f(v) dv + (1 + \lambda) q_0 v_0 - \lambda R_0$$

We call the quantities c_i^λ *virtual valuations*.

---

[8] When $\lambda = 0$, the PU constraint (13) is inactive and the optimum is attained at the Vickrey auction with no reserve price.

Definition 6 *For buyer i with valuation v_i drawn from distribution F_i, the* virtual valuation v_i *is*

$$c_i^\lambda(v) = c_i^\lambda(v_i) = (1+\lambda)v_i - \lambda \cdot \frac{1 - F_i(v_i)}{f_i(v_i)}$$

We now deviate from the main flow of this subsection and briefly compare our mechanism to that of Myerson, who introduced the use of virtual valuations in his analysis of expected revenue maximizing auctions. One of the differences between his auction and ours is in the form of virtual valuations. In the Myerson auction, a buyer's virtual valuation $c_i(v_i)$ is the difference between the buyer's real valuation v_i and the hazard rate:

$$c_i(v_i) = v_i - \frac{1 - F_i(v_i)}{f_i(v_i)} \tag{16}$$

The Myerson auction, operating on those virtual valuations $c_i(v_i)$ rather than on real bids, is biased in favor of disadvantaged buyers [5, p.73], thus creating an artificial competition between "weak" and "strong" buyers.[9] Such a mechanism allows the auctioneer to set a high sell price for a strong buyer while motivating him to stay truthful even if he is sure that his valuation exceeds any possible valuation of any other buyer. This approach provides the auctioneer with higher expected revenue. In our case, the virtual valuations depend on an additional parameter λ which controls the tradeoff between expected social welfare and seller's expected utility. For ease of comparison, our virtual valuations $c_i^\lambda(v_i)$ can be written as

$$c_i^\lambda(v_i) = (1+\lambda)\left(v_i - \frac{\lambda}{1+\lambda} \cdot \frac{1 - F_i(v_i)}{f_i(v_i)}\right) \tag{17}$$

We now return to the derivation of the optimal allocation rule. Despite the differences in virtual valuations and functionals being optimized, for any given λ, the optimal allocation rule $p^\lambda(v)$ can be derived similarly to the one in [9] and [7], without substantial changes in the argument.

In order to describe the optimal allocation rule we need a few more definitions. Let $\hat{c}_i^\lambda(v_i)$ be the closest *non-decreasing* continuous approximation for $v_i(v_i)$. Formally,

$$\hat{c}_i^\lambda(v_i) = \frac{d}{dq}G_i^\lambda(q), \quad \text{where } q = F_i(v_i) \tag{18}$$

$G_i^\lambda(q)$ is the lower convex hull of the function $H_i : [0, 1] \to \mathbf{R}$, defined as

$$H_i^\lambda(q) = \int_0^q c_i^\lambda(F_i^{-1}(r))dr \tag{19}$$

That is, $G_i^\lambda(q)$ is the highest convex function on $[0, 1]$,[10] such that

$$G_i^\lambda(q) \le H_i^\lambda(q)$$

---

[9] The terms "weak" and "strong" refer to buyers' valuation *distributions*. Distributions of "strong" buyers are concentrated around higher values.

[10] See [9] and [10, p.36] for details.

Redefined this way, virtual valuations are "ironed" over certain portions of the domain. The ironing procedure transforms the virtual valuations into non-decreasing functions, which is necessary to preserve incentive compatibility (see [9] for the discussion).

Theorem 1 *For any λ, $\hat{L}(p, \lambda)$ is maximized when the allocation rule is given by*

$$
p_i^\lambda(v) = \begin{cases} 1, & \text{if } \hat{c}_i^\lambda(v_i) \text{ is among } q_0 \text{ highest virtual valuations} \\ & \text{and } \hat{c}_i^\lambda(v_i) > (1+\lambda)v_0 \\ 0, & \text{otherwise.} \end{cases} \tag{20}
$$

Ties are broken by randomizing.

The proof follows that in [7] or [9] (except that it is for different virtual valuations).

Theorem 1 proves that for all λ, the optimal mechanism is integral, that is, the probability of a buyer getting an item is always 0/1 (except for the case of ties). The following provides some intuition behind the proof: integral allocation mechanisms can be thought of as "corners" of the feasible region, given by constraints. Since the objective is a linear functional and all the constraints are also linear in p, analogy with the linear programming problem suggests that the optimum should be in one of those "corners". It should be noted, that although the feasibility constraints (6, 7) are on expected utility of the buyer, Mechanism 20 is (ex post) incentive compatible and individually rational. The latter can be verified by substituting the payment rule (12) in the expression of buyer's utility.

The payment rule (12) means that the winning buyer pays the minimum valuation, required to win the item. Therefore Mechanism 20 can be viewed as a form of Vickrey auction, run on virtual, rather than real valuations. When $\lambda = 0$, Mechanism (20) yields the standard Vickrey auction.

3.3 Finding the Optimal Value for Lagrange Multiplier λ

Computing the optimal mechanism requires choosing a λ_{opt} so that the allocation rule $p^{\lambda_{opt}}$ maximizes expected social welfare over all allocation rules p^λ, which satisfy the PU constraint (13). (There is no need to account for feasibility constraints, since all p^λ satisfy them.) As we argued in the beginning Section 3, the optimal allocation rule satisfies (13) with equality and λ_{opt} is the solution to the integral equation

$$
\tilde{U}_0(\lambda_{opt}) = R_0 \tag{21}
$$

where $\tilde{U}_0$ is defined as

$$
\tilde{U}_0(\lambda_{opt}) = \hat{U}_0(\hat{p}^{\lambda_{opt}})
$$

Although $\tilde{U}_0(\lambda)$ can only be evaluated numerically, the following theorem states that $\tilde{U}_0$ is nicely behaved. The importance of this fact is that it makes Equation (21) easy to solve numerically (we present an algorithm for doing so in the next subsection).

Theorem 2 $\tilde{U}_0(\lambda)$ *is continuous and non-decreasing in λ.*

The proof of the theorem essentially relies on the fact that Mechanism 20 is (ex post) incentive compatible (the full proof is in the Appendix).

3.4   Algorithm for Computing the Optimal Allocation Rule

The optimal allocation rule can be computed with the following algorithm, where the optimal λ_{opt} is the root of $\tilde{U}_0(\lambda) - R_0$. It is easy to find because $\tilde{U}_0$ is continuous and increasing.

Algorithm 1 (Computing the optimal allocation rule)

1. *Check whether the Vickrey auction with reserve price equal to the seller's valuation satisfies the PU constraint (13). If it does, output it as a solution. Otherwise, go to 2.*
2. *Set λ_{min} to zero and λ_{max} to some positive number, such that $p^{\lambda_{max}}$, given by Mechanism (20), does not satisfy the PU constraint. The PU constraint is checked by evaluating $\tilde{U}_0(\lambda_{max})$ numerically.*
3. *Repeat the following step until $\lambda_{max} - \lambda_{min}$ converges to zero:*
   Set $\lambda_{new} = \frac{\lambda_{min}+\lambda_{max}}{2}$. Construct the allocation rule $p^{\lambda_{new}}$ and check the PU constraint. If it is satisfied, set $\lambda_{min} = \lambda_{new}$, otherwise set $\lambda_{max} = \lambda_{new}$.
4. *Set the allocation rule to $p^{\lambda_{opt}}$, where λ_{opt} is given by Step 3. Set the payment rule t according to 12:*

$$t_i(v) = p_i^{\lambda_{opt}}(v)v_i - \int_{a_i}^{v_i} p_i^{\lambda_{opt}}(v_{-i}, w_i)ds_i$$

$\tilde{U}_0$ is an n-dimensional integral over the allocation probabilities p^λ, but nevertheless it can be evaluated numerically. It can be estimated by sampling v and computing the Monte-Carlo sum, which converges to the true value of the integral. Sampling v is easy because the valuations v_i are drawn independently: v can be obtained by sampling individual valuations v_i from the distributions f_i.[11]

4   Randomized Mechanisms

When virtual valuations of the buyers c_i^λ given by (17) are non-decreasing and no ironing is needed,[12] there exist simple randomized mechanisms where the Vickrey rules are used w.p. t and the Myerson rules w.p. $1 - t$ that yield the same expected social welfare and seller's expected revenue as our mechanism.

Rather than computing the optimal λ using the algorithm above and running Mechanism (20), the seller can use the distributions f_i to evaluate the expected revenue of the Myerson auction and the Vickrey auction in advance, and use these revenue values to analytically determine t. When no ironing is applied this indeed yields the same expected revenue and social welfare as Mechanism 20.

However, randomization is often undesirable. In many settings an auction is only run once. For instance, each privatization auction usually has different participants and/or

---

[11] If one can solve for the inverse of F_i, it is possible to sample directly from f_i. Otherwise a technique such as importance sampling [4, p. 305] should be used.
[12] this is called a *regular* case in economics literature

a different object (company) for sale. Similarly, in Internet auctions, the set of buyers generally differs for every auction, as may the object for sale. Now, say that in a given setting, the auction designer is unsatisfied with the seller's expected utility in the Vickrey auction, and with the expected social welfare of the Myerson auction. Still, the designer can be satisfied with the seller's expected utility and expected social welfare in our deterministic mechanism. So, the deterministic mechanism is satisfactory, but the randomized mechanism would run an unsatisfactory auction for sure. (For randomization to really make sense, the designer would have to be able to repeat the random drawing multiple times, i.e., to repeat the same auction in the same setting.)

5   Prior-Free Mechanisms

The results of this paper are derived under the independent private values model, which assumes that the distributions of valuations (types) are common knowledge. However, in many practical application this assumption does not hold and the seller has no information about these distributions (for instance when the good on sale is new to the market). This raises the question of the possibility of prior-free mechanisms with desired properties, which is also motivated by the *Robert Wilson doctrine*. In the special case of symmetric valuations (the valuations of all buyers come from the same distribution F) and with more than one unit of the good on sale (i.e. $q_0 > 1$) it is possible to design a mechanism which does *not* use any prior knowledge about distributions, but still approaches the characteristics of WM-R_0 auction, derived in this paper, when the number of buyers is large.

Such a prior-free mechanism can be constructed, applying the idea of sampling, developed in [1]: since the valuations of buyers are independent draws from the same *unknown* distribution F, they can be used to estimate F, using the following technique:

$$F_n(t) = \frac{|j \in N, v_j < t|}{n - 1}$$

Then the estimates F_n can be used in place of the true distribution F in Mechanism (20) (the derivative of F, f can also be estimated from the sample, as discussed in [1]). The one issue remaining is incentive compatibility: when the reported valuation of buyer i is used to estimate F and f there exist an incentive to lie (since through F and f, buyer i gets a chance to manipulate the estimates of the virtual valuations for herself and the buyers, she is competing with. A solution to this problem is to apply the idea of dual-sampling auction from [3]:

1. Split the set of buyers randomly into two groups of size $\frac{n}{2}$ (if n is odd, place the remaining buyer into the first group).
2. Assign half of the units on sale ($\frac{q_0}{2}$ units) to group 1 and the other half to group 2.
3. Use the valuations of the buyers from group 1 to estimate F and f for the buyers from group 2 and vice versa.
4. Independently run the auctions among the buyers from group 1 and group 2.

Note that this way, buyers from different groups do not compete against each other and the report of any buyer does not affect the estimates of F and f used in her group. This property obviously makes the auction incentive-compatible. By the argument, using the law of large numbers, the expected efficiency of this mechanism approaches that of feasible WM-R_0 auction and expected revenue approaches R_0 when n (the number of buyers) goes to infinity (the proof closely follows that in Theorem 4 from [1]).[13]

The same idea can be trivially extended for the non-symmetric case (buyers' valuations are draws from different distributions), when there is sufficient number of buyers coming from each distribution.

6 Conclusions

We demonstrated that the auction, maximizing expected efficiency subject to a constraint on the seller's expected utility belongs to the family of dominant strategy mechanisms, parameterized with one free parameter and presented an algorithm for optimally choosing the value of the parameter. By running this auction the seller can expect to do well enough for himself, and maximize social welfare subject to that.

No matter how the tradeoff between efficiency and seller's utility is struck, the optimal auction has essentially the same form. Furthermore, except for the case of ties in virtual valuations the optimal auction does not rely on randomization, that is, given distinct bids the allocation probabilities are 0/1 (however, the winning bidder is not always the highest bidder).

It is important that the presented mechanism does not use randomization over different auction mechanisms (i.e. when the result is achieved by running different auctions with positive probability). The latter is inappropriate for the auction design problems, which motivate our work.

We derived our results under the asymmetric independent private values model. For the special case of symmetric distributions we also presented the approximation mechanism which does *not* use any prior knowledge about distributions. This mechanism approaches expected efficiency and expected seller's utility of the auction, designed with distributions known upfront, when the number of buyers, coming from every distribution tends to infinity.

References

1. Baliga S. and Vohra R. *Market Research and Market Design*, Advances in Theoretical Economics: Vol. 3: No. 1, 2003.
2. Conitzer, V., and Sandholm, V. *Complexity of Mechanism Design*, UAI 2002.
3. Fiat A., Goldberg A., Hartline J. and Karlin A., *Competitive Generalized Auctions*, STOC 2002.
4. Gelman A.B., Carlin J.S., Stern H.S., Rubin D.B. *Bayesian data analysis*, Chapman and Hall/CRC, 1995.

---

[13] It is well known that in symmetric setting with fixed number of goods and the number of bidders going to infinity, the Vickrey auction approaches the optimal revenue (for instance, [8] prove this statement for general combinatorial auctions). However the statement does not hold when the number of goods on sale is also increasing. This is exactly the case when the approximation technique of [1] is helpful.

5. Krishna V. *Auction theory*, Academic Press, 2002.
6. Krishna V., Perry M. *Efficient mechanism design*, Working Paper,1998.
7. E. S. Maskin and J. G. Riley. *Optimal multi-unit auctions*. The Economics of Missing Markets, Information, and Games. Oxford University Press, Clarendon Press, 1989.
8. Monderer D. and Tennenholtz M. *Asymptotically Optimal Multi-Object Auctions for Risk-Averse Agents*, manuscript, 2000.
9. Myerson, R. *Optimal auction design*, In Mathematics of operational research. Vol. 6, pp. 58-73, 1981.
10. Rockafellar, R.V. *Convex Analysis*, Princeton University Press, 1996.
11. Vickrey W. *Counterspeculation, auctions and competitive sealed tenders*. Journal of Finance, 16 pp.8-37, 1961.

Appendix

Proof of Theorem 2. Monotonicity of $\tilde{U}_0(\lambda) = \hat{U}_0(p^\lambda)$ can be proved as follows: Take arbitrary $\lambda_1 < \lambda_2$. Then, by definition of p^{λ_1}, p^{λ_2}

$$\begin{cases} \hat{L}(p^{\lambda_1}, \lambda_1) \geq SW(p^{\lambda_2}) + \lambda_1 \cdot \hat{U}_0(p^{\lambda_2}) \\ \hat{L}(p^{\lambda_2}, \lambda_2) \geq SW(p^{\lambda_1}) + \lambda_2 \cdot \hat{U}_0(p^{\lambda_1}) \end{cases} \tag{22}$$

Denote $\Delta p = p^{\lambda_2} - p^{\lambda_1}$ and $\Delta\lambda = \lambda_2 - \lambda_1$. Since SW, $\hat{U}_0$ and $\hat{L}$ are linear functionals, (22) implies

$$\begin{cases} \hat{L}(-\Delta p, \lambda_1) = -\hat{L}(\Delta p, \lambda_1) \geq 0 \\ \hat{L}(\Delta p, \lambda_2) \geq 0 \end{cases}$$

Therefore

$$\hat{L}(\Delta p, \lambda_2) - \hat{L}(\Delta p, \lambda_1) = (\lambda_2 - \lambda_1)\hat{U}_0(\Delta p) \geq 0$$

and

$$\hat{U}_0(\Delta p) = \hat{U}_0(p^{\lambda_2}) - \hat{U}_0(p^{\lambda_1}) \geq 0$$

Thus, $\tilde{U}_0(\lambda) = \hat{U}_0(p^\lambda)$ is non-decreasing in λ.

We now prove the continuity of $\tilde{U}_0(\lambda)$. The idea of the proof uses the (ex-post) incentive compatibility of the Mechanism 20 and shows that if $\tilde{U}_0(\lambda)$ is not continuous, the mechanism cannot be ex post incentive compatible.

$\tilde{U}_0$ is given by

$$\tilde{U}_0(\lambda) = \sum_{i=1}^{n} \left(\int_V \big(c_i(v_i) - v_0\big) p_i^\lambda(v) f(v) dv \right) + q_0 \cdot v_0$$

where c_i are the Myerson virtual valuations, defined in (16). For arbitrary λ_1, λ_2, we have

$$|\tilde{U}_0(\lambda_1) - \tilde{U}_0(\lambda_2)| \leq c_{max} \int_V \sum_{i=1}^{n} |p_i^{\lambda_1}(v) - p_i^{\lambda_2}(v)| f(v) dv$$

$$\leq 2 \cdot c_{max} \cdot \int_{V_{\lambda_1, \lambda_2}} f(v) dv \tag{23}$$

where

$$c_{max} = \max_{i \in N, v_i \in [a_i, b_i]} |c_i(v_i) - v_0|$$

and

$$V_{\lambda_1, \lambda_2} = \{v \in V| \quad p^{\lambda_1}(v) \neq p^{\lambda_2}(v)\}$$

is the set of valuation vectors where allocations $p^{\lambda_1}(v)$ and $p^{\lambda_2}(v)$ differ. We now show that $V_{\lambda_1, \lambda_2} = O(\Delta\lambda)$. By (17), for all i and v_i,

$$|v_i^{\lambda_1}(v_i) - v_i^{\lambda_2}(v_i)| = |c_i(v_i)\Delta\lambda| \leq |c_{max}\Delta\lambda|$$

Also, using the definition of $\hat{c}_i$ it is easy to show that for all i and v_i

$$\begin{cases} \hat{c}_i^{\lambda_1}(v_i) - |c_{max}\Delta\lambda| \leq \hat{c}_i^{\lambda_2}(v_i) \\ \hat{c}_i^{\lambda_2}(v_i) - |c_{max}\Delta\lambda| \leq \hat{c}_i^{\lambda_1}(v_i) \end{cases}$$

Therefore,

$$|\hat{c}_i^{\lambda_1}(v) - \hat{c}_i^{\lambda_2}(v)| \leq |c_{max}\Delta\lambda| \tag{24}$$

Mechanisms, using the payment rule (12) and with allocation rule, such that all $p_i(v_{-i}, s)$ are non-decreasing in s are *ex-post* incentive compatible (it can be verified by substituting the payment rule (12) into the definition of buyer's utility). Therefore, Mechanisms (20) are ex-post incentive-compatible. We show now that ex-post incentive compatibility together with (24) implies $V_{\lambda_1, \lambda_2} = O(\Delta\lambda)$ and therefore continuity of $\tilde{U}_0$.

We first demonstrate that utility of buyer i -

$$u_i(p^{\lambda}, t, v) = p_i^{\lambda}(v) \cdot v_i - t_i$$

is continuous in parameter λ for all λ and for all v. Assume the contrary: there exists v, λ_1 and ϵ_{λ_1}, such that for all $\delta > 0$, there exist some λ_2, satisfying

$$\begin{cases} |\lambda_2 - \lambda_1| < \delta \\ |u_i(p^{\lambda_1}, t, v) - u_i(p^{\lambda_2}, t, v)| > \epsilon_{\lambda_1} \end{cases}$$

We now show that such a mechanism is not ex-post incentive compatible. W.l.o.g. assume that the utility of buyer i under the allocation p^{λ_2} is higher than under the allocation p^{λ_1} (if this is not the case, interchange λ_1 and λ_2).

Non-continuity of u_i means that arbitrary small changes in λ yield substantial (at least ϵ_{λ_1}) increase in utility of buyer i. Mechanism (20) allocates the items to buyers with highest virtual valuations and by(24) the virtual valuations of *all* buyers change by at most $|c_{max}\Delta\lambda|$. Since $\hat{c}_i(v_i)$ s non-decreasing in v_i, there exists a type $\hat{v}_i$, such that when types of other buyers are given by v_{-i}, buyer i benefits from overbidding (i.e. mechanism is not ex-post IC).

More formally, by (24) $|\hat{c}_j^{\lambda_1}(v_j) - \hat{c}_j^{\lambda_2}(v_j)| \leq |c_{max}\Delta\lambda|$ for all j. Therefore, if $\hat{c}_i^{\lambda_1}(v_i)$ were at most $2 \cdot |c_{max}\Delta\lambda|$ higher, buyer i would get the same probability of winning an item as under allocation p^{λ_2}. Since $\hat{c}_i^{\lambda_1}(v_i)$ is a non-decreasing function of v_i, consider two cases:

1. $\hat{c}_i^{\lambda_1}(v_i)$ is increasing at v_i (i.e. $\hat{c}_i^{\lambda_1}(v_i) = c_i^{\lambda_1}(v_i)$). The derivative of $\hat{c}_i^{\lambda_1}$ is well-defined, positive and continuous in v_i (i.e. it is positive in some neighborhood of v_i). Therefore it is possible to choose $\Delta\lambda = |\lambda_2 - \lambda_1|$ small enough, so that there exist t_i', such that $0 < t_i' - v_i < \tau_{v_i}^{\lambda_1} \cdot \Delta\lambda$, for some constant $\tau_{v_i}^{\lambda_1}$ and $\hat{c}_i^{\lambda_1}(t_i') > c_i^{\lambda_1}(v_i) + 2 \cdot |c_{max}\Delta\lambda|$.
   If the true type of buyer i is v_i, then reporting t_i' yields an increase in utility of at least ϵ_{λ_1} (due to the increase of the probability of winning), while the payment of the bidder increases by at most $2\tau_{v_i}^{\lambda_1} \cdot \Delta\lambda$ (this can be verified by substituting v_i and $\hat{v}_i$ into the payment rule (12)). Therefore if $\Delta\lambda$ is sufficiently small, bidder i benefits from overbidding.
2. $\hat{c}_i^{\lambda_1}(v_i)$ is constant at v_i (i.e. v_i is on the flat (ironed) portion of the virtual valuation). Take $\hat{v}_i$ to be the highest type, such that $\hat{c}_i^{\lambda_1}(\hat{v}_i) = \hat{c}_i^{\lambda_1}(v_i)$ (i.e. $\hat{v}_i$ is at the end of the flat portion of $\hat{c}_i^{\lambda_1}$). It is easy to show that $\hat{v}_i$ has the same probability of winning an item as v_i and the same utility. Applying then the same argument as in the case of increasing $\hat{c}_i^{\lambda_1}(v_i)$ allows to show that $\hat{v}_i$ benefits from overbidding.

The argument yields a contradiction: (Mechanism (20) is not ex-post incentive compatible), which is due to our assumption about non-continuity of u_i. When the payment rule is set according to (12) the utility of buyer i is given by

$$u_i(p^\lambda, t, (v_{-i}, v_i)) = \int_{a_i}^{v_i} p_i(v_{-i}, w_i)ds_i$$

Therefore, since u_i is continuous in λ, and by (20) p_i takes values only in $\{0, \frac{1}{n}, \frac{1}{n-1}, \ldots, 1\}$ and is non-decreasing in v_i for all i we must have

$$\{v_i \in [a_i, b_i]| \quad p_i^{\lambda_1}(v_{-i}, v_i) \neq p_i^{\lambda_2}(v_{-i}, v_i)\} = O(\Delta\lambda), \quad \forall i, v_{-i}$$

It follows, that

$$V_{\lambda_1, \lambda_2} = \{v \in V| \quad p^{\lambda_1}(v) \neq p^{\lambda_2}(v)\} = O(\Delta\lambda)$$

Therefore, by (23), $\tilde{U}_0(\lambda)$ is continuous in λ.□

Choosing Samples to Compute Heuristic-Strategy Nash Equilibrium

William E. Walsh[1], David C. Parkes[2], and Rajarshi Das[1]

[1] IBM T. J. Watson Research Center
19 Skyline Dr., Hawthorne, NY 10532, USA
{wwalsh1,rajarshi}@us.ibm.com
[2] Division of Engineering and Applied Sciences,
Harvard University
33 Oxford St., Cambridge, MA 02138, USA
parkes@eecs.harvard.edu

Abstract. Auctions define games of incomplete information for which it is often too hard to compute the exact Bayesian-Nash equilibrium. Instead, the infinite strategy space is often populated with *heuristic strategies*, such as myopic best-response to prices. Given these heuristic strategies, it can be useful to evaluate the strategies and the auction design by computing a Nash equilibrium across the restricted strategy space. First, it is necessary to compute the expected payoff for each heuristic strategy profile. This step involves sampling the auction and averaging over multiple simulations, and its cost can dominate the cost of computing the equilibrium given a payoff matrix. In this paper, we propose two information theoretic approaches to determine the next sample through an interleaving of equilibrium calculations and payoff refinement. Initial experiments demonstrate that both methods reduce error in the computed Nash equilibrium as samples are performed at faster rates than naive uniform sampling. The second, faster method, has a lower metadeliberation cost and better scaling properties. We discuss how our sampling methodology could be used within *experimental* mechanism design.

1 Introduction

Agent-mediated electronic commerce advocates the design of markets in which automated trading agents will engage in dynamic negotiation over the prices and attributes of goods and services. Trading agents promise to remove the monitoring and transaction costs that make dynamic negotiation impractical in traditional commerce. However, before these automated markets are widely deployed, it will be necessary to design trading agents that can follow useful (perhaps even optimal) strategies.

Certainly, careful market design and mechanism design can help, through the design of systems with simple but useful agent strategies (e.g. [8, 9, 12]). However, many real-world problems are simply too complex to be amenable to the theoretical approach of mechanism design. First, the problem of optimal mechanism design is often not analytically tractable. Second, the result can be a mechanism that is not practical to deploy, either for reasons of communication complexity (e.g. [13]) or for reasons of computational complexity (e.g. [11]). Third, mechanism design is subject to known theoretical

P. Faratin et al. (Eds.): AMEC 2003, LNAI 3048, pp. 109–123, 2004.

impossibilities, and attempts to engineer tradeoffs have thus far produced somewhat limited results (e.g., [1, 14]). Simply stated, the cost of simplifying the strategic problem of agents through careful mechanism design is often too high.

For this reason we should expect electronic markets in which the equilibrium trading strategy for an agent is not a straightforward strategy, such as myopic best-response to prices or truthful bidding. As an example, consider a continuous double auction (CDA) in which agents dynamically enter a marketplace and trade goods over time. Computing the Bayesian-Nash equilibria directly for interesting auctions (e.g. the CDA) often proves to be impossible with current methods. Instead, a typical approach is to compute a Nash equilibrium across a space of *heuristic* trading strategies[5, 17]. Heuristic strategies define the actions an agent will take within the auction, e.g. "bid *b* at time *t*." For example, in an earlier study of CDAs, we generated a *heuristic payoff table*–an analog of the usual payoff table, except that the entries describe expected payoffs to each agent as a function of the strategies played by all other agents [22]. The heuristic payoff table was then used as the basis for several forms of analysis, including computation of the Nash equilibria with respect to the restricted strategy space, and the market efficiency at those equilibria.

Measuring the expected payoff to each agent in the auction for all strategy profiles and populating a payoff table is costly. This step involves sampling from a distribution of agent valuations, and then simulating a run of the auction mechanism with a particular profile of heuristic strategies in order to generate an additional sample in one cell of the payoff matrix. This step can be *much* more costly than computing the equilibrium. In the 2000 Trading Agent Competition [24], for instance, each run of the game requires 15 minutes, and the game must be run many times to fill out a payoff table. In contrast, it is possible to compute all equilibria for a small set of heuristic strategies within minutes [22].

In this paper, we address this problem by selecting samples more intelligently. We describe methods to *interleave* the sampling of the payoff in the underlying market game with the calculation of Nash equilibrium, and present an information-theoretic methodology to the sampling problem. The methods are designed to sample the strategy profile that is expected to provide the most value of information, measured in terms of beliefs about the effect that one more sample might have on the current decision about the equilibrium of the system. The difficulty in applying the framework is to develop appropriate models for the value of information, models that are principled, yet fast enough to be useful in practice.

It is useful to place this work in the context of a wider agenda of an *experimental* approach to computational mechanism design. Just as *experimental economics* [18] provides a "wind tunnel" to measure the performance of auctions with human participants, we need our own wind tunnel for an experimental approach to the design of agent-mediated mechanisms. Central to this experimental approach to agent-mediated mechanism design is the ability to compute the performance of a particular market-based system, given a realistic population of trading agents. There is already a rich tradition in performing experiments with automated trading agents, and more recently in using methods from evolutionary computing to compute approximate equilibrium strategies [7, 17, 22]. We believe that sophisticated methods to sample the underlying heuristic strategy space will be an important component in a framework for effective experimental mechanism design with automated agents.

Following is an outline for the rest of this paper. Section 2 delineates how a heuristic payoff table is created and the costs involved, and explains how this table is used to compute the Nash equilibria. Section 3 discusses our information-theoretic approach for payoff sampling, and presents an initial approach. Section 4 presents a faster method for determining how to sample, and Section 5 provides empirical results to compare our methods with that of uniform sampling in simple games. We conclude with a discussion of smart sampling methods in the context of experimental mechanism design.

2   Heuristic-Strategy Nash Equilibrium

We start with a game, such as an auction, that may include complex, repeated interactions between a finite set of agents. The underlying rules of the game are well-specified and common knowledge, but each agent has uncertain information about the types of the other agent. The rules specify particular *actions* that agents may take as a function of the state of the game. The *type* of an agent specifies individual, private characteristics of the agent, which, in the games we consider, specifies the agent's payoff for different outcomes in the game. It is instructive to consider an *ascending-price auction*: the *rules* specify closing rules and price dynamics; the *actions* allow an agent to bid at or above the current price; the *type* of an agent specifies its value for the item.

Many interesting and important games are too complex to compute Nash equilibria on the atomic actions with current game theory tools. This has led a number of researchers to devise innovative heuristic strategies—typically employing economic reasoning, optimization, and artificial intelligence techniques—to complex games including the Trading Agent Competitions [6, 20, 23], market-based scheduling [17], and the continuous double auction [3, 4, 21]. The key point is that the heuristic strategies are a subset of the (generally enormous) space of all strategies, and the set of heuristic strategies do not necessarily contain strategies that constitute an equilibrium of the underlying game (hence heuristic).

A heuristic strategy is simply an action policy specifying (generally complex) behavior for atomic actions in an underlying game. To give an example, in a continuous double auction (CDA), an agent's type specifies its value for the goods in the market. The underlying rules of the CDA allow agents to take actions of the form form "bid b at time t," while the heuristic strategies can be complex functions, expressed in hundreds or thousands of lines of code. One component of a CDA strategy could specify, for instance, to "place buy bid $s + \varepsilon$ when the lowest sell bid s is at most δ greater than the highest buy bid b."

Thus, diverging from standard Bayesian-Nash equilibrium analysis, we can assume that each agent has a choice of the *same* (exogenously specified,) *heuristic strategies*, and compute a Nash equilibrium across this restricted strategy space. Given the heuristic strategies, we transform the underlying game to one in which the agents' payoffs are the expected payoffs obtained by the heuristic strategies in the underlying game, computed with respect to a distribution of utility functions (or types) [17, 22]. We note that the approach we describe applies equally to any game in which there are a small number of strategies but whose payoffs cannot, in practice, be determined analytically.[3] An example is a proxy agent auction [15, 25], in which participating agents are allowed the choice of only a small set of proxy strategies, which are in turn implemented by proxy agents controlled by the auction.

Let H denote the space of heuristic strategies, and consider N agents. A pure *strategy profile* $a = (a^{j_1}, \cdots, a^{j_N})$ specifies, for each agent i, the pure strategy $a^{j_i} \in H$ played by the agent. A *payoff matrix* specifies the payoff to each agent for all possible strategy profiles. With $|H| = M$, the standard payoff table requires M^N entries which can be extremely large, even when M and N are moderate. To mitigate this problem, we restrict our analysis to symmetric games in in which each agent has the same set of strategies and the same distribution of types (and hence payoffs). Standard auction analyses often rely on the same symmetry assumption to simplify the problem. With this, we can merely compute the payoff for each strategy as a function of the *number* of agents playing each strategy, without being concerned about the individual identities of those agents. This gives us a much smaller payoff matrix, of size $\binom{N+M-1}{N}$. With the symmetry assumption, we generally dispense with the agent index.

Given a heuristic-strategy payoff matrix, mapping joint heuristic strategy choices to agent payoffs, we then compute a Nash equilibrium in the restricted space of heuristic strategies. Goldman et al. [5] have referred to this as an *experimental equilibrium*. We allow agent i to play a mixed strategy, and choose to play pure strategy $a^j \in H$ according to probability x_{ij}. Let $x_i = (x_{i1}, \ldots, x_{iM})$ denote the complete mixed strategy, with $x_{ij} \in [0,1]$ and $\sum_{j=1}^{M} x_{ij} = 1$. The vector of all agents' mixed strategies is denoted x and the vector of mixed strategies for all agents except i is denoted x_{-i}. We indicate by $x_i = a^j$, the special case when agent i plays pure strategy j with probability one.

We denote by $u(a^j, x_{-i})$ the *expected* payoff to an agent i for playing pure strategy j, given that all other agents play their mixed strategies x_{-i}. The expected payoff to agent i with mixed strategy x_i is then $u(x_i, x_{i-1}) = \sum_{j=1}^{M} u(a^j, x_{i-1}) x_{ij}$. In a Nash equilibrium, no one agent can receive a higher payoff by unilaterally deviating to another strategy, given fixed opponents' strategies. Formally, probabilities x^* constitute a *Nash equilibrium* iff for all agents i, and all $x_i \neq x_i^*$, $u(x_i, x_{-i}^*) \leq u(x_i^*, x_{-i}^*)$. To simplify the computation of equilibrium, in the remainder of this paper, we restrict our attention to symmetric mixed strategy equilibria, whereby $x_i^* = x_k^* = x^*$ for all agents i and k. It is known that symmetric Nash equilibria always exist for symmetric games.

An equilibrium computed with respect to expected payoffs, in the restricted strategy space, is not a Bayesian-Nash equilibrium (BNE) in the restricted strategy space because a full BNE would allow an agent to *choose* a different heuristic strategy for different realizations of its own type. Instead we require an agent to adopt the same heuristic strategy (e.g. "always bid at the price if the price is below my value and I am not currently winning") whatever its actual value. Thus, an agent plays an *ex ante* Nash equilibrium instead of an *interim*, or Bayesian-Nash, equilibrium. As the heuristic strategy space H becomes rich and contains arbitrarily complex strategies this distinction disappears because a heuristic strategy can simulate the effect of mapping from the multiple possible types of an agent in multiple different underlying strategies (e.g.

---

[3] We thank Tuomas Sandholm for brining this to our attention at the AMEC V workshop.

"if my value is less than \$5, then always bid at price if the price is below my value; otherwise, wait until the end of the auction and then snipe at 80% of my value.")[4]

To reiterate, the heuristic strategy approach is an approximation in which the designer of an auction consider only a very small subset of all possible strategies. As such, a Nash equilibrium in heuristic strategy space is *not* guaranteed to constitute an equilibrium in the underlying game.

3 An Information-Theoretic Approach

Before an equilibrium can be computed we require information about the payoffs of heuristic strategy profiles. But, because the underlying game is complex the payoffs are not analytically derivable and must be computed instead as average payoffs over repeated samples. It can be necessary to collect a large number of samples, each requiring a simulated run of the auction, to obtain sufficiently accurate payoff estimates. This is particularly expensive for games that must be run in real time, such as the Trading Agent Competition. However, it is not generally necessary to estimate all payoffs to the same degree of accuracy. For instance, if the unique equilibrium is for all agents to play the pure strategy a_j, then we need only *bound* the payoffs available from alternative strategies $a_k \neq a_j$ when every other agent plays a_j, to demonstrate a_j dominates. Thus, collecting samples uniformly for all strategy profiles may not be the most efficient method to arrive at an accurate equilibrium. In this section, we outline an information-theoretic approach to the problem of determining how to sample the underlying space of heuristic strategies, in which sampling is interleaved with Nash-equilibrium calculation.

Let S denote the set of all sample actions available, and let $\theta \in S^L$ denote a sequence of sample actions of length L. An example of a sample action could be "run the auction 10 times (each with agent values randomly chosen from the value distributions) in which agents follow (pure) strategy profile a". We find it convenient to also denote with θ the *information* that results from the new samples.

An information-theoretic approach to sampling requires three modeling assumptions. First, we need a *decision model*, $x(\theta)$, to denote the equilibrium selected, given information θ. Second, we need a *future information model* to predict the cumulative information that will be available after additional samples s, given current information θ. Third, we need an *error model* to estimate the error of the equilibrium selected due to current beliefs about the payoffs, with respect to the true equilibrium in the auction.

We define the error in terms of the gain in expected payoff that an agent can receive by deviating from the current equilibrium decision to a pure strategy, summed across all pure strategies. Clearly, in equilibrium this gain is zero because the agent has the same expected payoff for all pure strategies in the support, and less for other strategies. We can only *estimate* the true error, which we denote as $f_\pi(x)$, where π are the true payoffs, since the true equilibrium is what we are trying to compute in the first place! Instead, let $\hat{f}_\theta(x)$, denote the estimated error from decision x, as estimated with respect to information θ. We use this to guide sampling.

---

[4] We thank Michael Wellman for explaining this latter point.

The framework introduced by Russell & Wefald [19] for metadeliberation in time-critical decision problems with bounded-rational agents, estimates the *value of information*, $EVI(s|\theta)$, for sampling strategy s given information θ as:

$$EVI(s|\theta) = E_{s|\theta} \left[\hat{f}_{\theta.s}(x(\theta)) - \hat{f}_{\theta.s}(x(\theta.s)) \right]$$

where $E_{s|\theta}$ takes the expectation with respect to a model of the future samples s given current information θ. Here, $\theta.s$ indicates the information θ with the additional information acquired from samples s. Intuitively, $EVI(s|\theta)$ measures, in expectation, the degree to which further samples s will reduce the estimated error in the equilibrium choice. Notice that the first term is $\hat{f}_{\theta.s}(x(\theta))$ and not $\hat{f}_{\theta}(x(\theta))$, so that any effect that the information has on refining the *accuracy with which the error is computed* is factored out of this analysis. As observed by Russell & Wefald, this is important to maintain the useful property that the estimated value of information is positive for all possible sampling strategies.

In our model, the information θ that has already been accumulated through current samples provides a set of samples for each entry a in the payoff matrix. With this, the maximum likelihood estimator (MLE) for the *true mean*, $\mu(a)$, of strategy profile a, written $\mu_\theta(a)$, is computed as the sample mean. By the central limit theorem,[5] with sufficient number of samples (generally, 30 is considered sufficient) from any distribution, the true mean becomes normally distributed, with mean $\mu_\theta(a)$, and standard deviation $\sigma_{\mu_\theta(a)} = \sigma(a)/\sqrt{t_a}$, where $\sigma_\theta(a)$ is the standard deviation of the samples collected for a and t_a is the number of samples collected for a. We find it useful to refer to $\mu_\theta(a)$ and $\sigma_{\mu_\theta}(a)$ as the *observed mean*, and the *standard deviation over the observed mean*, given information θ. In the sequel, we drop the a indicator when the specific profile is understood, or immaterial to the discussion.

An optimal sampling strategy would take this definition of the expected value of information, and formulate an optimal *sequential* sampling strategy with future decisions contingent on the information returned from earlier decisions. One objective would sample payoffs to maximize the expected total decrease in decision error by the end of a fixed sampling period. Once determined, only the first step of the contingent sequential sampling strategy would be executed (e.g. *run the auction with all agents following strategy profile a*), at which point the complete sequential strategy would be reoptimized based on the new information. Berger [2, chapter 7] provides an extensive discussion of this methodology, which is central to statistical decision theory.

In practice, the best one can hope for is an approximation to this approach. Clearly metareasoning is valuable only to the extent that the time spent in metareasoning is less than the time saved through making better-informed sampling decisions. Russell & Wefald make a number of assumptions to keep metareasoning tractable for their setting of selective-search in adversarial search. Most importantly, they make a *single-step* assumption, which in our setting holds that the next sample is the last. This reduces the sampling decision to choosing the single best sampling action, to maximize $EVI(s|\theta)$.

---

[5] The central limit theorem assumes that samples are independent and of finite variance. The first assumption holds if strategies are static (they do not adapt) and the second assumption holds if payoffs in the underlying game are bounded.

The main problem with the single-step assumption in our setting is that it is often the case that *multiple* samples must be taken to have any effect on an estimated equilibrium. In our work, we instead estimate the value of performing a long sequence of the sample sampling action, $s \in S$, denoted s^∞. Once the optimal action is determined, we then *execute* a sequence of $K \geq 1$ of these samples, before reconsidering the value of making additional samples.

Given this, we define the three components of our information-theoretic model as follows:

Decision model. The equilibrium $x(\theta)$, given information θ, is computed as *one* of the mixed equilibria given the *mean* payoffs μ_θ in each entry in the payoff matrix. In particular, we select the equilibrium with the lowest error estimated from current information $\hat{f}_\theta(x)$.

Future information. Given the current information $(\mu_\theta, \sigma_\theta)$, we need a model for the effect that a large number of additional samples s^∞ on profile a will have on the future observed mean payoff, $\mu_{\theta.s^\infty}$, and the future standard deviation on observed mean, $\sigma_{\mu_{\theta.s^\infty}}$. We adopt two models for the future observed mean: (a) a *point*-estimate, with $\mu_{\theta.s^\infty} = \mu_\theta$; and (b) a *distributional*-estimate, with $\mu_{\theta.s^\infty} \sim N(\mu_\theta, \sigma_{\mu_\theta})$. We model the future standard deviation on the observed mean as $\sigma_{\mu_{\theta.s^\infty}} = \sigma_\theta / \sqrt{t_a + |s^\infty|}$, where t_a is the number of samples collected for a so far and $|s^\infty|$ is the number of samples in s^∞.

Error. As explained above, we define the true error function $f_\pi(x)$ with respect to payoffs π as $f_\pi(x) = \sum_{j=1}^{M} \max(0, u_i(a^j, x_{-i}) - u_i(x))$. We compute the estimated error, $\hat{f}_\theta(x)$, given information θ from Monte Carlo simulations on the actual error.

Looking at the two models of future information, the *point-estimate* of the future observed mean reflects the fact that our estimate of the true mean will remain the same in expectation. In comparison, the *distributional-estimate* considers that we expect the *observed mean* will converge to the true mean after many additional samples, and recognizes that the current information $(\mu_\theta, \sigma_{\mu_\theta})$ is the best current estimate for the true mean. The model for the future standard deviation on observed mean reflects an assumption that the standard deviation on the underlying payoff samples will remain the same as that for the current samples.

The complete algorithm for selecting the next samples is parameterized with K, C_f, and C_E, and defined as follows. First, compute the set of Nash equilibria NE given current information θ, and choose the $x(\theta) \in$ NE that minimizes estimated error $\hat{f}_\theta(x(\theta))$. Then choose the sampling action, $s \in S$, that maximizes EVI$(s^\infty | \theta)$. If EVI$(s^\infty | \theta) > 0$, perform those sample runs of the auction and continue the process. Otherwise, stop and return $x(\theta)$ as the chosen equilibrium.[6] Alternatively, continue to perform K samples

---

[6] With an explicit cost model, we would perform the samples only if EVI$(s^\infty | \theta)$ is greater than the cost of sampling. The model of cost and information value will depend heavily on the particular details of the problem, with the cost depending on the run time of the auction and the value of information depending on the importance of making an accurate decision. For example, in the context of an experimental approach to mechanism design we can interpret the value of a decision with respect to the goals of a mechanism designer, such as allocative efficiency.

from the most-preferred sampling action until no more samples can be made because
the algorithm must return an equilibrium (or set of equilibria).

To compute the estimated error $\hat{f}_{\theta.s}(x(\theta))$ for the current decision after additional information, we adopt the point-estimate model for the future observed mean after a large number s^{∞} of additional samples, together with the point-estimate model for the future standard deviation on observed mean. We average the results from C_f Monte Carlo simulations, with each simulation computing $f_{\hat{\pi}}(x(\theta))$ for a draw $\hat{\pi}$ of specific payoffs from the distribution $N(\mu_{\theta.s^{\infty}}, \sigma_{\mu_{\theta.s^{\infty}}})$ on true payoffs, with $\mu_{\theta.s^{\infty}} = \mu_{\theta}$ and $\sigma_{\mu_{\theta.s^{\infty}}} = \sigma_{\theta}/\sqrt{t_a + |s^{\infty}|}$.

To compute the estimated error $\hat{f}_{\theta.s}(x(\theta.s))$ for the new and improved decision after additional information, we must first estimate the future decision. For this, we adopt the distributional-estimate, $\mu_{\theta.s^{\infty}} \sim N(\mu_{\theta}, \sigma_{\mu_{\theta}})$, for the future observed mean. We sample C_E mean payoffs π' from this distribution, and compute a new equilibrium $x(\pi')$ for each. Then, we measure the estimated error for each of these decisions using the same model for future information as was adopted to compute the estimated error for the current decision, taking an additional C_f samples for each π'. Finally, we average this estimated error for future decision $x(\pi')$ across all C_E equilibrium samples.[7] For each of the $|H|$ possible heuristic strategies, the total number of equilibrium calculations performed are $C_E C_f$.

4   A Faster Approach

As we demonstrate in Section 5, EVI$(s|\theta)$ is an effective criterion for selecting a pure strategy profile to sample next. Unfortunately, EVI$(s|\theta)$ is slow to compute for even very small games, and impractically slow for moderately sized games. The problem lies in the fact that EVI$(s|\theta)$ must perform multiple equilibrium computations for each possible sample sequence. For each possible sample, s, we must compute multiple sample future equilibria to estimate the distribution of future equilibria. Although we have tricks to fairly quickly compute a future equilibrium based on the current equilibrium (see Section 5), the computational cost can still be prohibitively high, given that we perform C_E equilibrium computations for each strategy profile.

We have developed a much faster method for computing the value of performing a set of further samples that requires no additional equilibrium computations. The algorithm is the same as before, except that, instead of EVI$(s|\theta)$, we use the estimated *confirmational value of information*, ECVI$(s|\theta)$, of sampling action s given information θ, defined as:

$$\text{ECVI}(s|\theta) = E_{s|\theta}\left[\hat{f}_{\theta}(x(\theta)) - \hat{f}_{\theta.s}(x(\theta))\right]$$

---

[7] We note that an alternative model to compute the estimated error $\hat{f}_{\theta.s}(x(\theta.s))$ for the new decision after additional information would use a hybrid of the two models for future information. We could adopt the *same* sample π' that is used to compute a future equilibrium decision $x(\pi')$ to model the future observed mean for the purposes of computing the estimated error on that decision, but continue to adopt $\sigma_{\mu_{\theta.s^{\infty}}} = \sigma_{\theta}/\sqrt{t_a + |s^{\infty}|}$ to generate C_f samples for this error calculation. We plan to investigate this hybrid model in future work.

$\text{ECVI}(s|\theta)$ measures, in expectation, the degree to which further samples s would decrease the estimated error of the current equilibrium choice. Put another way, the sample s that maximizes $\text{ECVI}(s|\theta)$ provides the best evidence to confirm our current equilibrium choice.

We need not compute any future equilibria with this approach, but need only perform Monte Carlo simulations to estimate the expected error of the current equilibrium. Furthermore, we need perform significantly fewer of these Monte Carlo simulations than for $\text{EVI}(s|\theta)$. If we perform C_f Monte Carlo simulations to estimate the error for each future equilibrium, then $\text{EVI}(s|\theta)$ requires $C_E C_f$ simulations of $f_\pi(x)$, while $\text{ECVI}(s|\theta)$ requires only C_f.

Using $\text{ECVI}(s|\theta)$ appears to run counter to the methodology of Russell and Wefald, who argue that further samples are valuable only to the extent to which they may *change* the equilibrium choice. In fact, this is not the case. Based on some informal arguments, we can view the approach as a heuristic to choose the sampling action s that is most likely to change the estimated equilibrium, and as an approximate version of $\text{EVI}(s|\theta)$.

Recall that there is a continuum of mixed strategies that could potentially comprise a Nash equilibrium. Thus, so long as there remains "sufficient" uncertainty in the value of the payoffs in a cell c of the game matrix, we should expect that further samples of c will change the chosen equilibrium, however slightly. Thus, although we choose s to confirm that $x(\theta)$ is the correct equilibrium, sampling s will, in fact, generally change our decision.

Why should we expect that choosing s to increase our confidence in the current $x(\theta)$ would best help change the decision for the better? Since sample action s has the highest direct impact on reducing error for $x(\theta)$, we should expect that it also reduces error for some mixed strategies close to $x(\theta)$. And since $x(\theta)$ is our best estimate of the correct equilibrium, then we should expect the true equilibrium x^* to lie nearby. Thus, sample action s can be considered our best guess for reducing the error in our estimate of true equilibrium, x^*, hence making it a promising candidate for sampling.

Ultimately, the value of using $\text{ECVI}(s|\theta)$ is clearly borne out in our experiments. It is much faster than $\text{EVI}(s|\theta)$, yet reduces error in the chosen equilibrium at a rate comparable to $\text{EVI}(s|\theta)$.

5   Experiments

This section describes empirical results from using our methods to choose samples in stylized games. We compare our approach with a naive uniform-sampling approach. To chart the progress as more samples are performed, we compare with making uniform samples in a round-robin fashion. We report on results from two games: (i) one with $N = 1$ agent and $M = 5$ strategies, and (ii) one with $N = 8$ agents and $M = 3$ strategies. So that we could compare the results of the methods with the true equilibria of the games, we generated payoff samples directly from specified distributions, rather than from running a complex auction game.

For each game and each method, $\text{EVI}(s|\theta)$ and $\text{ECVI}(s|\theta)$, we collected 10 initial samples on each strategy profile to seed the payoff table, before applying the methods. The length of s^∞, which is used to estimate the value of additional sampling within metadeliberation, was 1000, and the length of s^K, the samples actually performed on one profile, was 10. We perform the same number of total samples with each sampling method and compare the true error in the equilibrium decision by comparing with the actual equilibrium (that we compute separately).

For game (i), we performed 1000 total samples, and for game (ii) we performed 2000 total samples. We ran each method 200 times on game (i), each time with a different random seed. Computing $EVI(s|\theta)$ is prohibitively expensive for game (ii), hence we ran only $ECVI(s|\theta)$ and uniform sampling (both for 200 times) but not $EVI(s|\theta)$.

For the purpose of the analysis, we graph two error measures of the chosen equilibrium x. Both are calculated with respect to the *true* game information, and as a function of the number of simulations performed and averaged over all runs. The first error measure is $f_\pi(x)$ discussed before, where π are the true payoffs. The second error measure considers the distance (in probability space) between the estimated equilibrium and a true equilibrium. For this, we adopt the L_2 norm, defined as $\sqrt{\sum(x_j - x_j^*)^2}$, where x_j is the probability of playing heuristic strategy a^j in profile x, and likewise for x^*, the true equilibrium. When multiple true equilibria exist, we compute the minimal L_2 norm across all equilibria.

Recall that our approaches require the repeated computation of Nash equilibrium. Nash equilibria can be formulated and computed in a variety of ways [10]. We use a formulation of Nash equilibrium as a non-linear optimization problem, in which the equilibria lie at the zero points of an appropriate objective function. We used *amoeba* [16], a non-linear, gradient-descent search algorithm to find the zero points. Although amoeba is not guaranteed to find all, or even any equilibria, we have found it effective in finding all equilibria for even reasonably large problems through restart (e.g. 20 agents and 3 strategies) [22].

In general, we find that the most costly step is not finding an equilibrium, but verifying to our satisfaction that all equilibria have been found, requiring that we restart at a number of random points. In our sample-selection algorithms, performing new samples does not move the equilibria too far from their previous location. Thus, we can start the search at the previously computed equilibrium points and amoeba's gradient-descent methods will often quickly converge to the new equilibrium.

5.1   Game 1: 1-Agent, 5-Strategies

This is a degenerate game with only one agent, where each strategy corresponds to a unique profile and the unique equilibrium is simply the (pure) strategy with the highest mean payoff. We define the game this way because the problem of equilibrium calculation reduces to determining the strategy with the highest expected payoff. This simplifies the computational problem and facilitates comparison between $EVI(s|\theta)$ and $ECVI(s|\theta)$, and also allows informal validation of our methods by inspection of this simple game.

We model the true payoff distribution in each of the 5 entries in the payoff table as Normal(μ, σ), with parameters defined as:

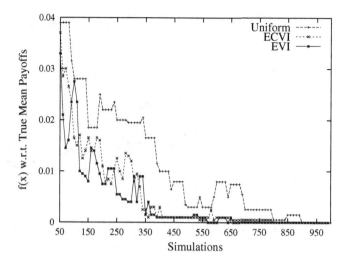

Fig. 1. True error $f_\pi(x)$ of the computed equilibrium x with respect to true mean payoffs from the three sampling methods on the 1-agent 5-strategies game. The three sampling methods are uniform, EVI$(s|\theta)$, and ECVI$(s|\theta)$. Results shown here are averaged over 200 separate runs, where each run consist of a total of 1000 samples.

Strategy	μ	σ
1	1.0	0.5
2	0.9	0.5
3	0.5	0.1
4	0.3	0.3
5	0.35	0.4

The expected-utility maximizing strategy is to play strategy 1. Strategy 2 is the most-likely candidate for the optimal strategy after strategy 1. A few samples would distinguish quickly that strategy 1 and 2 are the top two strategies, hence we would hope that our methods assign most samples to these two strategies.

In fact, in this game it is common that both methods EVI$(s|\theta)$ and ECVI$(s|\theta)$ predict that additional sampling will have zero value, long before 1000 samples are collected (within an average of 163 samples for EVI$(s|\theta)$ and 304 samples for ECVI$(s|\theta)$). This is a consequence of the approximations made in their model for the value of information. When this occurs we continue sampling by adopting a simple heuristic that chooses the profile with the smallest L_2 norm to the current equilibrium.

Figure 1 shows the $f_\pi(x)$ error measure for the three methods. As expected, after an initial 50 samples, all three methods find equilibria that have roughly the same magnitude of $f_\pi(x)$. After this initial stage, $f_\pi(x)$ of the ECVI$(s|\theta)$ and EVI$(s|\theta)$ methods decrease more rapidly and reach zero error faster than the uniform sampling method. Method EVI$(s|\theta)$ has a somewhat lower $f_\pi(x)$ than ECVI$(s|\theta)$ through most of the samples, although both methods reach near zero error at near the same point. For this game the L_2 norm is identical to error $f_\pi(x)$ (after some rescaling).

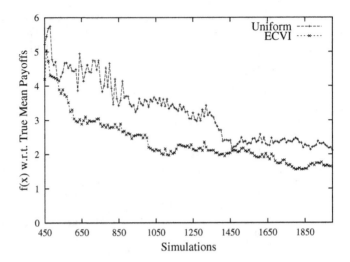

Fig. 2. True error $f_\pi(x)$ of the computed equilibrium x with respect to true mean payoffs from sampling methods uniform and ECVI$(s|\theta)$ on the 8-agents 3-strategies game. Results shown here are averaged over 200 separate runs, where each run consist of a total of 2000 samples.

We notice that the methods are selective in assigning samples: EVI$(s|\theta)$ assigns on average 50.3% and 49.6% of samples to strategy 1 and 2 respectively, likewise 51.2% and 46.5% for ECVI$(s|\theta)$ (we took these measures only for samples performed by the two approaches after the initial samples and only while there was a positive value for sampling). Thus, the methods make decisions that correspond to the intuitively correct distribution of samples.

5.2 Game 2: 8-Agents and 3-Strategies

This game has 8 agents and 3 strategies, and a total of 45 different strategy profiles. The true mean payoff, $\mu(a)$, for each strategy a, was chosen randomly from a uniform distribution [300, 600], with $\sigma = 50$ for all payoffs. The three (exact) mixed-strategy Nash equilibria in this game are: $(0.4114, 0.0000, 0.5886), (0.0000, 0.5213, 0.4787)$, and $(0.0268, 0.0877, 0.8856)$.

We only present results for ECVI$(s|\theta)$ in Game 2, because EVI$(s|\theta)$ is too expensive to compute. Figure 2 plots $f_\pi(x)$ for the ECVI$(s|\theta)$ and uniform sampling methods. As with the 1-agent, 5-strategy game, using ECVI$(s|\theta)$ gives a smaller error across all numbers of samples. We see similar, but more pronounced results when comparing with the L_2 norm, as shown in Figure 3. The rather small L_2 norm of ≈ 0.0005 after 1050 samples with the ECVI$(s|\theta)$ method indicates that the estimated equilibrium is very close to an exact Nash equilibria (c.f. ≈ 0.005 for uniform-sampling).

The ECVI$(s|\theta)$ method chooses samples very non-uniformly between the strategy profiles. Strategy profiles that are closer to one of the true Nash equilibria (in terms of

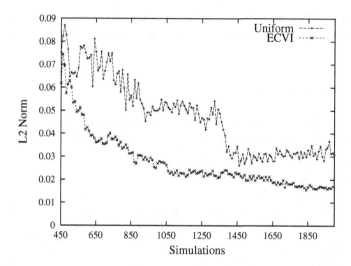

Fig. 3. L_2-norm of two sampling methods on the 8-agents 3-strategies game. Results shown here are averaged over the same 200 runs reported in Figure 2.

L_2 norm) received 5% to 10% of the 2000 samples, while some profiles were assigned virtually no new samples after their initial set of 10 samples.

6   Discussion

We have presented information-theoretic methods to choose the samples necessary to compute a Nash equilibrium with respect to *ex ante* payoffs of heuristic strategies. The first method is more principled, but is impractically slow. We were not able to run the method even on our 8-agents and 3-strategies problem. The second method approximates the first, but is much faster because it avoids additional equilibrium calculations during metadeliberation. Our initial experiments suggest that these approaches give us an equilibrium with less error from fewer samples than with uniform sampling.

Our immediate next step is to run the second information-theoretic method, $\text{ECVI}(s|\theta)$, in the setting of a Continuous Double Auction, or for the Trading Agent Competition. More broadly, we believe these methods are relevant to the problem of *Experimental Mechanism Design*, in which computational methods are used in a closed loop to evaluate alternative designs for electronic markets. Rather than modeling agents as game-theoretic, as in classic mechanism design and auction theory, we can consider a parameterized class of markets and experimentally validate the performance of a market with respect to a set of desiderata. Our approach extends to determine how to allocate samples *across multiple designs*, in addition to across strategies within a particular design. The goals of a mechanism designer, for example allocative efficiency, provide a metric with which to define the decision error. Additional samples can then be allocated to best improve the decision made about the final market design, in terms of its actual efficiency. This integration of information-theoretic sampling methods, within agent-based methods for electronic market design, provides an interesting direction for future work.

Acknowledgments

We thank Daniel Reeves for his helpful discussions on this topic and comments on this paper. David Parkes was supported in this work by an IBM Faculty Award.

References

[1] Moshe Babaioff and William E. Walsh. Incentive-compatible, budget-balanced, yet highly efficient auctions for supply chain formation. *Decision Support Systems, to appear.*

[2] James O Berger. *Statistical Decision Theory and Bayesian Analysis.* Springer-Verlag, 1985.

[3] D. Cliff and J. Bruten. Minimal-intelligence agents for bargaining behaviors in market-based environments. Technical Report HPL-97-91, Hewlett Packard Labs, 1997.

[4] S. Gjerstad and J. Dickhaut. Price formation in double auctions. *Games and Economic Behavior*, 22:1–29, 1998.

[5] Claudia V. Goldman, Sarit Kraus, and Onn Shehory. Agent strategies: for sellers to satisfy purchase-orders, for buyers to select sellers. In *Tenth European Workshop on Modeling Autonomous Agents in a Multiagent World*, 2001.

[6] Amy Greenwald. The 2002 trading agent competition: An overview of agent strategies. *AI Magazine*, 24(1):77–82, Spring 2003.

[7] Jeffrey O. Kephart and Amy Greenwald. Shopbot economics. *Autonomous Agents and Multi-Agent Systems*, 3(3-4):245–276, 2003.

[8] Anshul Kothari, David C. Parkes, and Subhash Suri. Approximately-strategyproof and tractable multi-unit auctions. In *Fourth ACM Conf. on Electronic Commerce (EC'03)*, 2003. To appear.

[9] Daniel Lehmann, Liadan Ita O'Callaghan, and Yoav Shoham. Truth revelation in approximately efficient combinatorial auctions. *Journal of the ACM*, 49(5):577–602, September 2002.

[10] Richard D. McKelvey and Andrew McLennan. Computation of equilibria in finite games. In *Handbook of Computational Economics*, volume 1. Elsevier Science B. V., 1996.

[11] Noam Nisan and Amir Ronen. Computationally feasible VCG mechanisms. In *Proc. 2nd ACM Conf. on Electronic Commerce (EC-00)*, pages 242–252, 2000.

[12] Noam Nisan and Amir Ronen. Algorithmic mechanism design. *Games and Economic Behavior*, 35:166–196, 2001.

[13] Noam Nisan and I Segal. The communication complexity of efficient allocation problems. Technical report, Hebrew University and Stanford University, 2002.

[14] David C Parkes, Jayant R Kalagnanam, and Marta Eso. Achieving budget-balance with Vickrey-based payment schemes in exchanges. In *Proc. 17th International Joint Conference on Artificial Intelligence (IJCAI-01)*, 2001.

[15] David C. Parkes and Lyle H. Ungar. Preventing strategic manipulation in iterative auctions: Proxy-Agents and price-adjustment. In *Seventeenth National Conference on Artificial Intelligence*, pages 82–89, 2000.

[16] W. Press, S. Teukolsky, W. Vetterling, and B . Flannery. *Numerical recipes in C.* Cambridge University Press, 1992.

[17] Daniel M. Reeves, Michael P. Wellman, Jeffrey K. MacKie-Mason, and Anna Ospayshvili. Exploring bidding strategies for market-based scheduling. *Decision Support Systems, to appear.*

[18] A E Roth. The economist as engineer. *Econometrica*, 70:1341–1378, 2002.

[19] Stuart Russell and Eric Wefald. Principles of metareasoning. *Artificial Intelligence*, 49:361–395, 1991.

[20] Peter Stone and Amy Greenwald. The first international trading agent competition: Autonomous bidding agents. *Electronic Commerce Research*, 5(1), 2005.

[21] Gerald Tesauro and Rajarshi Das. High-performance bidding agents for the continuous double auction. In *Third ACM Conference on Electronic Commerce*, pages 206–209, 2001.

[22] William E. Walsh, Rajarshi Das, Gerald Tesauro, and Jeffrey O. Kephart. Analyzing complex strategic interactions in multi-agent systems. In *AAAI-03 Workshop on Game Theoretic and Decision Theoretic Agents*, pages 109–118, 2002.

[23] Michael P. Wellman, Amy Greenwald, Peter Stone, and Peter R. Wurman. The 2001 trading agent competition. *Electronic Markets*, 13(1):4–12, 2003.

[24] Michael P. Wellman, Peter R. Wurman, Kevin O'Malley, Roshan Bangera, Shoude Lin, Daniel Reeves, and William E. Walsh. Designing the market game for a trading agent competition. *IEEE Internet Computing*, 5(2):43–51, 2001.

[25] Peter R. Wurman, Gangshu Cai, Jie Zhong, and Ashish Sureka. An algorithm for computing the outcome of combinatorial auctions with proxy bidding. In *Fifth International Conference on Electronic Commerce*, pages 1–8, 2003.

Improving Learning Performance by Applying Economic Knowledge

Christopher H. Brooks[1], Robert S. Gazzale[2], Jeffrey K. MacKie Mason[2], and
Edmund H. Durfee[3]*

[1] Computer Science Department, University of San Francisco, San Francisco, CA 94117-1080
cbrooks@usfca.edu
[2] Department of Economics, University of Michigan, Ann Arbor, MI 48109
{rgazzale,jmm}@umich.edu
[3] EECS Department, University of Michigan, Ann Arbor, MI 48109
durfee@umich.edu

Abstract. Digital information economies require information goods producers to learn how to position themselves within a potentially vast product space. Further, the topography of this space is often nonstationary, due to the interactive dynamics of multiple producers changing their positions as they try to learn the distribution of consumer preferences and other features of the problem's economic structure. This presents a producer or its agent with a difficult learning problem: how to locate profitable niches in a very large space.

In this paper, we present a model of an information goods duopoly and show that, under complete information, producers would prefer not to compete, instead acting as local monopolists and targeting separate niches in the consumer population. However, when producers have no information about the problem they are solving, it can be quite difficult for them to converge on this solution. We show how a modest amount of economic knowledge about the problem can make it much easier, either by reducing the search space, starting in a useful area of the space, or introducing a gradient. These experiments support the hypothesis that a producer using some knowledge of a problem's (economic) structure can outperform a producer that is performing a naive, knowledge-free form of learning.

1 Introduction

Recent advances in networked information technology have led to the emergence of a digital economy. This is an economy in which digital goods, in particular information goods, are traded online. In these environments, a producer of information goods is faced with a potentially daunting problem: how to position itself within a large and dynamic product space. In addition, many of the participants in this information economy are computational agents, which leads us to examine automated techniques for solving this problem.

The large product space is in many ways a result of the characteristics of digital information goods. They can be easily unbundled and re-bundled to create different products. In addition to a pre-defined "newspaper" for example, a producer can sell the

---

* This work was supported in part by NSF grants IIS-9872057 and IIS-0112669.

P. Faratin et al. (Eds.): AMEC 2003, LNAI 3048, pp. 124–144, 2004.

whole news collection, categories of articles, individual articles, graphics, data tables, etc. Digital goods typically have low marginal cost: once the first copy is produced, subsequent copies can be reproduced essentially for free. This makes *bundling* of goods a particularly attractive strategy [7]. The effect of unbundling and re-bundling is to exponentially proliferate possible product configurations.

In addition, the economy is likely to be highly dynamic. First, the enormous size of the product configuration space implies that producers will need to *search* for good configurations. If there are competing producers also searching, then a second dynamic is introduced, since the path followed by competitors will affect profits and learning for a producer. Third, the composition of the consumer population or the preferences of individual consumers may be nonstationary. These factors imply that firms must engage in active learning in order to determine what to offer and what price to charge. It is thus important to understand the system's dynamics, in addition to its equilibria.

In this paper, we consider the problem of competing information producers positioning their offerings when faced with a heterogeneous consumer population. We focus on the role that economic knowledge can play in reducing the producers' search burden. When producers must simultaneously learn what to offer and how to price it, the naive learning problem becomes very difficult. However, if producers use even a limited amount of economic knowledge, they can sharply reduce the difficulty of each learning problem, locating a profitable niche and extracting a significant fraction of the equilibrium profit.

"Economic knowledge" is a broad term, and such knowledge can take on a variety of forms. We take the position that economic knowledge is information that allows a producer to more effectively or efficiently learn what good to sell or how to price a good. Much of our research (e.g. [3]) has examined producers at either extreme of the spectrum of knowledge. On one end, economic knowledge can mean complete information about consumer preferences and the strategies of all other producers. This is the classical analytic assumption taken in section 3. At the other extreme, a producer has no knowledge about the problem whatsoever. Even in this case, some basic economic knowledge (for example, that prices must be nonnegative) will likely be built in. In this paper, we explore the space between these two extremes, beginning with the relatively well-understood full-information solution and then progressively weakening the information these producers have. One of our goals in this paper is to study the way in which different sorts of economic knowledge alter the solution space, and the resulting problem difficulty.

Other researchers have considered the problem of producers attempting to locate suitable niches in a high-dimensional product space. Chang and Harrington [4] study conditions under which a chain ought to allow individual stores find profitable niches in 'idea space' and when it ought to centrally supply ideas. They find that when consumers are sufficiently heterogeneous, allowing each store to learn simultaneously provides higher profits than a centralized search.

Several researchers, including ourselves, have studied the problem of "zero-knowledge" agents, meaning agents that learn without taking advantage of the economic aspects of the learning problem. Our previous work examined zero-knowledge monopolists trading off the precision of a price schedule against the difficulty of learning that schedule [3] and zero-knowledge duopolists attempting to discover whether to compete directly or target separate niches [2]. In both cases, the learning agents did not attempt to exploit any economic knowledge about the structure of the problem.

Kephart, et al [9], and Dasgupta and Das [6] have examined economies in which zero-knowledge agents adaptively adjust the prices they offer in an attempt to maximize aggregate profit. These sorts of systems often exhibit *price wars*, in which producers repeatedly undercut each other, driving prices down to marginal cost and profits to zero; a focus of these papers is on developing learning algorithms that can avoid price wars. We argue that a relatively small amount of economic knowledge can also serve this purpose, and that the paucity of information available in the zero-knowledge setting makes the learning problem overly difficult for each producer.

In this paper we analytically derive optimal producer behavior in a full-information static environment, then use agent simulations to study behavior in an incomplete-information dynamic environment with learning. In Section 2, we present the details of our model of an information market. In Section 3, we derive the static equilibrium conditions and profits, both for a monopolist and for multiple strategic firms. Next, in Section 4, we examine the problem of zero-knowledge duopolists learning what bundle to offer and show that naive learning performs quite poorly. Then, in Section 5, we show that a learning producer with even a limited amount of economic knowledge is able to extract a significant fraction of the available profit. Finally, we discuss our results and future directions in Section 6.

2   Modeling

In this section, we present our model of consumer preferences, describe the structure of the consumer population, and then characterize the resulting behavior of both consumers and producers.

2.1   Consumer Preferences

We assume that there is set of Γ disjoint information categories. Each consumer is willing to pay w for each article in her favorite category, γ^*. All consumers agree that the relationship between categories can be expressed by ordering them from $\gamma_1, ..., \gamma_\Gamma$.[4] We label categories by their index. Each consumer values a fraction $k < 1$ of the categories.[5] We assume that values for articles in particular categories fall off linearly from γ^*. The value that consumer j places on category γ_i is thus:

$$\mu_j(\gamma) = \begin{cases} w_j(1 - \frac{2(|\gamma_i - \gamma_j^*|)}{k_j \Gamma}) & \text{if } |\gamma - \gamma_j^*| \leq \frac{k_j \Gamma}{2} \\ 0 & \text{otherwise} \end{cases} \quad (1)$$

Figure 1 illustrates the value that consumers place on articles in categories.

---

[4] That all consumers agree on the relationship between categories is an admittedly large assumption.

[5] Our formulation of consumer demand is similar to that introduced by Chuang and Sirbu [5].

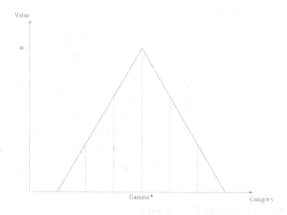

Fig. 1. Consumer valuations of articles in different categories.

A bundle is a collection of articles partitioned into categories. Bundles are useful for producers in this scenario, in that they allow a producer to extract greater profit from a heterogeneous consumer population. We define the size of a bundle as $|B| = \sum_{i=1}^{\Gamma} n_i$, where n_i is the number of articles in category j. While Equation 1 expresses the value of a single article, we wish to capture the notion that large bundles can place a burden upon the consumer due to the scarcity value of the consumer's attention. We refer to this as clutter cost, $\alpha(|B|)$. We assume that this cost function is exponential (and thus convex): $\alpha(|B|) = e^{\lambda|B|}$. In practice producers may endogenously influence this cost function by providing search and indexing features, thereby changing λ. In this paper, we assume that λ is exogenous and common across all consumers.

Thus, a consumer j's valuation for a given bundle is

$$V_j(B) = \sum_{\gamma=1}^{\Gamma} n_\gamma \mu_j(\gamma) - e^{\lambda|B|}. \tag{2}$$

2.2   Consumer Population Structure

We assume that w and λ are common across consumers, so a consumer is fully specified by her values of γ^* and k. We also assume there is a finite number of k values, denoted by $\bar{k}$. We call each unique pair a "niche", and label a pair by $c_l \equiv \{\gamma_l^*, k_l\}$, with $l = 1, \ldots, \Gamma \times \bar{k}$. We assume that there is the same number of consumers in each niche.

2.3   Consumer Behavior

Consumers perfectly evaluate bundles before purchase. Each period, a consumer purchases a bundle which gives her the highest non-negative surplus, if at least one such bundle exists. All consumers in a niche purchase the same bundle except when multiple bundles offer the highest non-negative surplus, in which case each chooses randomly.

2.4   Producer Behavior

The producer's goal is to maximize cumulative (discounted) profits. In each period, each of M producers offers a single bundle, which consists of a number of articles in each category and a price for the bundle. We assume that consumers are anonymous; producers are unable to identify which consumers have purchased their bundles. Instead, each producer only receives its aggregate profit. [6]

We represent producer m's offer as a vector of length $\Gamma + 1$, $\{n_{m1}, n_{m2}, ..., n_{m\Gamma}, p_m\} = \{\vec{n}_m, p_m\}$, indicating the number of articles in each category and the bundle price. The producer chooses $n_i \in (0, \bar{n})$, where $\bar{n}$ is the maximum number of articles a producer can offer in a single category,[7] and chooses $p_i \in [0, \bar{p}]$.[8]

3   Full-Information Equilibria

In this section we characterize the solution of the firm's product configuration and pricing problem in a static, full-information environment. We assume that producers know the values of Γ, w, and λ, and know the distributions of k and γ^*. We first solve the problem for a monopolist, and then characterize the pure-strategy [9] Nash equilibria when there are multiple complete-information firms.

3.1   One Firm Optimization

In order to provide insights into the effects of consumer demand on the producer's incentives, we first look at the case of a monopolist.[10] The results derived for $M = 1$ are also useful for the analysis when $M \geq 2$.

Lemma 1 *If there is a single producing firm, then p is optimal for $\vec{n}$ only if at least one niche receives zero surplus.*

---

[6] This assumption makes offering multiple bundles simultaneously less appealing when a producer must learn, as it becomes more difficult to accurately assess the value of a bundle.

[7] We set this to be a non-binding constraint for any profit-maximizing firm. For example, we can set $\bar{n}$ to be the positive n such that $w*n - e^{\lambda *n} = 0$. For analytic convenience we assume that the number of articles offered in a category, n_i, has a continuous support. Imposing an integer constraint would greatly complicate the analysis and statement of results without changing their qualitative nature.

[8] We set $\bar{p}$ to be the maximal willingness to pay possible. As $k < 1$, for any bundle size, a consumer strictly prefers a bundle consisting only of articles in her most-preferred category to any other distribution of $|B|$. The willingness to pay of this consumer is $V = |B|w - e^{\lambda|B|}$. Maximizing this value with respect to $|B|$, and substituting back into the value function results in a willingness to pay equal to $\bar{p} = \frac{w(log(\frac{w}{\lambda})-1)}{\lambda}$.

[9] We have not analyzed the mixed-strategy solutions for this problem; this remains a topic for future work.

[10] We assume, for analytical convenience, that optimal bundles are not constrained by the number of categories. That is, if consumers in a niche with $\gamma^* = \Gamma$ purchase, a producer would not change her offering to attract consumers with $\gamma^* = \Gamma + 1$, if they existed.

Proof: Assume not. Let c_l receive the smallest positive surplus from $\{\vec{n}, p\}$. By continuity of p, there exists a $\hat{p}$ such that c_l receives zero surplus. With a higher price and equal demand, profits must increase, and so $\{\vec{n}, p\}$ cannot be optimal.   ∎

Lemma 2 *Assuming $\bar{k} \geq 2$, if $\{\vec{n}, p\}$ is the optimal offering for a monopolist, then at least 2 niches receive zero surplus.*

Proof: By Lemma 1, we know that at least one niche must receive zero surplus. We show that at least one other niche must receive zero surplus.

Assume that $n_j < |B|$ and that the only zero-surplus niche has $\gamma^* = \gamma_j$. By continuity of n, we can reallocate ϵ articles from γ_i to a category closer or equal to γ_j, for ϵ small. As this increases the surplus of $\gamma^* = \gamma_j$, p can be increased without changing total demand, and therefore $\{\vec{n}, p\}$ cannot not be optimal.

If $n_j = |B|$, all niches with $\gamma^* = \gamma_j$ receive the same surplus, regardless of k, and therefore receive zero surplus.   ∎

We can now characterize more completely the optimal offering by a monopolist. We assume that there are at least $2\, k$ values, and from Lemma 2 we know that at least two niches receive zero net surplus. We call the two outermost niches, c_a and c_b, the *target niches*. We assume that the most-favored category of c_a is to the left of or the same as that of c_b, or $\gamma_a^* \leq \gamma_b^*$. We first show that given two target niches, it is optimal for the firm to restrict itself to choosing amongst a subset of bundle distributions, i.e. percentages of total articles in each category. Given that the monopolist chooses from this subset, the revenue that it receives is a function only of bundle size. The problem of choosing an optimal bundle and price, *conditional on a pair of target niches*, thus reduces to choosing the appropriate bundle size $|B|$.

At least one combination of target niches, when optimally targeted, must result in the highest profit. We call this combination of niches, c_a^* and c_b^*, the *optimal target niches*.

We start by characterizing optimal bundle distributions given a pair of target niches.

Lemma 3 *If $\{\vec{n}, p\}$ is optimal for a monopolist conditional on $V_{c_a} = V_{c_b} = 0$, then $n_i = 0 \ \forall \gamma_i < \gamma_a$ and $\gamma_i > \gamma_b$.*

Proof: Assume not, and that $n_i = 0$ for all $\gamma_i < \gamma_a$. Let γ_k be rightmost category with $n_k > 0$. By continuity of n_i, reallocating ϵ from γ_k to γ_{k-1} increases the surplus of c_a and c_b to $\hat{p}$. Only those with $\gamma^* \geq \gamma_k$ are worse off. All of these niches received positive surplus if they purchased the original bundle. Therefore, $p = \hat{p}$ strictly increases profits as all niches with positive surplus at $\{\vec{n}, p\}$ still have non-negative surplus. Therefore, $\{\vec{n}, p\}$ could not have been optimal.   ∎

Thus by Lemma 3, conditional on particular niches receiving zero surplus, only bundles where no articles are to the outside of either niche can be optimal. We now show that the set of all "interior" bundles which deliver zero surplus to the target niches are characterized by the mean category of the bundle, $\hat{\gamma} \equiv \sum_{i=1}^{\Gamma} \gamma_i \frac{n_i}{|B|}$, and show for which niches this characterization, together with the bundle size, is sufficient to determine gross surplus.

Lemma 4 *If $n_i = 0$ for all $i < \gamma^*$ ($i > \gamma^*$) then $V_j(B) + e^{\lambda|B|} = |B|w(1 - \frac{\hat{\gamma} - \gamma^*}{k_j \Gamma})$*
$(= |B|w(1 - \frac{\gamma^* - \hat{\gamma}}{k_j \Gamma}))$.

Proof: We show that this is true for if $n_i = 0$ for all $i < \gamma^*$. The proof when $n_i = 0$ for all $i > \gamma^*$ is analogous.

As all articles are to the right of the consumer:

$$V_j(B) + e^{\lambda|B|} = \sum_{i=\gamma_j^*}^{\Gamma} n_i w \left(1 - \frac{2(\gamma_i - \gamma_j^*)}{k_j \Gamma}\right)$$

$$= \sum_{i=\gamma_j^*}^{\Gamma} n_i w + \sum_{i=\gamma_j^*}^{\Gamma} \frac{2wn_i\gamma^*}{k_j \Gamma} - \sum_{i=\gamma_j^*}^{\Gamma} \frac{2wn_i\gamma_i}{k_j \Gamma}$$

$$= |B|w + \frac{2w|B|\gamma^*}{k_j \Gamma} - \frac{2w|B|\hat{\gamma}}{k_j \Gamma}$$

$$= |B|w \left(1 - \frac{2(\hat{\gamma} - \gamma^*)}{k_j \Gamma}\right), \tag{3}$$

using the definition of $\hat{\gamma}$ and $\sum n_i = |B|$ on the third line. ∎

Lemma 4 shows that assuming that all articles in a bundle are on one side of a niche's γ^*, that niche's value of that bundle depends *only* on the size of the bundle and the mean category. By Lemma 3, this result applies to the target niches. Our next result shows that for given target niches, there is a unique mean bundle category ($\hat{\gamma}$) that satisfies $V_{c_a}(B) = V_{c_b}(B)$.

Lemma 5 *If $n_i = 0$ for all $\gamma_i < \gamma_a$ and all $\gamma_i > \gamma_b$, then $V_{c_a}(B) = V_{c_b}(B)$ if and only if $\hat{\gamma} = \gamma_a + (\gamma_b - \gamma_a) \frac{1/(k_a \Gamma)}{1/(k_a \Gamma) + 1/(k_b \Gamma)}$.*

Proof: First, if $\gamma_a^* = \gamma_b^*$, then $n_{\gamma_a^*} = |B|$, and $\hat{\gamma} = \gamma_a^*$.

Now assume that $\gamma_a^* \neq \gamma_b^*$. By Lemma 4, $\hat{\gamma} \in [\gamma_a^*, \gamma_b^*]$. By Equation 3, the value of c_b is increasing on this interval, and that of c_a decreasing. Therefore, if there exists a $\hat{\gamma}$ such that $V_{c_a}(\hat{\gamma}) = V_{c_b}(\hat{\gamma})$, it will be unique. To find this $\hat{\gamma}$:

$$V_{c_a}(B) = V_{c_b}(B)$$

$$|B|w \left(1 - \frac{2(\hat{\gamma} - \gamma_a^*)}{k_a \Gamma}\right) = |B|w \left(1 - \frac{2(\gamma_b^* - \hat{\gamma})}{k_a \Gamma}\right)$$

$$\hat{\gamma} = \gamma_a + (\gamma_b - \gamma_a) \left(\frac{1}{k_a \Gamma}\right)\left(1/\left(\frac{1}{k_a \Gamma} + \frac{1}{k_b \Gamma}\right)\right),$$

where the final row is the result of tedious algebra. ∎

Therefore, given two target niches, $\hat{\gamma}$ characterizes any interior bundle satisfying $V_{c_a}(B) = V_{c_b}(B)$. By Equation 3, bundle size alone determines value of these bundles, and thus the price. We now show that, given two target niches receiving zero surplus, the surplus received by niches whose γ^* is exterior to a bundle is *independent* of bundle size.

Lemma 6 *Given a bundle interior to target niches, the identity of the two target niches, c_a and c_b, is sufficient to determine the surplus of niche c_d if $n_i = 0$ for all $i < (>)\gamma_d^*$.*

Proof: Assume that $\gamma_d^* > \hat{\gamma}$. As $surplus(c_b) = 0$, $surplus(c_d) = surplus(c_d) - surplus(c_b)$. As prices and clutter costs will be the same for both niches, we can simplify as follows:

$$surplus(c_d) = |B|w \left(\left(1 - \frac{2(\gamma_d^* - \hat{\gamma})}{k_d \Gamma} \right) - \left(1 - \frac{2(\gamma_b^* - \hat{\gamma})}{k_b \Gamma} \right) \right)$$

$$= \frac{2|B|w(\hat{\gamma}(k_b - k_d) + \gamma_b^* k_d - \gamma_d^* k_b)}{k_b k_d \Gamma}. \tag{4}$$

All parameters positive by assumption, the sign of the surplus is the same as the sign of the outer parentheses of equation 4, the sign of which is determined solely by the niches. The proof for $\gamma_d^* < \hat{\gamma}$, using c_a, is analogous. ∎

We can thus tell *a priori* which niches outside of the target niches will purchase the bundle. This is not the case for those niches for whom $\gamma^* \in (\gamma_a^*, \gamma_b^*)$. For example, if $\hat{\gamma} = 3$, then those niches for whom $\gamma^* = 3$ will certainly prefer a bundle of only category 3 to one of the same size with half in category 2 and half in category 4. Our next result shows that surplus of these consumers depends only on the distribution of articles, and not the size of the bundle.

Lemma 7 *Given a bundle interior to target niches c_a and c_b, the share of the bundle in each γ_i is sufficient to determine the surplus of niche c_d.*

Proof: We show for $\hat{\gamma}$ fixed and $n_i = 0$ for all $\gamma_i \notin [\gamma_a^*, \gamma_b^*]$, niche surplus does not depend on the size of the bundle.

The share in each category is equal to $s_i \equiv \frac{n_i}{|B|}$. Further define $\alpha = \sum_{i=\gamma_a^*}^{\gamma_d^*} s_i$, $\hat{\gamma}_l \equiv \sum_{i=\gamma_a^*}^{\gamma_d^*} s_i n_i$ and $\hat{\gamma}_r \equiv \sum_{i=\gamma_d^*+1}^{\gamma_b^*} s_i n_i$. The value of a bundle for any c_d is:

$$V_{c_d} + e^{\lambda|B|} = |B|w\alpha \left(1 - \frac{2(\gamma_d^* - \hat{\gamma}_l)}{k_d \Gamma} \right) +$$

$$+ |B|w(1 - \alpha) \left(1 - \frac{2(\hat{\gamma}_r - \gamma_d^*)}{k_d \Gamma} \right)$$

$$= |B|w \left(1 + \frac{2((1 - 2\alpha)\gamma_d^* - \hat{\gamma}_r + \hat{\gamma})}{k_d \Gamma} \right)$$

where the first equation is a result of algebra similar to that in the proof of Lemma 4 and the last line is the result of straightforward but tedious algebra and $\hat{\gamma} = \alpha\hat{\gamma}_l + (1-\alpha)\hat{\gamma}_r$.

Subtracting $surplus(c_b) = 0$ from $surplus(c_d)$ gives us:

$$surplus(c_d) = \frac{|B|w \left((\hat{\gamma} + \gamma_d^* - 2\alpha\gamma_d^* - \hat{\gamma}_r) \gamma_b^* + (\gamma_b^* - \hat{\gamma})k_d \right)}{k_b k_d \Gamma},$$

the sign of which is entirely determined by the sign of the outer parentheses of the numerator, a function of the niches and the distribution of the bundle. ∎

We can now characterize the optimal offering for a monopolist given two target niches.

Proposition 1 *Given two target niches, c_a and c_b, the monopolist's optimal bundle configuration solves:*

$$\max_{|B|} V_{c_a}(|B|) \text{ subject to } V_{c_a}(|B|) = V_{c_b}(|B|),$$

and the optimal price for the bundle is $p = V_{c_a}$.

Proof: Lemma 2 implies that $V_{c_a} = V_{c_b}$. Setting surplus equal to zero, the optimal price must be $p = V_{c_a} = V_{c_b}$.

Given c_a and c_b, the distribution of the optimal bundle must be of a certain form. For any offering, let the number of purchasing niches be $c^\#$. By Lemma 3, we know all articles are interior and are characterized by $\hat{\gamma}$ as defined by Lemma 5. We further restrict our subset to those distributions for which $c^\#$ achieves its maximal value on the set. This highest total demand subset is independent of bundle size and thus price by Lemma 7. As the set for which $c^\#$ is maximal is independent of bundle size, profit is maximized by choosing the bundle size $|B|$ that maximizes $p = V_{c_a}(|B|)$ and allocating this bundle by any of the distributions in our non-empty highest total demand subset. ∎

bundle	1	2	3	4	5	6
k high	C	+	+	+	C	C
k med	-	0	+	0	-	-
k low	-	-	C,D	-	-	-

0: Target Niche, Will Purchase
+: Will Purchase
-: Will Not Purchase
C: Purchase depends on niche characteristics
D: Purchase depends on article distribution

Fig. 2. Consumer demand given two target niches. Each square is a niche defined by $\{\gamma^*, k\}$. All articles are in categories 2,3, and 4, with a mean category of 3 and a price equal to the willingness to pay of the targets.

Figure 2 demonstrates the link between characteristics of the target niche and the surplus that other niches get, regardless of bundle size. First, note that niches with most-favored categories outside of the target niches and smaller breadth of interest than the target niches do not purchase the bundle. Similarly, those whose breadth of interest is not smaller than the targets and whose ideal category is at least as close to 3 as the targets will purchase. Those consumers outside the targets but with higher k (denoted by C) might purchase. Finally, we look at the niche denoted by C, D. Note that only bundles of the form $\{0, \frac{\alpha}{2}|B|, (1 - \alpha)|B|, \frac{\alpha}{2}|B|, 0, 0\}$ are interior and satisfy equality of the targets. Regardless of α, the willingness to pay of the targets depends only upon $|B|$. The willingness to pay of C, D does depend on α. At $\alpha = 0$, this niche has positive surplus. At $\alpha = 1$, this niche receives negative surplus as the sum of differences between most-preferred category and bundle category is the same as it is for the targets, yet this niche has a lower k.

Proposition 1 tells the firm how to find the optimal bundle conditional on any two target niches, c_a and c_b. By Lemma 2, the optimal offering for a monopolist will consist of a pair of target niches. To find the optimal target niches, the firm can find the optimal bundle and associated profit for each candidate pair of target niches, and then from this set choose the bundle and price that yield the highest overall profit.

3.2   Multi-firm Equilibrium

In this section, we analyze multiple interacting firms. Our goal is to characterize, to the extent possible, equilibrium outcomes.

Define the offerings of the M firms by $\vec{N}$, an $M \times \Gamma$ matrix with $N_{m,i}$ the number of articles from firm m in category i, and $\vec{p}$, a $M \times 1$ column vector where p_m is firm m's price. Denote producer i's profits as $\pi_i(\vec{N}, \vec{p})$. The next lemma gives a strong characterization of any equilibrium resulting from pure strategies.

Lemma 8 *In any pure-strategy Nash equilibrium,* $\pi_i(\vec{N}, \vec{p}) = \pi_j(\vec{N}, \vec{p})$ $\forall i, j \in \{1, 2, \ldots, M\}$.

Proof: If $\pi_i(\vec{N}, \vec{p}) > \pi_j(\vec{N}, \vec{p})$, then j could deviate by offering $\{\vec{n}_i, p_i - \epsilon\}$ for ϵ arbitrarily small. Therefore, $\{\vec{N}, \vec{p}\}$ cannot be an equilibrium.   ∎

Lemma 8 is a direct result of firms being unconstrained in the categories in which they can offer items. We shall show that such an equilibrium exists only if the category space is wide enough to accommodate M local monopolists. Letting Γ^m correspond to the number of γ^*-types that would be served by a monopolist, we define a local monopolist as one whose offering is optimal for $\Gamma = g < \Gamma^m$. The next proposition gives conditions sufficient for the existence of a multi-firm Nash equilibrium.

Proposition 2 *A pure strategy Nash equilibria exists if* λ, w, Γ *and* $\hat{k}$ *are such that* $\Gamma^m \leq \frac{\Gamma}{M}$.

Proof: Assume a monopolist in a market characterized by the parameters would optimally serve no more that $\frac{\Gamma}{M}$ distinct γ^*-types. Let firm i configure the optimal monopolist bundle such the left-most niche served has $\gamma^* = (i - 1) * \Gamma^m + 1$. As all receive the monopolist profit, none has an incentive to deviate.   ∎

We now look at the case where all firms cannot act as monopolists. The next two lemmas greatly restrict the space of possible equilibria outcomes.

Lemma 9 *In no pure-strategy Nash equilibria are any consumers indifferent between the offerings of the two firms.*

Proof: An ϵ decrease in price by either firm leads to a discrete increase in demand, as all consumers in the previously indifferent niche now all purchase from the same firm. ∎

Lemma 10 *In any pure-strategy Nash equilibrium, a niche gets positive surplus from at most one producer's offering.*

Proof: Assume not. By Lemma 8, we know that all firms earn equal profit. Let firms i and j provide positive surplus to the niche c_d. By Lemma 9, c_d is not indifferent. If c_d purchases from j, j offering $\{\vec{n}_i, p_{i-\epsilon}\}$ increases profits. ∎

Therefore, all niches with the same γ^* that do purchase will purchase purchase from the same firm, implying that each firm serves a unique subset of γ^*-types. We can now provide necessary conditions for the existence of a Nash equilibrium.

Proposition 3 *A pure-strategy Nash equilibrium exists only if each firm is a local monopolist such that $\pi_i = \pi_j \ \forall i, j$.*

Proof: By Lemma 10, each firm serves a unique subset of γ^*-types. Given this subset, the firm selects the optimal offering. By Lemma 8, all firms' profits must be equal. ∎

Thus the addition of firms in our environment need not lead to firms directly competing over the same consumers. However, in searching for a profitable niche, even the monopolist producer needs to search over a very large product space to find an optimal bundle and price as detailed in Section 3. The addition of other firms aggravates this already difficult problem. When a producer uses profits as a guide to finding a good bundle, these profits will be affected by the actions of other learning producers. The ability to find a profitable niche and avoid competition requires a great deal of knowledge not only about both consumer preferences and the strategies of other firms.

4   Zero-Knowledge Learning

In the previous section, we showed that the optimal strategy for duopolist producers, when they know the distribution of consumer preferences and understand the economic structure of the problem, is for each to target a separate consumer niche, acting as a local monopolist. We expect that firms (and their computational agents) will not typically have complete information about the distribution of consumer preferences, nor about the economic structure of the problem. Therefore, we now examine what happens when the producers are learning what bundle to offer and how to price it. We are interested in examining whether learning producers can locate the equilibrium solution, and in characterizing the extent to which economic knowledge can help in locating profitable niches more easily, particularly in the face of competing producers.

We model the learning of each producer using a genetic algorithm (GA).[11] We chose to use GAs primarily because of their effectiveness at learning in high-dimensional, nonstationary problems. GAs are also commonly used [1,4] to study the adaptive behaviors of agents in a multi-agent systems. We cannot claim that a GA is the optimal algorithm for this problem, or even that the parameters or encoding we have chosen are ideal. Our goal is to identify the sorts of knowledge that will help a producer locate profitable niches, given that it has adopted a widely-used off-the-shelf learning algorithm, rather than determining and optimizing a particular algorithm to fit this particular problem.

We encode the number of articles in each category as a gene. A bundle is then represented as a chromosome: a list of the articles in each category, plus a price, encoded

---

[11] Goldberg [8] provides a comprehensive introduction to genetic algorithms.

as a binary string. The *fitness* of a bundle is the profit that that bundle receives when it is offered to the consumer population. We refer to the set of bundles that a producer's GA is currently evaluating as its *pool*. Note that each producer is learning simultaneously; this means that each producer's target (the function it is optimizing) is potentially changing. It is helpful in visualizing this learning process to realize that each producer is learning a mixed strategy, represented by the elements of its pool.

In the following experiments, we consider the following situation: a population of 100 consumers, with k (the fraction of categories valued) drawn uniformly from $[0.2, 0.8]$ and $\Gamma = 9$. Each consumer's γ^* is drawn from a uniform distribution, and all consumers have valuation $w = 10$ for their favorite category. This leads to an equilibrium in which each of two producers acts as a local monopolist, selling a bundle of 2 categories, with 113 articles in one category, 169 articles in the adjacent category, and a price of 1286. In expectation, if k is completely uniformly distributed, each producer will earn a profit of 36008.

We begin with the situation in which both producers are zero-knowledge producers. Each producer begins with a pool of 50 bundles in which the number of articles is drawn from $[0, \hat{n}]$ and the price is drawn from $[0, 2048]$. In this experiment, as well as the following ones, $\hat{n}$ is set to 128.[12] In Section 5.5, we vary this parameter and discuss the implications of this choice. Once the experiment has begun, the GA allows producers to select any possible bundle and price; a producer's only feedback is the profit that a bundle earns. The results of this experiment are shown in Figure 3. The error bars indicate 95% confidence intervals for the data; that is, 95% of the data points for that iteration fall within the indicated range. As we see from Figure 3, when the producers are asked to locate equilibria without any other knowledge, they fail spectacularly. There are two potential reasons for this. First, the search space is extremely large. If we assume that a producer can offer 256 articles in a bundle, the maximum price is 2048, and prices are integers, then there are $256^9 \times 2048 \approx 9.6 \times 10^{22}$ bundles. Second, a large fraction of these bundles produce no profit. A random sample of one million bundles in this landscape reveals that only 55, or 0.005%, of the bundles have non-zero profit. This leaves a learning algorithm such as a GA, which depends upon a gradient, with little help in escaping zero-profit plateaus and locating optima. Even in those cases where producers are able to locate positively-valued bundles, the bundles they find are far from optimal. This indicates that the search space is pocked with plateaus and local optima.

It seems unlikely that information goods producers would have absolutely no knowledge of the goods they were selling or the preferences of the consumer population. More likely, they would have some (potentially uncertain) information that they could apply to their learning problem. In the following section, we examine the consequences of applying different sorts of economic knowledge on this learning problem.

5   Injecting Economic Knowledge

In real markets, even those in which consumers are anonymous and the consumer population is rapidly changing, producers typically have some knowledge about their learn-

---

[12] Note that $\hat{n}$ limits the maximum number of articles in a category at *the beginning* of an experiment; the maximum possible number of articles in a category was set to 1024.

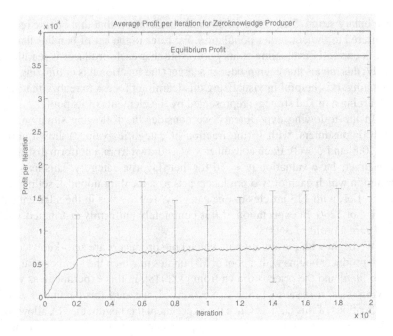

Fig. 3. Moving average of profit for zero knowledge Producers. Producers can only capture a small fraction of the surplus.

ing problem. At the very least, they know that their problem is an economic one, and so it will obey some simple criteria, such as that demand is non-increasing *ceteris paribus* as price increases.

This knowledge allows a producer to prune its search space in a way that a knowledge-free algorithm such as a GA, or optimization algorithms such as amoeba, which we have used in previous work [3], cannot. This leads us to suspect that results generated with zero-knowledge producers may be overly naive.

The experiments in this section map out some of the space between the full-information producers described in Section 3 and the zero-knowledge producers described in Section 4. In particular, we examine three ways in which economic knowledge can transform a learning producer's search problem: it can reduce the size of the search space; it can transform the landscape, introducing a gradient that aids adaptive algorithms such as GAs; or it can allow the producer to start in a more effective region of the search space.

5.1   Equilibrium Stability

We begin with producers that have near-perfect information. In this experiment, each producer's pool is seeded with all elements in the pool equal to the equilibrium solution. This provides the equivalent of the perfect information used to derive the analytic results in section 3. On every iteration, we increase the GA's mutation rate until it reaches 30%.

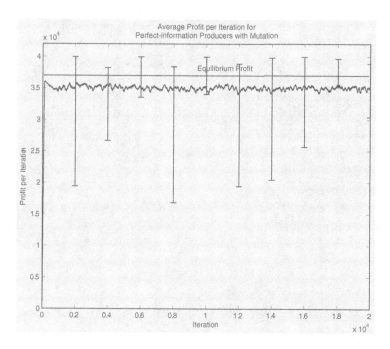

Fig. 4. Moving average of profit for perfect-information producers with mutation. Despite large amounts of mutation, producers are able to maintain the equilibrium solution.

This is meant to represent the situation where producers know what they "should" do, but occasionally make mistakes. It is also intended to help understand the nature of the equilibrium basin. It was not clear whether the difficulty in the zero-knowledge case was due to the size of the search space or the structure of the equilibrium. When producers are pushed off the equilibrium, are they able to easily return? Figure 4 shows the results of this experiment. Once again, error bars indicate a 95% confidence interval.[13] As we see in Figure 4, the equilibrium solution is quite resistant to the introduction of mutation. The error bounds show that mutation can push the producer quite far from the equilibrium solution, yet it is able to return to the equilibrium. This implies that the basin of attraction around the solution is quite broad; even when producers are pushed away from it, there is a natural gradient they can follow to return back to the equilibrium.

Another way to understand this is to consider the change in each producer's search space. The zero-knowledge agent searched over all possible bundles, which produced a vast space overwhelmingly filled with bundles that yielded zero profit. In contrast, the initial search space here consists of one bundle: the equilibrium bundle. As we increase the mutation rate, the GA considers more bundles, and so the search space will grow. At its highest, the mutation rate reaches 30%, meaning that there is a 0.3 probability

---

[13] Since the experiments are conducted on a finite, randomly generated population, it is possible that, in a particular run, the equilibrium solution will differ slightly from the theoretical solution, allowing producers to earn slightly more than the theoretical profit.

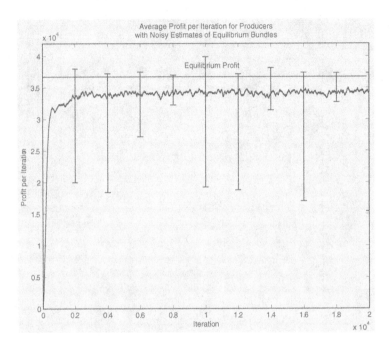

Fig. 5. Moving average of profit for producers with uncertainty over consumer valuation for each category. Producers are still able to capture a large fraction of equilibrium profit.

that a bundle in a producer's pool will be mutated. In expectation, 15 new bundles will be added to the search space every time mutation is applied. At this rate, it would take approximately 6.6×10^{21} rounds of mutation, or 3×10^{23} iterations (since mutation is applied after all 50 bundles in a pool are evaluated) to sample all possible bundles.

5.2   Uncertainty over Consumer Valuation

In this section, we further weaken each producer's knowledge about the consumer population. In particular, we assume that they no longer know exactly how many articles to sell in each category. To achieve this, we seed each producer's pool with copies of the equilibrium bundle, and then apply Gaussian noise (mean 0, standard deviation 50) to the number of articles in each category for each of the bundles in the pool. This gives a producer a pool of approximate solutions. We continue to apply mutation as in the previous experiment. The results of this experiment are shown in Figure 5.

As we can see in Figure 5, applying significant amounts of Gaussian noise does not affect each producer's ability to return to the equilibrium solution. Although average profits decrease slightly, and we see the introduction of an initial transient in which producers are converging on a solution, the application of noise is not enough to push producers out of the basin of attraction of the equilibrium.

In this case, we have not reduced the total search space, since it is possible for Gaussian noise to produce any possible bundle. Instead, each producer starts its search in a profitable area of the search space, namely one that has a gradient. Random sampling of one million initial bundles generated according to this procedure shows that 27.5% of them have a non-zero profit. In a pool of 50 initial bundles, 13 of them will have non-zero profit, which provides the GA with a sufficient gradient for learning.

5.3   Adjacent Categories

In the previous experiment, we applied noise to each producer's solution, but we still seeded the producers with the proper coordination knowledge. That is, producer 1 was seeded with bundles that tended to have large numbers of articles in categories 2 and 3, and producer 2 was seeded with bundles that tended to have large numbers of articles in categories 7 and 8. In this experiment, we remove that knowledge. However, we allow producers to retain the knowledge that the consumer valuation of categories exist on a line, and so they are best off offering adjacent categories. In this sort of environment, 'general interest' bundles containing a wide variety of articles are not highly valued.

We implement this by seeding each producer's pool with the equilibrium bundle and applying noise, as above, and then rotating the categories in each bundle by a random amount. This produces a pool in which bundles tend to have large numbers of articles in adjacent categories, but the favorite category is distributed uniformly throughout the pool. Again, mutation is applied. The results of this experiment are shown in Figure 6. We see that the producers in this experiment suffer a loss in profit when compared to the producers shown in Figure 5. We have not changed the nonzero fraction of the search space relative to the previous experiment, but we have removed the initial coordination of solutions between producers. This can create inadvertent competition. Since the producers no longer start out in separate areas of the search space, there are cases in which they mis-coordinate and offer the same bundle. In fact, if each producer is choosing two adjacent categories at random, there is a $\frac{3}{8}$ chance that the producers will offer at least one category in common. Given this, it would seem that the producers still seem to do a relatively good job of coordinating, which implies that there is a strong 'learning gradient' toward acting as a local monopolist.

5.4   Bundle Diversity

In the following experiment, we further weaken each producer's knowledge by removing the assumption that producers know that categories are arranged on a line. Instead, we assume that they only know the approximate diversity of the bundle; that is, how many categories they should offer articles in. We implement this by seeding each pool with copies of the equilibrium bundle, applying Gaussian noise, and then permuting the articles offered in each category within each bundle. This produces a pool of bundles that tend to have two categories that contain a large number of articles, but which are not necessarily adjacent. The results of this experiment are shown in Figure 7. The profits in this experiment are very similar to those shown in Figure 6. This serves as an indicator that the knowledge that categories are arranged on a line may not be that essential to producer performance. Instead, knowing the number of categories to offer articles

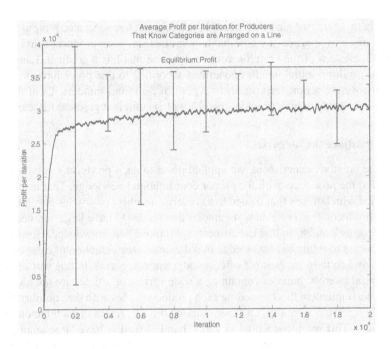

Fig. 6. Moving average of profit for producers that know that category values are arranged on a line. Lack of coordination lowers profits slightly.

in may be a more useful piece of knowledge. Interestingly, by removing the adjacency knowledge, we reduce the probability that two random bundles will compete directly (to $\frac{17}{81}$, or 21%). However, random sampling of one million random bundles reveals that only 17% of them yield positive profit. So the reduction in potential competition is canceled out by the increasingly poor starting bundles.

An alternative explanation for why adjacency knowledge doesn't produce a significant improvement in performance might lie in the way in which GAs search for solutions. GAs build up solutions by composing contiguous sub-solutions (sometimes referred to as building blocks) that tend to perform well. This produces a selection bias toward solutions in which adjacent genes (or numbers of articles, in our case), both produce a high fitness. So the fact that the articles are encoded on a line on the gene may be enough for the producer to exploit that relationship within the model of consumer preferences, even without being given that knowledge in the form of initial conditions.

5.5   Total Bundle Size

As we have pointed out, the greatest challenge that these producers face in locating a suitable bundle to offer is the incredibly large search space. Many of the previous experiments have focused on ways in which a producer can apply economic knowledge to reduce the size of the search space. In this experiment, we allow each producer to exploit economic knowledge to instead start its search in useful areas of the search

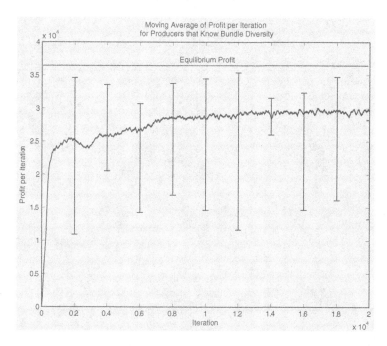

Fig. 7. Moving average of profit for producers that know bundle diversity. Even though producers no longer know that categories are arranged on a line, profits remain at a level consistent with the previous experiment.

space. We do this by modifying the number of articles in each category that a producer will initially offer. Smaller initial bundles will be more likely to yield nonzero profit, but may potentially trap the producer in a local optimum.

In Section 4, we seeded the producers' pools with bundles containing a random number of articles in each category, where this number was drawn from $[0, \hat{n}]$, with $\hat{n} = 128$. In this experiment, we begin with the zero-knowledge producers from section 4. We then vary $\hat{n}$, thereby changing the region of the search space in which the producers can start. In Figure 8, we show the results of experiments in which the number of articles in each category of a producer's initial bundle were drawn from $[0, \hat{n}]$ with $\hat{n}$ set to $\hat{n} = 25$, 64, 128, 192, and 256, respectively. As we can see from this experiment, starting with a smaller bundle definitely allows a producer to achieve better profits. In addition, when $\hat{n}$ becomes too large (greater than 128), profits are either very low or zero, implying that the producers never find their way out of zero-profit regions of the search space. However, even a small $\hat{n}$ is not enough to move the producers all the way to the equilibrium. This implies that there are local optima within the landscape in which producers can become stuck. In addition, we can see that the transient is different for the $\hat{n} = 25$ and $\hat{n} = 64$ cases. In the $\hat{n} = 25$ case, the initial bundles were simply too small, and so time (and a larger number of mutations) was needed to make the bundles large enough to extract significant profit. Beyond $\hat{n} = 128$, most of the initial bundles occur in zero-profit areas of the landscape, and so producers do quite poorly. This tells us that

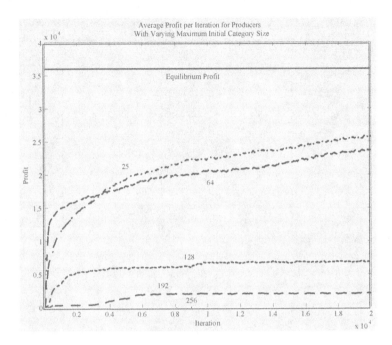

Fig. 8. Moving average of profit for producers with different initial numbers of articles in each category. Smaller initial numbers of articles allow producers to locate solutions, but overly small bundles introduce longer learning transients.

knowing something about where to start one's search is a useful piece of knowledge, but by itself it is not a replacement for more detailed economic knowledge about the behavior of either consumers or competing producers.

5.6   Introducing a Gradient

Another way in which producers can make their search problem easier is to transform the landscape so that it contains more of a gradient. One way to do this is to get feedback from the consumer population about how much they value a bundle, as opposed to only what they purchase. This allows a producer to distinguish between those bundles that receive zero profit because they're slightly undesirable and those bundles that receive zero profit because they're extremely undesirable.

In this experiment, we provide producers with a gradient by altering the way in which the GA assigns fitness to a bundle. Rather than using the profit that a bundle earns, we use the valuation that the five most-satisfied consumers assign to the bundle, even if some or all of these are negative.[14] While the size of the search space does not

---

[14] The assumption that producers can discover how negatively a bundle is valued is admittedly a bit artificial, although a clever producer might be able to estimate this quantity, either through offering rebates or cash to consumers, or packaging this bundle with another good whose value is known and observing the difference in demand.

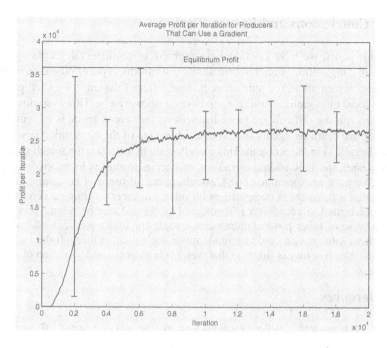

Fig. 9. Moving average of profit for producers with a gradient.

change at all, the underlying landscape is transformed, as there are (almost) no areas of zero profit. Instead, most of the large zero-profit plateaus will now be populated with valleys corresponding to negative valuations. This provides a gradient-using algorithm (such as a GA) with the feedback needed to learn effectively. By using only the valuations of the most-satisfied consumers, a producer is encouraged to adapt its bundle to better satisfy those consumers that are most inclined to buy its bundle, as opposed to consumers who would need drastic changes in order to purchase.

One potential complication that comes from using consumer surplus, rather than profit, as a measure of bundle fitness is that bundles that are priced at zero will be highly valued by the consumer (since they yield high surplus), even though they are not particularly useful solutions for the producer. We avoid this problem by fixing prices for this experiment and having producers learn only bundle contents. This solution is only partly satisfactory; a more comprehensive approach would combine both profit and consumer satisfaction in estimating bundle fitness.

Figure 9 shows the results of this experiment. There is still a significant transient period when producers are searching through low-profit areas of the landscape, but after about 400 iterations, a producer is able (on average) to extract about 70% of the equilibrium profit, which is a distinct improvement over the experiments in Section 4, where a producer was unable to extract any significant profit. As in the previous experiment, this tuning of the learning algorithm helps, but not as much as the application of specific domain knowledge, which can be used to drastically prune the search space.

6   Conclusions and Future Work

In this paper, we have examined the problem of producers determining where to locate in a high-dimensional information-goods product space. When the producers have perfect information, the pure-strategy equilibrium solution is for each producer to act as a local monopolist, serving a separate consumer niche. However, discovering those niches is quite difficult for naive learners, as the search space is incredibly large. We argue that learning agents should take advantage of the economic knowledge implicit (and explicit) in the problem. This can allow them to reduce the search space, transform the search space by adding a gradient, or start in promising locations.

We have not examined one particularly useful piece of economic knowledge: the fact that a producer is competing with other producers. Adding a layer of reflectivity, in which the GA's feedback is modulated by the distance between a producer's bundle and those of other producers, remains a topic for future work. In addition, the use of gradient information could be made more sophisticated through the introduction of a multi-objective fitness function that weights both profit and valuation of a bundle.

References

1. J. Andreoni and J. Miller. Auctions with artificial adaptive agents. *Games and Economic Behavior*, 10:39–64, 1995.
2. C. H. Brooks, E. H. Durfee, and R. Das. Price wars and niche discovery in an information economy. In *Proceedings of the 2nd ACM Conference on Electronic Commerce (EC-00)*, pages 95–106, Minneapolis, MN, October 2000.
3. C. H. Brooks, R. S. Gazzale, R. Das, J. O. Kephart, J. K. MacKie Mason, and E. H. Durfee. Model selection in an information economy: Choosing what to learn. *Computational Intelligence*, 18(4), 2002.
4. M. Chang and J. E. Harrington. Centralization vs. decentralization in a multi-unit organization: A computational model of a retail chain as a multi-agent adaptive system. *Management Science*, 46(11):1427–1440, November 2000.
5. J. C. Chuang and M. A. Sirbu. Network delivery of information goods: Optimal pricing of articles and subscriptions. Available at: http://ksgwww.harvard.edu/iip/econ/chuang.html, 1998.
6. P. Dasgupta and R. Das. Dynamic pricing with limited competitor information in a multi-agent economy. In *Proceedings of the Fifth International Conference on Cooperative Information Systems*, 2000.
7. S. A. Fay and J. MacKie Mason. Competition between firms that bundle information goods. In *Proceedings of the 27th Annual Telecom Policy Research Conference*, Alexandria, VA, September 1999.
8. D. E. Goldberg. *Genetic Algorithms in Search, Optimization and Machine Learning*. Addison Wesley, Boston, 1989.
9. J. O. Kephart, J. E. Hanson, and J. Sairamesh. Price and niche wars in a free-market economy of software agents. *Artificial Life*, 4:1–23, 1998.

Handling Resource Use Oscillation in Multi-agent Markets

Mark Klein[1] and Yaneer Bar-Yam[2]

[1] Massachusetts Institute of Technology, NE20-336, Cambridge MA 02132
m_klein@mit.edu
[2] New England Complex Systems Institute, 24 Mt. Auburn Street, Cambridge, MA 02138
yaneer@necsi.org

Abstract. When resource consumers select among competing providers based on delayed information, inefficient oscillations in resource utilization can emerge. This paper describes an approach, based on selective stochastic resource request rejection, for dealing with this emergent dysfunction.

1. The Challenge

The convergence of ubiquitous electronic communications such as the Internet, software agents, and web/grid service standards such as XML is rapidly ushering in a world where hordes of agents, potentially acting for humans, can rapidly select among multitudes of competing providers offering almost every imaginable service. This is inherently an "open" world, a marketplace where the agents operate as peers, neither designed nor operated under central control. Such a world offers the potential for unprecedented speed and efficiency in getting work done.

In such open markets we face, however, the potential of highly dysfunctional dynamics emerging as the result of many locally reasonable agent decisions [1]. Such "emergent dysfunctions" can take many forms, ranging from inefficient resource allocation [2] to chaotic inventory fluctuations [3] [4] to non-convergent collective decision processes [5]. This problem is exacerbated by the fact that agent societies operate in a realm whose communication and computational costs and capabilities are radically different from those in human society, leading to collective behaviors with which we may have little previous experience. It has been argued, for example, that the 1987 stock crash was due in part to the action of computer-based "program traders" that were able to execute trade decisions at unprecedented speed and volume, leading to unprecedented stock market volatility [6].

Let us focus on one specific example of emergent dysfunctional behavior: resource use oscillation in request-based resource sharing. Imagine that we have a collection of consumer agents faced with a range of competing providers for a given resource (e.g. a piece of information such as a weather report, a sensor or effector, a communication link, a storage or computational capability, or some kind of data analysis). Typically, though not exclusively, the utility offered by a resource is inversely related to how many consumers are using it. Each agent strives to select the resource with the highest utility (e.g. response time or quality), and resources are allocated first-come first-

P. Faratin et al. (Eds.): AMEC 2003, LNAI 3048, pp. 145-153, 2004.

served to those who request them. This is a peer-to-peer mechanism: there is no one 'in charge'. This kind of resource allocation is widely used in settings that include fixed-price markets, internet routing, and so on. It is simple to implement, makes minimal bandwidth requirements, and - in the absence of delays in resource status information – allows consumers to quickly converge to a near optimal distribution across resources (see figure 1).

Consumers, however, will often have a delayed picture of how busy each resource is. Agents could imaginably poll every resource before every request. This would cause, however, a N-fold increase in number of required messages for N servers, and does not eliminate the delays caused by the travel time for status messages. In a realistic open system context, moreover, consumers probably cannot fully rely on resource providers to accurately characterize the utility of their own offerings (in a way that is comparable, moreover, across providers). Resource providers may be self-interested and thus reluctant to release utilization information for fear of compromising their competitive advantage. In that case, agents will need to estimate resource utilization using other criteria such as their own previous experience, consulting reputation services, or watching what other consumers are doing. Such estimates are almost certain to lag at times behind the actual resource utility.

When status information is delayed in some way, we find that resource use oscillations emerge, potentially reducing the utility achieved by the consumer agents far below the optimal value predicted by an equilibrium analysis [7].What happens is the following. Imagine for simplicity that we have just two equivalent resources, R1 and R2. We can expect that at some point one of the resources, say R1, will be utilized less than the other due to the ebb and flow of demand. Consumer agents at that point will of course tend to select R1. The problem is that, since their image of resource utilization is delayed, they will continue to select R1 even after it is no longer the less utilized resource, leading to an "overshoot" in R1's utilization. When the agents finally realize that R2 is now the better choice, they will tend to select R2 with the same delay-induced overshoot. The net result is that the utilization of R1 and R2 will oscillate around the optimal equilibrium value. The range of the oscillations, moreover, increases with the delay, to the extent that all the consumers may at times select one server when the other is idle:

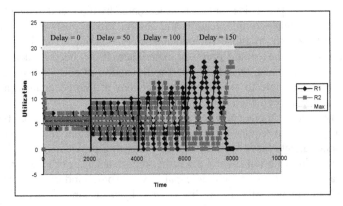

Fig. 1. The tilization of two equivalent resources with and without delays in status information.

Oscillations have two undesirable effects. One is that they can reduce the utility received by consumers below optimal values. The other is that they can increase the variability of the utility achieved by the consumers, which may be significant in domains where consistency is important. The precise impact of oscillations is driven by the relationship between resource utilization and utility. Let us consider several scenarios to help make this more clear.

Imagine we have grocery store customers (consumers) choosing from two checkout lines (resources). Their utility is inversely related to how long they have to wait. The time needed to check out each customer is not affected by the length of a line, so the wait at each line is *negatively* and *linearly* impacted by its length. As long as both checkout lines remain busy, oscillations in the distribution of customers across lines do not affect average check out times. The longer waits faced by customers in one line are exactly offset by the shorter waits enjoyed by the customers in the other line. The *variance* of checkout times will, of course, be wider if there are oscillations. Note, also, that if the oscillations are so severe that one line goes idle while the other has customers, the average waiting times will increase because only one resource is active.

Now consider, by contrast, movie goers faced with a choice of theatres to attend. Each movie goer wants the best seat possible. The fuller the theatre, the poorer the seats that remain, so the utility of the seats is *negatively* and *non-linearly* impacted by the number of people using the theatre. There is one optimal distribution of movie goers across theatres (50-50 in this case), and oscillations in the actual distribution reduce the average utility because much of the time is spent at a non-optimal distribution. Oscillations increase the variance in this case as well.

A third scenarios involves TV viewers (consumers) with a choice of shows (resources) to watch. The utility of a show for a given consumer is *not* impacted by who else happens to be watching it. In this case we would expect no persistent oscillations to occur, because changing viewership does not impact the movement of viewers among shows. Any variations that do occur would, in any case, have no impact on the utility received by the consumers.

The last scenario involves club goers (consumers) with a choice of night clubs (resources) they can attend. The value of a club to them is given by how many other people are there. The resource utility is thus *positively* impacted by the number of consumers. In this scenario, there will be no persistent oscillations because whatever club achieves an initial advantage in number of participants will eventually get all of the club goers.

We can therefore distinguish four scenarios for request-based resource sharing. All are potentially important in open agent system contexts. Network routers operate using the "Grocery Checkout" model. A broadcast operates using the "TV show" model. Auctions arguably fit into the "Nightclub" model. And providers of varying utility resources such as sensors, effectors, or storage capacity fit into the "Movie Theatre" model. These scenarios vary however in their susceptibility to the emergent dysfunction of resource use oscillation. The key factor concerns how the utility offered by a resource varies with its utilization:

Table 1. The cases for how resource utility is affected by utilization.

	Linear Relationship	Non-linear Relationship
Positive Impact	Nightclub	
Zero Impact	TV Show	
Negative Impact	Grocery Checkout	Movie Theatre

When resource utility is a constant or positive function of resource utilization, resource use oscillation will not occur and/or have no impact. In the remaining scenarios, however, oscillations can occur and negatively impact the consistency and/or average value of the utility achieved by consumers. We will confine our attention to these latter cases in the remainder of the paper.

2. Previous Work

What can be done about resource use oscillation in request-based systems? This problem has been studied in some depth, most notably in the literature on "minority games" [8] [9]. This line of work has investigated how to design agents so that their local decisions no longer interact to produce substantial resource use oscillations. One example involves designing agents that make resource selection decisions using historical resource utilization values [7]. If the agents look an appropriate distance into the past, they will be looking at the resource state one oscillation back in time, which should be a good approximation of the current resource utilization. The agent's delay parameter is tuned using survival of the fittest: agents with a range of delay factors are created, and the ones that get the highest utility survive and reproduce, while others do not. With this in place the resource utilization, under some conditions, settles down to near-optimal values.

Any approach predicated on the careful design of agent resource selection strategies, however, faces a fundamental flaw in an open systems context. In open systems, we do not control the design or operation of the consumer agents and can not be assured that they will adopt strategies that avoid emergent dysfunctions. Our challenge, therefore, is to find an approach that moderates or eliminates oscillatory resource utilization dynamics without needing to control the design or operation of the consumer agents.

3. Our Approach

Our approach to this problem is inspired by a scheme developed to improve the allocation of network router bandwidth (the resource) to client computers (the consumers). Routers currently operate as follows. Clients send packets to routers, and routers then forward the packets on towards their final destination. Every router has a buffer where it stores the packets that arrive when the router is busy. If any packets arrive when the buffer is full, the routers send a 'packet drop' message to the originating clients, at which point they immediately drop their data send rate to some minimal value, and then gradually increase it. This scheme is prone to inefficient router use oscillations because clients can synchronize their data send rate changes. If several get a packet dropped message from the router at about the same time, they all slow down and potentially under-utilize the router until their data rates ramp up enough to overload it, at which point they all drop their rates again.

A scheme called "Random Early Detect" (RED) has been proposed to address this problem [10]. The idea is simple. Rather than dropping packets only when the buffer is full, the router drops them stochastically with a probability proportional to how full the buffer is (e.g. 50% full results in a 50% chance of a packet being dropped). RED is successful at damping oscillations in router utilization because it de-synchronizes the data send rate changes across clients. While it does increase client-side message traffic by increasing the number of reject messages, it has no negative impact on total throughput because it is very unlikely to cause the buffers to empty out and leave a router needlessly unutilized.

We have adapted this idea for the context of request-based resource sharing in open agent systems. We call our technique 'stochastic request rejection', or SRR. Imagine that every resource stochastically rejects new requests with a probability proportional to its current load. This can be implemented by the resource itself, or by 'sentinel' agents that track the number of consumers each resource is currently serving, and stochastically intercept/reject consumer requests with a probability proportional to that load. When oscillations occur, we would predict that the increased level of rejections from the currently more heavily utilized resource will shift the requests to the less-utilized resource, thereby damping the oscillations and ameliorating their negative impact on the utility and consistency experienced by consumer agents.

4. The Grocery Checkout Case

Our first set of tests studied the value of SRR when applied to "grocery checkout" scenario. The experimental setup was as follows. There were 20 consumers and 2 resources. Each consumer sends a 'request' message to the resource it believes has the smallest backlog, waits until it receives a 'job completed' message from the resource, and then after a randomized delay sends the next 'request' message. The consumers' estimate of a resources' utility may lag the correct value. Resources may either take on requests or reject them. If a consumer receives a 'reject' message, it sends the request to the other resource. Messages take 20 units of time to travel, resources require 20 units of time to perform each task, and consumers have a normally distributed delay at 40 ticks, with a standard deviation of 10, between receiving one result and submitting the next request. The aggregate results reported below represent averages over 100 simulation runs, each 4000 ticks long, and all the conclusions we make were statistically significant at $p < 0.01$.

The impact of applying SRR in this scenario can be visualized as follows:

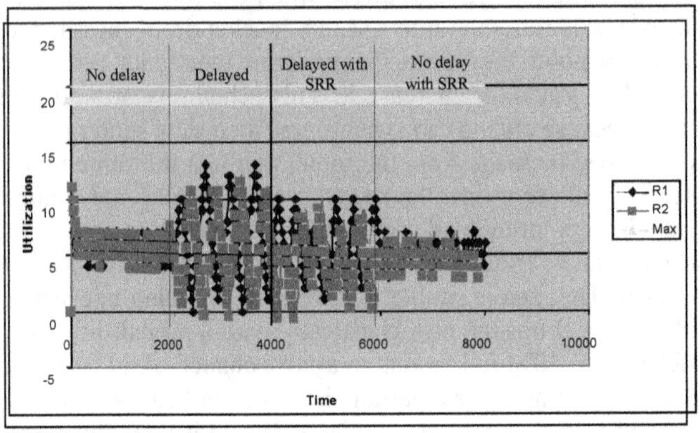

Fig. 2. The impact of SRR on resource oscillations.

In this simulation run, the agents initially made their resource requests using current information on the length of each resources' backlog. As we can see, in this case the resource utilization clusters tightly around the optimal distribution of 50-50 across resources. At T = 2000, the backlog information provided to the consumers was made 100 time units out of date, rapidly leading to large resource use oscillations. At T = 4000, SRR was turned on, resulting in substantial damping in the magnitude of these oscillations. At T = 6000, the delay was removed but SRR was left on, whereupon the resource utilization returns to clustering tightly around the optimal distribution. The aggregate results confirm the patterns suggested by this example:

Table 2. Task completion times +/ 1 standard deviation, as well as reject rates, for different delays, with and without SRR.

	Null	SRR
No delay	160 +/- 4 0%	160 +/- 6 33%
Short Delay (50)	160 +/- 7 0%	160 +/- 6 34%
Long Delay (100)	167 +/- 8 0%	161 +/- 6 35%

As we would expect for the grocery checkout scenario, the variability in task completion times without SRR increases with the delay in status information, and if the delay is long enough, the average task completion time can increase as well. If we turn on SRR, we find that it significantly reduces the variability in task completion times in the delayed cases, and almost eliminates the increase in task completion times in the long delay case. Rejecting some requests can thus, paradoxically, actually speed up task completion when delay-induced oscillations occur. But this does come at a cost. Message traffic is increased: roughly $1/3^{rd}$ of the consumer requests elicit a reject message and must be re-sent. The variability of task completion times in the no delay case is also increased by SRR. This is because many resource requests that would otherwise simply have been queued up incur the additional delay of being rejected and re-submitted. The absolute size of these effects, of course, can be expected to vary with the ratio of task and messaging times. Ideally, we would be able to enable SRR only when it is needed, so we can avoid incurring its costs in the no-oscillation contexts where it is not helpful. We will return to this point later.

5. The Movie Theatre Case

The parameters for the movie theatre simulations were the same as in the grocery store case, except for the following changes. Resources do not have a waiting line, but instead offer concurrent access to 15 different 'slots' with varying utility (the first slot has value 15, the second has value 14, and so on). Tasks take 160 ticks to perform. The aggregate results for this case are as follows:

Table 3. Average quality +/- 1 standard deviation, as well as reject rates and number of completed requests, for different delays, with and without SRR.

	Null	SRR
No delay	9.6 +/- 1.5	9.7 +/- 1.2
	0%	59%
	331	303
Short Delay (50)	9.1 +/- 1.9	9.8 +/- 1.4
	0%	60%
	332	303
Long Delay (100)	7.6 +/- 2.1	9.6 +/- 1.4
	3%	66%
	331	300

As we can see, SRR is also effective in this scenario. Delay-induced oscillations cause consumers to often select the resource that is actually more heavily utilized and thus lower in quality, resulting in a reduction of the average achieved quality. Using SRR eliminates this problem, but with the cost of increasing message traffic, as well as reducing the rate of task completion (since every time a task is rejected a delay is incurred while the request is re-submitted). As in the "grocery checkout" case, we would ideally prefer to be able to apply SRR selectively, so we do not incur these costs when oscillations are not occurring. Can this be done?

6. Selective SRR

It is in fact straightforward to use spectral analysis to determine if persistent oscillations are occurring in resource utilization. In our implementation, each resource periodically (every 20 ticks) sampled its utilization and submitted the last 30 data points to a Fourier analysis. SRR was turned on if above-threshold values were encountered in the power spectrum so determined. The threshold was determined empirically. This approach proved to be successful. In the grocery checkout scenario, selective SRR was as effective as SRR in maintaining throughput and task duration consistency while avoiding increases in message traffic in the no-delay case:

Table 4. Task completion times +/ 1 standard deviation, as well as reject rates, for different delays, with and without [selective] SRR.

	Null	SRR	Selective SRR
No delay	160 +/- 4 0%	160 +/- 6 33%	160 +/- 4 0%
No delay	160 +/- 4 0%	160 +/- 6 33%	160 +/- 4 0%
Short Delay (50)	160 +/- 7 0%	160 +/- 6 34%	160 +/- 6 29%
Long Delay (100)	167 +/- 8 0%	161 +/- 6 35%	161 +/- 6 33%

In the movie theatre scenario, selective SRR was as effective as SRR in maintaining task quality while almost eliminating increases in message traffic and task time in the no-delay case:

Table 5. Average quality +/- 1 standard deviation, as well as reject rates and number of completed requests, for different delays, with and without [selective] SRR.

	Null	SRR	Selective SRR
No delay	9.6 +/- 1.5 0% 331	9.7 +/- 1.2 59% 303	9.5 +/- 1.4 6% 327
Short Delay (50)	9.1 +/- 1.9 0% 332	9.8 +/- 1.4 60% 303	9.6 +/- 1.5 41% 311
Long Delay (100)	7.6 +/- 2.1 3% 331	9.6 +/- 1.4 66% 300	9.3 +/- 1.6 54% 305

This simple spectral analysis approach can be fooled, of course, into triggering SRR when resource use oscillations are due to variations in aggregate demand rather than status information delays. This problem, however, is easily addressed: whenever a resource detects significant usage oscillations, it analyzes the correlation of it's utilization with that of the other resource. Variations in aggregate demand will show a positive correlation, while delay-caused oscillations show a negative one. We have implemented this approach and found that it successfully avoids triggering SRR for aggregate demand variations while remaining effective in responding to delay-induced oscillations.

7. Contributions and Next Steps

We have presented a promising approach for mitigating the deleterious effects of delay-induced resource-use oscillations on request-based resource sharing. It differs from previous techniques in that it is designed to be appropriate for the important context of open agent systems, where we can not rely on being able to control the design or operation of the resource consumers. The key elements of this approach involve the stochastic load-proportional rejection of resource requests, triggered selectively when spectral and cross-resource correlation analyses reveal that delay-induced oscillations are actually taking place.

Next steps for this work include evaluating the selective SRR approach when there are more than two resources. This research is part of the author's long-standing efforts to develop a systematic enumeration of the different multi-agent system exception types as well as how they can be addressed in open systems contexts [11] [12]. See for further details on this work.

8. Acknowledgements

This work was supported by the NSF Computational and Social Systems program as well as the DARPA Control of Agent-Based Systems program.

9. References

1. Jensen, D. and V. Lesser. Social pathologies of adaptive agents. In the proceedings of Safe Learning Agents Workshop in the 2002 AAAI Spring Symposium. 2002: AAAI Press.
2. Chia, M.H., D.E. Neiman, and V.R. Lesser. Poaching and distraction in asynchronous agent activities. In the proceedings of Proceedings of the Third International Conference on Multi-Agent Systems. 1998. Paris, France.
3. Youssefmir, M. and B. Huberman. Resource contention in multi-agent systems. In the proceedings of First International Conference on Multi-Agent Systems (ICMAS-95). 1995. San Francisco, CA, USA: AAAI Press.
4. Sterman, J.D., Learning in and about complex systems. 1994, Cambridge, Mass.: Alfred P. Sloan School of Management, Massachusetts Institute of Technology. 51.
5. Klein, M., H. Sayama, P. Faratin, and Y. Bar-Yam, The Dynamics of Collaborative Design: Insights From Complex Systems and Negotiation Research. Concurrent Engineering Research & Applications, 2003. **In press**.
6. Waldrop, M., Computers amplify Black Monday. Science, 1987. **238**: p. 602-604.
7. Hogg, T., Controlling chaos in distributed computational systems. SMC'98 Conference Proceedings, 1998(98CH36218): p. 632-7.
8. Challet, D. and Y.-C. Zhang, Emergence of Cooperation and Organization in an Evolutionary Game. arXiv:adap-org/9708006, 1997. **2**(3).
9. Zhang, Y.-C., Modeling Market Mechanism with Evolutionary Games. arXiv:cond-mat/9803308, 1998. **1**(25).
10. Braden, B., D. Clark, J. Crowcroft, B. Davie, S. Deering, D. Estrin, S. Floyd, V. Jacobson, G. Minshall, C. Partridge, L. Peterson, K. Ramakrishnan, S. Shenker, J. Wroclawski, and L. Zhang, Recommendations on Queue Management and Congestion Avoidance in the Internet. 1998, Network Working Group.
11. Klein, M. and C. Dellarocas. Exception Handling in Agent Systems. In the proceedings of Proceedings of the Third International Conference on AUTONOMOUS AGENTS (Agents '99). 1999. Seattle, Washington.
12. Klein, M., J.A. Rodriguez-Aguilar, and C. Dellarocas, Using Domain-Independent Exception Handling Services to Enable Robust Open Multi-Agent Systems: The Case of Agent Death. Autonomous Agents and Multi-Agent Systems, 2003. **7**(1/2).